Early Acclaim

'In a world of much turbulence and rapid changes, *Spirituality at Work* can help us find our own inner strength and serve as an inspiration to find new gateways. I thank Devdas Menon for sharing his deep insight and wisdom, and I very much recommend this book to anyone interested in self-development. This book is based on the wisdom from the ancient Indian scripture, *Bhagavad Gita*. It draws inspiration from the famous sage of India, Sri Aurobindo, and the author's own experiences and interpretations. The author makes the Gita come alive with his profound and inspiring way of presenting the message. He has introduced courses such as *Self Awareness* and *Integral Karmayoga* at IIT Madras with great success, and knows how to present ancient wisdom to young people in a modern world.'

– Christian Thaulow,
Professor, NTNU Norway

'Spirituality is often, mistakenly, associated with withdrawal from life and action. This book comes as a refreshing reminder to show us that not only can our daily work be a means for spiritual progress, but the very spiritual progress is our most effective means to excel in our field of work and live a deeply fulfilling life, contributing to the general progress of humanity. Devdas Menon has done a masterful rendering of the essential wisdom of the *Bhagavad Gita* for the new generation in a language that is simple, practical and rooted in his own spiritual and professional experience. It is a great joy to see that this book is coming from someone who is living the teachings of the Gita. This is an essential book for all aspirants who want to transform their daily life activities into a field of *Karmayoga*.'

– Manoj Pavitran,
Film Director, Auroville

'I have truly learned a great deal about myself after taking the *Integral Karmayoga* course at IIT Madras. A big shift in my attitude has also happened. Now, whenever my routine is disturbed or I am stuck in unhealthy habits, I am able to come out of that ignorance quickly. I am not easily let down by external challenges, and feel more focussed and efficient at work. I have also been able to quit unhealthy habits (such as addiction to social networking, net-surfing, pornography), and to nurture healthy ones (getting up early every morning, exercising, meditating). All this has brought more energy, enthusiasm and vitality in my life. I feel more peaceful and grounded after meditation.'

– Ganesh Bapat,
PhD research scholar, IIT Madras

'Life moves at an incredibly fast pace in today's highly competitive world, and we feel stressed and confused when we (especially women) have to manage both career and home. This book really helps one explore and understand one's own self, realise one's inner strength and find inspiration for meaningful and healthy living. The depiction and descriptions of the three *gunas* pinpoint with clarity as to exactly how we normally function in the lower nature, unconsciously. We realise clearly what needs to be done for us to drop dysfunctional habits and to evolve consciously. I find myself to be a much happier, contented and inspired person after the living experience of reading and re-reading this book.'

– Ambili Mechoor,
Biotechnology Research Head, Sahrdaya CET, Thrissur

'I highly recommend this book to get the most out of one's life. It is a "how to" book on realising Peace, Satisfaction and Happiness in Life. I understand that this book is a compilation of the notes the author uses in his class to teach students in their early twenties. I found it equally absorbing, thought-provoking and useful for my generation of retired folks in their seventies. This book indeed is a classic for people of all ages.'

– K. Ramachandran,
retired Researcher, Boeing and Bell System, USA and alumnus, IIT Madras

'This wonderful book makes it clear that the solutions to all our problems are to be found through the problems themselves. The choice to challenge our lower self and make progress has to be taken right now, not later. This book has made me become more resolute. My decision-making is now wiser and firmer. It has also made me more compassionate and kinder to my fellow beings. I may never "finish reading" this book. I have to go over it, again and again, till it helps me truly evolve and ascend into higher nature.'

– Vijay Kumar Nair,
Airside Operations Manager, Dubai Airports

'Devdas Menon is a world-class structural engineering professor. But his mission is much larger: to help awaken self-awareness and Self-realization in students, professionals, teachers and others. He does this with profound passion and selflessness. His earlier book, *Stop Sleep Walking Through Life!*, is bringing about transformation in many students and professionals, as they make choices during their life. His latest work, *Spirituality at Work*, based on the Gita, will help seekers with valuable guidance on many of the issues we face in what he calls a 'Living Battlefield' of life. His words and wisdom have positively impacted me and several of my colleagues at all levels at our R&D center in India, enhancing not only productivity at work but also fulfilment in personal life. The way he brings equanimity and peace into tough situations using the 'inner meaning' from the Gita quenches many boiling issues. Embracing the teachings from this book will help in transforming the corporate soldiers of our industry from a self-centered short-term results pursuit to a deeper fulfilment, by addressing the burning needs of the society, and meeting customer demands in a highly ethical, moral, meaningful and fulfilling way. I am personally grateful for his teachings and interventions during many challenging situations at work.'

– Anand Tanikella,
Managing Director, Saint Gobain Research India Pvt Ltd

Dedicated to

Sri Aurobindo

ॐ

वासुदेवः सर्वमिति

SPIRITUALITY AT WORK

The Inspiring Message of the Bhagavad Gita

Devdas Menon

YogiImpressions®

SPIRITUALTIY AT WORK
First published in India in 2016 by
Yogi Impressions LLP
1711, Centre 1, World Trade Centre,
Cuffe Parade, Mumbai 400 005, India.
Website: www.yogiimpressions.com

First Edition, June 2016
Seventh reprint, January 2024

ISBN 978-93-82742-52-4

Printed at: TACT Print

Contents

Foreword

In professional education today, we place, or misplace, emphasis on getting jobs and pay packages. We miss out on inner development, which is essential to find fulfilment and deal effectively with the demands and challenges of society around us. All around, we see a 'rat race' culture: desperation, selfishness, lack of concern for others, greed, corruption, frustration and despondency (including suicidal tendencies). We need a holistic development of the individual, with spirituality at the core. Unfortunately, this is not actively patronised or even discussed in our modern temples of learning, in sharp contrast to our more renowned ancient universities at Takshashila and Nalanda.

In an attempt to fill this vital gap in education, my esteemed colleague, Prof. Devdas Menon, author of this book (and also of *Stop sleepwalking through life!*) has introduced 'elective' courses titled *Self-awareness* and *Integral Karmayoga* at IIT Madras. These have turned out to be popular and transformative courses at our Institute, and some of us have had the good fortune of attending them. The teaching notes related to the timeless wisdom of the *Bhagavad Gita* have been carefully worked upon by the author to result in this seminal work, titled *Spirituality at Work*. This is a sacred offering of a truly learned person, who has experienced the nectar of the Gita and has chosen to share his insights and joy with those who seek a truly meaningful and fulfilling existence. He is also widely known as a teacher, researcher, consultant and author of popular textbooks in structural engineering.

This book, like the Gita, comprises eighteen chapters, each devoted to a particular theme, based on a careful selection of key verses from the Gita. Each chapter is replete with insights worthy of deep rumination, containing the essence of the Gita, made relevant to modern times. The analysis of human psychology and the presentation of ancient Indian wisdom is deep and awe-inspiring, particularly because it also includes actionable items of the *yoga* of the Gita for authentic transformation. Clearly, we are all in need of clear insight, self-awareness, inspiration and strong inner motivation to do the 'right thing', our *dharma*. The Gita's *yoga* shows a way to realise complete fulfilment through union with our Divine Source. This book advocates an integral approach, with *Karmayoga* as the fundamental basis, and with our actions supported by the wisdom of *Jnanayoga* and the devotion of *Bhaktiyoga*. It is pointed out that the best place to seek the Divine is in our innermost being, in the cave of our hearts. For it is there that we can truly find an inner delight and ease of being, as well as an inner radiance that can show us with certitude the 'right way' amidst all confusions.

We are urged to excel at work, to self-actualise and bring our inherent talents and potential to fruition, dedicating all our work to the Divine, and eventually transcending the ego-centred notion of 'doership'. We are urged to discover our true inner calling and life purpose, to achieve mastery and serve as instruments of the omniscient Divine. We will then find ourselves frequently in a 'flow' state of perfect action. This is referred to as our 'higher nature', and it is here that we can find enduring fulfilment and consummation of our life purpose.

But attaining to that state of perfection and union is not easy. We find ourselves pulled down, time and again, by various forces (inner and outer) beyond our control. These can be well understood in terms of the three *gunas* (qualities) of nature: *tamas* (inertia, ignorance), *rajas* (dynamism, restlessness) and *sattva* (lucidity, balance). The inter-play of these three *gunas*, and our total identification with a narrow separate ego-self keep us trapped in 'lower nature' (*Prakriti*). In order to see this play objectively (without getting affected) and to discover our hidden True Self (*Purusha, Atman*), we need to withdraw periodically into the stillness of deep meditation. We can then contact the divinity hidden in our innermost being, and remain free from the tumultuous world around and inside us. This is true freedom.

However, we are likely to lose that freedom when we re-engage with the world. There are cravings that spring up, and we find ourselves getting entrapped again in the *karmic* cycles of action and reaction. Through insight and practice, we begin to gain better control over ourselves. While acknowledging that there are authentic 'deficiency needs' in us that need to be satisfied ethically, we realise how easily 'need' can change into 'greed'. We also gain increasing understanding of how the three *gunas* operate, and we work towards increasing *sattva-guna* in our being, becoming more and more selfless in our actions and compassionate in our relationships.

Yet, there are limits to our efforts, because our capacities seem to be limited. We need help, and that help is always available to us in the form of *Divine grace*, which manifests mysteriously, especially when there is a strong aspiration and devotion (*bhakti*). In this regard, the Divine Teacher of the Gita gives a guarantee that regardless of the stage of spiritual evolution of the aspirant, as long as there is steadfast faith and diligence in the practice of *yoga*, the goal will be realised. As we progress along the path of *Integral Karmayoga*, we tend to place more and more reliance on the One Divine Source, and aided by Divine grace, are bound to ascend from our lower nature to the higher nature. This brings to us fulfilment and maximises our contribution to the well-being of the world.

May this book inspire you, dear reader, to discover fulfilment in life in all its dimensions: in *being*, in *doing*, in *knowing* and in *loving*!

– A. Meher Prasad,
Professor and Head, Department of Civil Engineering, IIT Madras

Acknowledgements

This book has come into being, thanks to the inspiration and support offered by many individuals, past and present.

I wish to first offer my obeisance to the teachers who revealed the Gita to me: Sri Aurobindo, Swami Krishnananda and Sri A.D. Pisharody. I also wish to express my love and gratitude to my first teachers: my dear parents, Madhavi and Achutha Menon. I thank my dear wife, Roshni, for her loving support and for constantly inspiring my own practice of the *yoga* of the Gita.

I am indebted to A.P. Nandini, Ananda Wood, Christian Thaulow, Manoj Pavitran, Arul Dev, V. Vijayalakshmi, Meher Prasad, Senthil Kumar, K.B.M. Nambudiripad, P.M. Gopalan, S. Achuthan Nair, M.P. Singhal, P. Gopinathan, Swati Bali, Bijily B., Anusha Chavva, K. Ramachandran, Shiv Sharma and Gautam Sachdeva for their helpful suggestions. I thank my dear sister, Girija, for her loving encouragement.

Thanks to all my dear students, colleagues and friends!

Finally, I offer my obeisance to the Divine Teacher of the Gita!

– Devdas Menon

Preface

Spirituality may not be a popular word in today's technological world. It is considered 'unscientific' and often viewed with suspicion and scepticism. Whether we are spiritually inclined or not, we all basically seem to want to be happy and successful, be inspired and find fulfilment in our lives. That indeed is the very objective of *Spirituality at Work*, properly understood and lived.

Sadly, the harsh reality is that we are rarely able to find and sustain such fulfilment at work and in our relationships. Stephen Covey summarises this human condition in modern times in his book, *The 8th Habit*, based on decades of research conducted worldwide: 'Despite all our gains in technology, product innovation and world markets, most people are not thriving in the organisations they work for. They are neither fulfilled nor excited. They are frustrated. They are not clear about where the organisation is headed or what its highest priorities are. They are bogged down and distracted. Most of all, they don't feel they can change much.'

Clearly, in order to live life whole-heartedly, and to enjoy what we do, we need to be motivated by some inner inspiration or meaningful purpose in life. Mostly, we are driven by short-term goals, but the motivation is *extrinsic*, and the promise of enduring fulfilment does not come to us. We need to have clarity on the very purpose of our lives, our *dharma*, on *who we are* and *why we are here*. We need *spirituality*.

Spirit is what keeps us *inspired* — a word that in fact is derived from spirit! We need daily inspiration to keep us motivated and to sustain our enthusiasm. We also need to develop the unique skills and potentials that lie latent in us, and put these into creative use for a higher purpose. We need to *individuate* and *self-actualise*, so that the unique potential given to each one of us is authentically realised — which means not just being part of the herd, or caught in some rat race. In the process of growing self-awareness, we will naturally discover the need of our higher nature to *unify* with the universe around us. This is the kind of spirituality explored in this book. Our inner transformation gets increasingly reflected in outer expressions of light, love, joy, beauty and creativity in all our work and our relationships.

The *Bhagavad Gita* is a resource that gives inspiring guidance to us on all the above issues. The *yoga* of the Gita reflects a profound spirituality, not only aiming at ego-transcendence and *unification* (called *Self-realisation*), but also authentic *individuation* and excellence in performance at work. The integrated practice of spirituality through work (*karma*), knowledge (*jnana*) and devotion (*bhakti*) — referred to as *Integral Karmayoga* in this book — is the way recommended in the Gita. The Gita does not support the view that spiritual salvation implies abdication of responsibilities in life or doing just the minimal work needed for sustenance, and that too half-heartedly, not seeing any higher purpose in creation. It is not renunciation of work and life that the Gita advocates, but the higher renunciation of ego-centred desire and attachment to the fruits of action. Unfortunately, this fundamental message of the Gita seems to have got lost in the very country of its origin! The message of *Integral Karmayoga* in the Gita is meant for immediate practice, while working and living in the world, and not something to be dabbled with, post-retirement!

Sri Aurobindo referred to the Bhagavad Gita as '*our chief national heritage, our hope for the future*'. Composed several thousand years ago, it has been recognised worldwide as a classic text and scripture, giving the gist of ancient Indian wisdom. However, it remains largely unknown to most Indians, and is not easily accessible in education, even in our leading institutions. It is with the objective of rediscovering the inspiring message of the Gita in a modern context that a 'free elective' course on *Integral Karmayoga* was introduced in the curriculum at IIT Madras in 2014. The focus is on finding fulfilment in life through the application of conscious will — through *Karmayoga* — in a way that is also integrated with knowledge and devotion. This book has emerged from the lecture notes prepared for this course, and its contents are based on a theme-wise selection of 162 verses spread across the Gita, which comprises 700 verses. The interpretation is primarily based on Sri Aurobindo's *Essays on the Gita* and his other writings. In each of the 162 selected Gita verses, the translation is preceded by the original Sanskrit verse (in *Devanagari* script). Corresponding to every line in the 'free verse' English translation, the relevant Sanskrit phrase is also shown in Devanagari.

For a deep and experiential understanding, the Gita needs to be studied and contemplated upon, again and again. Every time, it is likely to reveal a deeper understanding to the sincere aspirant, resulting in a growing inner wakefulness, calm, communion, integral knowledge, harmony, love and compassion, as well as a more purposeful and fulfilling engagement in the world. The spiritual journey cannot be said to be complete until we get to see and feel the One Divine Presence in everything and every being — always, everywhere.

In the spiritual journey, it is helpful to be able to maintain an earnest, humble and ever-learning beginner's mind. This journey is typically full of ups and downs, and often after making seemingly rapid progress initially, we tend to slow down, hit plateaus and sometimes even descend into delusion and cynicism. Spiritual knowledge of the academic or dogmatic kind sometimes proves to be a burden, closing us to fresh learning and giving us a foolish know-it-all arrogance. True knowing is not separate from being; it has to be experiential — as implied by the term, *Self-realisation*.

May we be inspired and initiated by the selected Gita verses in this book into a daily spiritual practice that is likely to unfold uniquely for each of us!

1

The Setting and Purpose of the Gita

धृतराष्ट्र उवाच ।
धर्मक्षेत्रे कुरुक्षेत्रे समवेता युयुत्सवः ।
मामकाः पाण्डवाश्चैव किमकुर्वत सञ्जय ।।1.1।।

Dhritarashtra said:	धृतराष्ट्रः उवाच
At Kurukshetra, the field of dharma,	धर्म क्षेत्रे कुरु क्षेत्रे
Where my folks and the Pandavas	मामकाः पाण्डवाः च एव
Have assembled, eager to fight,	समवेताः युयुत्सवः
What did they do, O Sanjaya?	किम् अकुर्वत सञ्जय

Thus begins the *Bhagavad Gita*.

It is indeed a most unusual setting for one of the most celebrated and timeless scriptures of India to begin! The setting is a battlefield at Kurukshetra, where a terrible and violent war is about to begin. The theme of *dharma* is invoked in the very first lines of the Gita, spoken by Dhritarashtra, the blind king in the great Indian epic, *Mahabharata*. Dhritarashtra is stationed within the confines of his palace, but he is constantly updated about the happenings at the distant battlefield, through his assistant, Sanjaya.

In the opening verse, Dhritarashtra refers to the conflict between his sons (whom he openly refers to as 'my folks') and the Pandavas, the five sons of his late brother and former king, Pandu. It is ironic that Dhritarashtra should talk about *dharma* (law of righteousness). Blinded by his affection for his sons (especially the eldest one, Duryodhana), he finds himself helpless in correcting their evil ways, having no control over their criminal nature. The Pandavas had to face a series of many acts of injustice, but it is the final act of driving them away from the kingdom (based on Duryodhana's insistence) that led to the war. It was to be a disastrous war, afflicting many kingdoms in North India. Thousands of inter-related family members and friends, along with their armies, had to choose sides between the Pandavas and the Kauravas and take part in this war.

The main protagonist in the Gita is Arjuna, one of the five Pandavas, recognised to be perhaps the greatest warrior of his time. At the battlefield of Kurukshetra, just before the battle is about to commence, he finds himself challenged, unexpectedly, by a terrible conflict in terms of his dharma. Unlike Dhritarashtra and Duryodhana, here is a heroic man, who strives to live according to the highest ideals of his age and culture. He sincerely wants to do the right thing, but is now bewildered and disturbed by the enormity of the destruction that this war is about to unleash on his own people — an ethical dilemma or *dharma sankatam*! He is so disturbed, that he is tempted to drop everything and quit the battlefield.

Fortunately, Arjuna is aware of his confusion and dejection, and intuitively knows that it would be wrong to make impulsive decisions in his confused state. He is wise enough to seek the advice of Krishna, who happens to be a cousin and mentor of the Pandavas, now serving as Arjuna's charioteer at the battlefield. However, unknown to most people of his time, Krishna was also a great *Avatar*, the Supreme Divine descended in human form.

The replies given by Krishna to Arjuna's many queries take the form of a spiritual discourse, in poetic verse. This constitutes the *Srimad Bhagavad Gita* (literally, the *Divine Song*). Spread over 700 verses, it contains the essential spiritual wisdom of the ancient *Upanishads* (synthesised with *Sankhya* philosophy), referred to as *brahma vidya*. Yet, the

Gita has much more to offer than theoretical knowledge leading to Self-realisation. It is also a manual of practice (*yoga shastra*) that demonstrates how spirituality can be, and should be, practised in our day-to-day lives.

Spirituality is something that is commonly associated with peace and non-violence: with temples, ashrams, monasteries, churches and mosques, and with serene landscapes. We feel uplifted in such sublime settings, which provide an ambience that feels significantly different from the hustle and bustle of our daily lives. Yet, we find it difficult to invoke that sublime peace in our habitual circumstances. Especially, when we find ourselves placed in challenging situations. So, for the majority of us, spirituality and living in the world seem to be rather mutually opposed. It is difficult, and sometimes impossible, to be *spiritual* in our day-to-day work and relationships. Even in those precious moments when we do get a glimpse of what it means to be spiritual, we find that we are not quite rightly engaging with the world! Paradoxically, we need to retreat from the world outside, physically and psychologically, especially from any kind of ugliness or violence, in order to contact the Spirit.

Indeed, traditionally, spirituality has been often associated with renunciation and asceticism, with abandoning this world, and thereby its ugliness and miseries in order to seek and hopefully find, the 'other' world of heavenly bliss. In the Gita itself, there is a clear acceptance of the harsh reality of living in this world, the very nature of which appears to be transient and unhappy, *anityam-asukham lokam* (verse 9.33). Yet, the Gita does not advocate outer renunciation. It points to a way of living spiritually in this world through day-to-day activities and relationships, and especially while facing critical moments in our lives.

Perhaps, for this very reason, the most unlikely of all places and occasions has been chosen for rendering this unique spiritual discourse. For, if spirituality can be practised in a living battlefield, with one's inner being remaining supremely at peace, in communion with the Divine, amidst the most difficult turmoils and violent happenings in our outer circumstances, then it certainly can be practised easily anywhere and at any time. It is this that makes the teachings of the Gita so significant and relevant for all of us. Although it dates back many thousand years ago, its appeal is universal, immediate and untiringly fresh.

Dharmakshetra and Kurukshetra

The term *dharma* refers to the basis or principle or law of being, which sustains and regulates the functioning of everything in this cosmos. The term *kuru*, which is closely linked to and derived from the same root as the term *karma*, refers to any work or action, including the underlying intent. Thus, *dharmakshetre kurukshetre* refers to a generic human setting, a *kshetra*, where we are all required to perform our respective *karma* appropriately — for sustaining ourselves and the universe in a right and harmonious manner, for *dharma*. For harmony and order to prevail in this evolving universe, all beings need to conduct themselves in accordance with dharma, which simply put, means doing the right thing. However, what is this *dharma*? This points to a fundamental question in life: *What indeed is the purpose of all existence, of creation? What is the purpose of our life, of my life?*

We shall see in the chapters to follow, how the theme of dharma is unravelled in the Gita, leading to a climax in the closing verses. Although Arjuna's concerns are primarily limited to his own dharma and are based on the anguish that he personally feels at this critical moment in his life, the very nature of his questions calls for a deeper and wider understanding, as brought out in the 700 verses of the Gita. Naturally, the questions and answers span over a wide spectrum of topics, covering spirituality, philosophy, psychology and work ethics.

Indeed, in line with all other scriptures all over the world, the Gita does urge us to purify ourselves of all evil and to be good and to do good. It does uphold, for example, non-injuring and non-killing — *ahimsa* — to be of extreme importance in spiritual conduct. It also upholds ascetic renunciation as a valid way of spiritual salvation, for those who are so inclined. Equally, it upholds the social dharma of all individuals living in the world. In the case of Arjuna-like *Kshatriya* warriors, this dharma would be to fight for the protection of the good and destruction of evil, whenever this is required — something that Arjuna himself was well aware of, and extremely skilled at.

However, all actions have consequences, and hence it is important that our karma be aligned to our dharma. When we act in violation of dharma and enagage in *adharma*, we tend to generate chaos and disorder, within us and outside us. The misalignment between our karma and dharma occurs typically when we are driven by our selfishness and self-interest, by lust and greed, to transgress on the rights and well-being of others (including the environment), and when we fail to carry out our responsibilities and obligations. Often we do this, even when we know that this is adharma — out of a sense of helplessness, driven by habits, impulses or cravings over which we seem to have little control. The personal cravings are characteristically driven by self-centred feelings of 'I' and 'mine'.

Each one of us is made up of many parts of being (physical, vital and mental), which often pull us in different directions. There is a need for proper governance, for kingship, and ideally this should come from an awakened intelligence in us. Unfortunately, very often, we are confused with regard to our dharma, and even when doing the right thing stares at us clearly in the face, like Dhritarashtra, we succumb to the pulls of our lower nature, over which we have little or no control. In the absence of integrity and self-mastery, knowledge and will are not aligned with each other, and the will may execute a wrong action that can have disastrous consequences. Thus for example, various forms of corruption — such as giving and taking bribes, for even small matters such as getting a driving licence — are rampant in countries like India, because we succumb to the temptation of easy, quick and sure returns without having to put in the required effort or having to wait, despite knowing that this is wrong. When we tend to feel some prick of conscience about our wrong-doing, the same intellect is now put to use in self-defence and rationalisation of that action.

'As you sow, so shall you reap' is a famous Biblical saying. In the same vein, according to traditional Indian wisdom, every karma is bound to generate a reaction. This is believed to manifest as a *karmic force*, which influences the future of not only the *doer* (*karta*), who will reap or suffer the consequences, but also the collective future of others, as well as the environment. Thus, we create our own destiny, individually and collectively! This is depicted throughout the *Mahabharata* story — how the collective destiny of countless people is affected by the actions and decisions made by a few individuals.

Conflicts in our dharma can arise in various ways. Typically, this happens when we feel obliged to do two different things, or cater to the needs of two different persons at the same time, but have to forego one of them. This may cause us and others considerable distress. The conflict takes the shape of an ethical dilemma when we are troubled by a realisation that the action we are about to take up is a violation of some value or ideal that we hold dear. This realisation may even come upon us suddenly, as with Arjuna at Kurukshetra, despite the fact that he was an accomplished warrior who had successfully fought many wars.

Let us consider situations we can relate to in modern times. What happens when we come to realise that the products we manufacture or sell have some seriously damaging effects or clearly violate ethical norms? What happens to a criminal lawyer, if he were to awaken to a sense of guilt in having to resort to lies in the courtroom, just to acquit his client (whom he knows to be guilty), or worse, to convict someone innocent? More commonly, we feel this dilemma when we end up paying a bribe, either directly or indirectly, to get some work done.

We encounter such conflicts in issues involving technological and economical development versus destruction of environment and ecology and displacement of human habitat — for example, in the construction of a large dam, or in mining of minerals in tribal and forested areas, or in real estate development involving conversion of agricultural land to profitable construction. All such 'developments' are generally carried out based on the argument that this is for the 'greater good', even if it implies loss or sacrifice by a few. Frequently, such arguments are specious, covering up several inconvenient truths — such as environmental and social costs, the narrow and greedy interests of a few individuals or corporations, and the pressures that are inevitably brought upon the political ruling class who are funded by such groups.

Thus a wide range of *dharmic* conflicts are possible at various levels — global, national, regional, communal, at the workplace, within the family, within the individual. An example of a dharmic conflict within an individual occurs with respect to time management. Students typically know that they should be spending more time at studies and self-development, but these priorities give way to lazy ways, to fooling around, watching films, gossiping, excessive playing, etc. — and even worse, they end up cheating, and copying assignments, submitted at the last minute. The conflict, in such cases, is invariably between the pull of some practical necessity, calling for appropriate outer action, and the inner resistance or recoil we feel on account of some ethical sense in us, which perceives inappropriateness or a sense of sin or wrong-doing in the *means* adopted. The ends do not always justify the means! At the same time, if no action is taken or the action taken is inadequate, the ends may not get achieved, and if they have wider social or global implications, the consequences arising from our inaction could well be disastrous!

How does one resolve this issue of dharma satisfactorily — in such a way that we are left with no doubt that we are indeed doing the right thing? There is no easy solution, as Arjuna indeed discovers. However, he is fortunate to have the guidance of Krishna, whom he later discovers beyond doubt to be the embodiment of the Supreme Divine, called *Purushottama* in the Gita. The Gita points out that there is such a Divine guide ever accessible to us — not outside, but in our innermost being, as the *Antaryami*, who dwells in the very hearts of all beings: *ishvarah sarvabhutanam hriddeshe tishthati* (verse 18.61). It is this portion of the Supreme Divine, hidden in the depths of our soul, that can not only give us all the knowledge, love and happiness we seek, but can also divinise our lives and actions, so that we live in fulfilment — in being, in knowing, in doing and in loving.

Thus, those of us who have deeply realised the import of the Gita, know that this is not just some spiritual discourse given in the remote past to some historical (or perhaps mythical) character called Arjuna. It is a direct message intended for you and me, from the Supreme Divine, showing us how we can live life in fulfilment, moment-to-moment. Indeed, you and I are the Arjuna of the Gita, and Krishna resides in our soul.

The battlefield setting of the Gita is symbolic of the challenges that life presents to all of us through conflicts. In every instance, we are required to make a choice and to act decisively. What is represented here as a battle between the righteous Pandavas and the evil Kauravas is often interpreted as being symbolic of the eternal conflict between the so-called forces of good and evil. However, that would be a simplistic reading of the true import of the Gita, whose verses ring with a deeper meaning.

The Hidden Purpose of any Conflict

The Gita suggests that every situation in life, especially moments of apparent crisis, are in fact invitations to us to rise from our lower nature into our higher Divine nature. They are to be perceived, not as threats, but as God-given opportunities, for us to make an evolutionary leap in our consciousness — something that we are actually capable of doing, but generally keep evading and postponing. What is needed is an integral transformation, of all the different parts of our being. Sometimes we feel inspired by one of these parts (perhaps our conscience or intellect), to take the initiative to make the change. It is then that we find there are other parts of our being (governed by the ego-self), which refuse to budge. They then seem to behave like the Kauravas led by Duryodhana, who declared that he will not yield even the space of a needle-tip to the Pandavas. Thus the external wars depicted in the Mahabharata story mirror the relentless battles that go on in our inner being. This is the deeper meaning that we will do well to discern.

Who wins in these battles raging within us? Do we seize the opportunities for inner transformation and fight valiantly to emerge victorious, periodically making the breakthroughs we are meant to in the evolutionary journey of life? Or do we give up early, without even putting up a fight (as Arjuna was tempted to at Kurukshetra), fearful of a breakdown or confused about how to deal with the forces within and around us, thereby remaining untransformed? We then miss the Divine purpose and the 'big picture' (the relationship between the part and the whole) hidden in any conflict. Sri Aurobindo explains: 'All kinds of conflicting qualities, powers, values meet together and run into each other to make up our action, life, nature. We can only understand entirely if we get to some sense of the Absolute and yet look at its workings in all the relativities which are being manifested... For behind all relativities there is this Absolute which gives them their being and their justification.'[1.1]

Abdul Kalam, the illustrious former President of India, and a source of tremendous inspiration to our youth, had this to say about difficulties in life: 'Difficulties in your life do not come to destroy you, but to help you realise your hidden potential and power.' He also linked this potentiality to overcome challenges to a Divine fire in us: 'We are all born with a Divine fire in us. Our efforts should be to give wings to this fire and fill the world with the glow of its goodness.'[1.2]

Science and Spirituality, Evolution and Education

It is important to recognise that in traditional India, there was truly no conflict between science and spirituality. There was an implicit understanding and reverential acceptance of Spirit as being the basis of all existence — from which emerged Mind, Life-energy and Matter, as differently graded forms of consciousness, ranging from the subtle to the gross. While the gross includes the subtle, the gross remains inferior to the subtle in terms of grade of consciousness, and so cannot 'grasp' it.

Indeed, human reason and intellect provide us reliable and indispensable means to comprehend the material world, and even the biological world. The psychological world is perhaps less amenable to us, and clearly, the spiritual realm is well beyond the scope of science. Peering through even the most sophisticated microscopes and telescopes is not likely to detect pure Spirit, which transcends our sensory perception. Scientific discoveries using such sophisticated instruments (which are but extensions of our senses) and powerful mathematical logic can evoke a profound sense of wonder in the scientist — a sense that has a mystical quality that could be termed spiritual. Carl Sagan, astrophysicist and strong advocate of critical scientific enquiry, had this to say in this regard, 'Science is not only compatible with spirituality; it is a profound source of spirituality. When we recognise our place in an immensity of light-years and in the passage of ages, when we grasp the intricacy, beauty, and subtlety of life, then that soaring feeling, that sense of elation and humility combined, is surely spiritual.'[1.3]

What many scientists like him are strongly averse to is 'pseudoscience', religious dogma and superstition, including the popular notion of an anthropomorphic God (out there in the sky) behaving like a feudal lord. Yet, to condemn the varied religious belief systems of all humanity spread over diverse cultures across millennia as something naive and stupid, simply because they do not conform to one's reason and the tests of the modern 'scientific method' (which is no more than 400 years old), is perhaps akin to throwing out the baby with the bathwater.

We need to acknowledge that our ancestors may not have been as stupid as we may deem them to be. We are dealing here with a supreme mystery, and so will do well to remain open even to views that presently may not conform to our rational beliefs. What we often tend to dismiss as nonsense merely points to domains that lie beyond our current sense. What we consider to be irrational could well be something trans-rational. Indeed, this is the approach adopted in the highest spiritual pursuits, where everything is acknowledged to be a supremely mysterious Divine manifestation. This is the concept of *Brahman* in the ancient Indian wisdom teachings. There are indeed levels of ignorance (*avidya*) in our limited understanding, but there is a core goodness, sacredness, peace and joy underlying it all — something that countless mystics worldwide have testified.

In primordial times, when primitive man lived in awe of nature, ever-fearing imminent threats against survival, there arose naturally the tendency to worship various powers in nature, primarily out of fear. The purpose of such worship was essentially to appease these powers — to prevent destruction, to ensure survival and to gain prosperity. To this day, such fear-based worship, is widely prevalent across the world — whether it be of many gods in pantheism or of the 'one and only true God' in monotheistic religions.

With human evolution and gain in scientific knowledge, our fears of physical survival have reduced considerably. Our fear of nature has been replaced by an arrogance. We now feel rather confident of controlling and harnessing nature's powers to our material advantage. Here, sadly, an uncontrolled arrogance has led to mindless exploitation of natural resources. Paradoxically, the same science that has enabled more comfortable lifestyles compared to previous generations has also unleashed environmental disasters. We are now rapidly running out of conventional energy resources to sustain our unsustainable lifestyles. We have polluted our planet to such an irretrievable degree that what the future has in store is something even scientists are unable to predict. This, of course, is no fault of science. It is clear that our progress in external development has not been matched by similar progress inwardly. We have missed out on a deeper spiritual realisation of how we are connected integrally with the rest of nature.

To make matters worse, we live in an era where developments in science and technology provide access to weapons of mass destruction, and it is increasingly difficult to ensure that these weapons do not reach evil forces who will not hesitate to use them indiscriminately. As the integral philosopher Ken Wilber puts it, 'You can only inflict so much damage on the biosphere, and on other human beings, with a bow and arrow. But with the emergence of modernity and its sweeping scientific capacities... global catastrophes, for the first time in history, became possible and even likely. From atomic holocaust to ecological suicide, humanity began facing on a massive scale its single most fundamental problem: lack of integral development.'[1.4]

Our root problem is the one recognised in ancient Indian wisdom — it is ignorance, *avidya*. Modern education, research and science have not succeeded in addressing this. The pioneering scientist, Albert Einstein, put it succinctly, 'A human being is a part of the whole, called by us 'Universe': a part limited in time and space. He experiences himself, his thoughts and feelings, as something separated from the rest – a kind of optical delusion of his consciousness. This delusion is a kind of prison for us, restricting us to our personal desires and affection for a few persons nearest us. Our task must be to free ourselves from this prison…'[1.5] We need to break the mind-made walls of this prison that separates us from not only the rest of humanity, but the entire Universe, which is the dwelling place of the One Divine. When we attain this realisation, we make the all-important shift from fear to love. For indeed, love is the healing of separation.

Einstein went on to suggest, very insightfully, that we need solutions from a higher level of consciousness to resolve problems that we have created at our current level. The Gita certainly provides us that access to higher consciousness. In it, we see a compassionate understanding of the world situation across the ages, embracing all things, people, cultures and ideologies in a loving Divine understanding. Most important, we see that there is an evolution in consciousness. We are presently living in times where we have people at different stages of evolution in different parts of the world, living simultaneously along with other sentient beings, sharing one common Divine space.

While we may have progressed significantly from primordial times with regard to our understanding of nature, thereby losing much of our fear of survival, we have remained enmeshed in the ego-centred entrapment of nature (*Prakriti*). Fear of physical survival has been replaced by fear of ego-survival. The aim of the Gita is precisely to bridge the gulf between the separate ego-centred self and the One Divine Source of all existence, between man and God. This union with the Divine Oneness is the deeper meaning implied by the term *yoga*. It is also used to refer to any practice or discipline (*yoga-abhyasa*) that leads to this union. The Gita advocates an integration of three such disciplines — related to work (*Karma-yoga*), knowledge (*Jnana-yoga*) and devotion (*Bhakti-yoga*) — involving a combination of physical, psychological and spiritual practices (*sadhana*) to achieve this. We need to turn inwards, and realise our true Divine Self, and thereby see its Divine presence everywhere around us.

Clearly, the subjective world presently lies beyond the domain of objective science. Yet, it is precisely in that subjective inner world that we find our happiness and meaning in existence. It is also in that realm that we find ourselves caught up in conflict and disharmony, individually and collectively. If we are to know and understand reality, we must remain open to discovering truths and relationships in the realms of both the subjective and the objective, the individual and the collective. We need both science and spirituality, for they are complementary quests for knowledge.

The current approach of science is to perceive matter as the fundamental reality. The manifestation of life on earth and biological evolution are seen as extensions of chemical evolution in matter, occurring by chance and 'natural selection'. Evolution, according to traditional Indian wisdom, is essentially a progressive development of consciousness. In the evolving human being, it manifests through increasing self-awareness, individuation and unification with the One Divine Source from which everything has emerged. Man is still bound by entrapment to the ignorance of a lower nature, and it is through an evolution in consciousness that he can rise to his rightful higher Divine nature. This fundamental spiritual urge is reflected in a traditional Indian prayer:

ॐ असतो मा सद्गमय । तमसो मा ज्योतिर्गमय ।
मृत्योर्मा अमृतं गमय ।

Lead us from the unreal (asat) to the real (sat)!
Lead us from darkness (tamas) to light (jyoti)!
Lead us from death (mrityu) to immortal bliss (amritam)!

The very purpose of the Gita is to empower us with the basic recognition of our status and direction. Where are we presently stationed in this spectrum of consciousness? Are we ascending towards true reality, enlightenment and fulfilment (*sat*, *jyoti*, *amritam*)? Or are we stagnating, or worse, descending (perhaps unconsciously and inadvertently), towards *asat*, *tamas* and *mrityu*? The *Katha Upanishad* offers another insightful way of looking at this spiritual journey — in terms of the paths of *shreyas* (truly good) and *preyas* (the ephemeral pleasant). The former is the ascending path taken by the *dhira* (heroic wise man), while the latter is followed by the *manda* (the unwise).

Both 'shreyas' and 'preyas' present themselves before man.
The 'dhira' carefully discriminates
And then chooses shreyas over preyas.
The 'manda' chooses preyas, seeking only material well-being.
– Katha Upanishad

This Upanishadic message, supposedly conveyed by Lord Yama to the young truth-seeker, Nachiketa, according to ancient fable, points to a great truth: one that is universal and timeless, and indeed very relevant in education. Are we preparing our youth — at least, the best among them — to take to the heroic wise path of the *dhira*, the fulfilling path of *shreyas*? The evidence, unfortunately, does not point in this direction. The vast majority of our educated population are clearly on the *manda's* path of *preyas* — with a self-centred focus almost entirely, and endlessly, on satisfying the basic deficiency needs. Regardless of the noble visions and missions proclaimed with regard to education, in practice, a student takes up formal education mainly to get a degree certificate, in order to gain a livelihood, and thereby, amass wealth, enjoy the pleasures of materialistic living, and gain status and power — often at any cost. Cynical as it may sound, there is truth in Theodore Roosevelt's famous remark, 'A man who has never gone to school may steal from a freight car; but if he has a university education, he may steal the whole railroad.' The wisdom of *shreyas*, of developing discrimination between need and greed, and thereby discovering higher needs, of living authentically and purposefully — for fulfilment and well-being of all — appears to be missing in education, as practised worldwide today.

The root cause for this may be attributed to the fact that the noble goals of *shreyas* seem to be in the long term, and appear to be distant. In contrast, the short-term goals of *preyas*, promising immediate sense-gratification, turn out to be far more appealing. It takes wisdom to realise that although all our actions (*karma*) are required to be done in the present, they have long-term consequences, which affect our future — individual and collective. Life is not a short-term sprint; it is more akin to a long-distance marathon! The challenge before us is to live in such a healthy and perfect way, as to ensure not only a fulfilling future for all, but also to enjoy living fully in the present. The Gita clearly and unambiguously points to the road to *shreyas*, and also the dangers of taking the alternative, though the far more popular, road to *preyas*. It is a journey, that calls for a long preparation, involving development and purification of all parts of our being — which is indeed the very purpose of education. It is a challenging journey that takes the shape of a joyful adventure, as one travels, guided by the light within.

Unlike other journeys, the spiritual journey is unique for each one of us, the path and the goal being equally important (as symbolised by the word *gati* used in the Gita). One realises, sooner or later, that the Divine is the *gati*, unfolding uniquely, mysteriously and delightfully for each one of us. Indeed, texts like the Gita serve as very useful roadmaps in this journey — but, as described in the Gita itself, the true

Divine guide abides within our deepest core, and it is this that we need to awaken to and realise. All knowledge serves to be useless, unless made experiential. Fulfilment lies in realisation, and not in theory.

Aspiration and Faith, *Shraddha*

Aspiration and faith have a key role to play in the integral practice of the *yoga* of the Gita that we call *Integral Karmayoga* in this book. For success in this journey, the aspirant needs to aim high and have absolute faith and dedication, called *shraddha*. As one progresses and gains insights and undergoes inner transformation, the *shraddha* gets reinforced naturally.

It is good to raise questions, as Arjuna does, and seek answers to clarify one's doubts, but we must realise the limitations of our own rational minds, especially when we seek deeper insights. The Indian wisdom tradition refers to *dharmas* (universal laws of being), associated with the physical, vital and mental realms. Among these, the laws of the *hard sciences* (such as the law of gravity in physics) are easier for us to establish, compared to the laws relating to how our minds function. In order to understand these fully, and even to glimpse the one over-arching *Dharma*, subservient to which all these *dharmas* operate, one needs to invoke intuitive levels of understanding that transcend the reasoning intellect. There is no room for any doubt or scepticism with regard to the reality of Spirit here. Sri Aurobindo points out, '...in the lower knowledge, doubt and scepticism have their temporary uses; in the higher they are stumbling-blocks: for there the whole secret is not the balancing of truth and error, but a constantly progressing realisation of revealed truth.'[1.6]

He goes on to add insightfully, 'Whatever incompleteness there is in the knowledge attained, it must be got rid of, not by questioning in its roots what has already been realised, but by proceeding to further and more complete realisation through a deeper, higher and wider living in the Spirit. What is not yet realised must be prepared for by faith, not by sceptical questioning... it is not a truth which has to be proved, but a truth which has to be lived inwardly, a greater reality into which we have to grow.'[1.6]

अज्ञश्चाश्रद्दधानश्च संशयात्मा विनश्यति ।
नायं लोकोऽस्ति न परः न सुखं संशयात्मनः ||4.40||

One who is ignorant and faithless,	अज्ञः च अश्रद्दधानः च
Always doubting, not trusting, is lost.	संशय आत्मा विनश्यति
No stability in this world or beyond,	न अयं लोकः न परः
Nor joy is there for the doubting soul.	न सुखं संशय आत्मनः अस्ति

In the absence of such aspiration and faith, the teachings of the Gita would not serve much purpose. In one of the concluding verses, the Divine Teacher of the Gita Himself gives some sound advice on this.

इदं ते नातपस्काय नाभक्ताय कदाचन ।
न चाशुश्रूषवे वाच्यं न च मां योऽभ्यसूयति ||18.67||

Never is this to be taught by you to one	इदं ते न वाच्यं कदाचन
Who is lacking in austerity and devotion,	न अतपस्काय न अभक्ताय
Or does not wish to listen,	न अशुश्रूषवे
Or who speaks ill of Me.	न च मां यः अभ्यसूयति

Thus, we observe that the teachings of the Gita are certainly not meant to be imposed on anyone. They are not to be wasted on those who are not yet ready or who lack the required aspiration and faith, *shraddha*. Those who are likely to benefit enormously, experiencing a profound transformation in their lives, are those who feel a strong inner calling for learning and living these teachings.

This book is intended to serve such individuals.

2

Arjuna's Dejection

कृपया परयाविष्टः विषीदन्निदमब्रवीत् ।
दृष्ट्वेमं स्वजनं कृष्ण युयुत्सुं समुपस्थितम् ||1.28||

Overwhelmed by pity, dejected,	कृपया परयाविष्टः विषीदन्
He (Arjuna) spoke thus: O Krishna!	इदम् अब्रवीत् कृष्ण
I see but my own kith and kin,	दृष्ट्वा इमं स्वजनं
Assembled here, eager to battle!	युयुत्सुं समुपस्थितम्

We need to understand the immediate background of Arjuna's dejection. At the Kurukshetra battlefield, the warriors have all blown their conches, thus showing their readiness for the battle to commence. It is at this juncture that the Bhagavad Gita dialogue between Arjuna and Krishna is about to start.

Arjuna tells Krishna — who plays the role of the charioteer — to take the chariot to the front lines, from where Arjuna can survey the enemy formation and plan his moves. Krishna drives the chariot to a position between the two armies, directly in front of the two senior-most warriors, his great grand-father, Bhishma, and his teacher, Drona. Seeing these two beloved and revered elders, Arjuna is quite unnerved. It is to the invincible grand old warrior Bhishma that he owes his inherited nobility, and it is under the tutelage of the great teacher Drona that his warrior skills have been nurtured and perfected. He is thus dazed by the grave implications of engaging in battle with such beloved family elders and respected kith and kin, whom he must now strive with his utmost capability to defeat and destroy.

He then looks around to see that all the warriors are related to him in some way or the other, or are his associates and friends. The horror of this war creeps into him, as he foresees that the inevitable outcome will be death and destruction on a massive scale — a case of close relatives and friends killing one another!

Arjuna is stunned by this realisation, and he gives expression to his feelings of despair. The wickedness of his cousins (which led to the war) has now receded into the background, and moved by his feelings, he is inclined to see them more compassionately. He is dejected (*vishidan*) to see his own role as the chief instrument of a likely holocaust.

Sensational, Emotional, Mental and Moral Recoil

सीदन्ति मम गात्राणि मुखं च परिशुष्यति ।
वेपथुश्च शरीरे मे रोमहर्षश्च जायते ||1.29||

My legs are giving way,	सीदन्ति मम गात्राणि
My mouth is going dry,	मुखं च परिशुष्यति
My body is trembling,	वेपथुः च शरीरे मे
My hairs are bristling!	रोमहर्षः च जायते

Arjuna describes the effects of his feelings as reflected in his body: a description that reveals significant self-awareness! Being a skilled and accomplished warrior, these are unusual sensations that he encounters — and that too at a most awkward moment, just before the battle! A clear sense of physical recoil is revealed to him through his sensations.

गाण्डीवं स्रंसते हस्तात् त्वक्चैव परिदह्यते ।
न च शक्नोम्यवस्थातुं भ्रमतीव च मे मनः ||1.30||

Gandiva slips my grip,*	गाण्डीवं स्रंसते हस्तात्
My skin is burning.	त्वक् च एव परिदह्यते
I cannot stand firm,	न च शक्नोमि अवस्थातुं
My mind is reeling!	भ्रमति इव च मे मनः

* Arjuna's special bow

These physical reactions next trigger a sequence of emotional and mental responses, all signifying and enhancing the feeling of recoil. He, who earlier had no issues with enjoying the pleasures of kingship, suddenly finds these repulsive! His outpouring reveals a loss of attraction for all worldly pursuits and pleasures. Sri Aurobindo refers to this as a recoil of the vital being.

अहो बत महत्पापं कर्तुं व्यवसिता वयम् ।
यद्राज्यसुखलोभेन हन्तुं स्वजनमुद्यताः ||1.45||

Alas! Great is the evil crime	अहो बत महत् पापं
We have resolved to commit,	कर्तुं व्यवसिताः वयम्
Intent on killing our own kinsmen,	हन्तुं स्वजनम् उद्यताः
To enjoy the pleasures of kingship!	यत् राज्य सुख लोभेन

Arjuna is so overwhelmed by his state of dejection that he continues to support the claims of his vital being, visualising all kinds of horrors. He now sees the gains from the war as blood-stained pleasures. With his heart and mind losing their balance, he even makes a virtue of living the life of a beggar.

In this dejected state, he goes on to say many things to Krishna, reflecting a sense of mental and moral recoil.

गुरूनहत्वा हि महानुभावान् श्रेयो भोक्तुं भैक्ष्यमपीह लोके ।
हत्वार्थकामांस्तु गुरूनिहैव भुञ्जीय भोगान् रुधिरप्रदिग्धान् ।।2.5।।

Instead of killing our noble gurus,	गुरून् अहत्वा हि महानुभावान्
It is better to live here as beggars.	श्रेयः भोक्तुं भैक्ष्यम् अपि इह लोके
Else, we will be killing our elders	हत्वा तु गुरून् इह एव
For the sake of our enjoyments,	भुञ्जीय भोगान्
Wealth and pleasures,	अर्थ कामान्
Stained by their blood.	रुधिर प्रदिग्धान्

The last few verses of the Gita's first chapter (continuing into the next chapter) sound like a discourse on morality. Arjuna lectures on how the evil crime that they are about to commit will lead to the destruction of family values and corruption of all kinds, leading to chaos and disorder in society in times to come. He grieves for a meaningless and desolate existence, and he predicts doom for all. Arjuna ends his outpouring, laying down his weapons and slumping into the chariot seat, unarmed and ready to be killed, somewhat like a martyr.

Arise, *Uttishtha!*

Krishna, who has been quietly observing Arjuna's reactions, tries to provoke him with a strong reprimand, and with a clear message that is directed to us all. It is noteworthy that from the very beginning, whenever Krishna speaks, he is referred to in the Gita as *Sribhagavan* or the *Blessed Lord*, in recognition of his status as the *Divine Avatar*. However, this Divine identity of Krishna was not known to people of his time, even to the Pandavas, who mostly saw him as their close friend and well-wisher, a wise leader and a brave warrior, who had accomplished many miraculous deeds, even as a child. Indeed, even in his role in the Gita as the Divine Teacher, he does not depict the gentle saintliness and advocacy of peace and goodness that some would normally expect from a Divine personality. Here he reminds Arjuna of his role as a warrior, and conveys that his dejected outpouring is most unbecoming of the brave and heroic *Aryan* warrior that Arjuna is known to be.

श्रीभगवानुवाच ।
कुतस्त्वा कश्मलमिदं विषमे समुपस्थितम् ।
अनार्यजुष्टमस्वर्ग्यम् अकीर्तिकरमर्जुन ||2.2||

The Blessed Lord said:	श्रीभगवान् उवाच
How come this weakness arises	कुतः कश्मलम् इदं समुपस्थितम्
In you, at this critical moment?	त्वा विषमे
This is ignoble and disgraceful,	अनार्य जुष्टम् अकीर्ति करम्
Not leading to heaven, Arjuna!	अस्वर्ग्यम् अर्जुन

क्लैब्यं मा स्म गमः पार्थ नैतत्त्वय्युपपद्यते ।
क्षुद्रं हृदयदौर्बल्यं त्यक्त्वोत्तिष्ठ परन्तप ||2.3||

Arjuna, yield not to such impotence,	क्लैब्यं मा स्म गमः पार्थ
Unbecoming of a warrior like you!	न एतत् त्वयि उपपद्यते
Give up this petty faint-heartedness,	क्षुद्रं हृदयदौर्बल्यं त्यक्त्वा
And stand up, O Scorcher of foes!	उत्तिष्ठ परन्तप

Stand up! (*uttishtha*) is the simple and powerful message that the Divine Teacher tries to convey. It is a strong message conveyed to us all, when we find ourselves overwhelmed by dejection and inadequacy. Here, it takes a special meaning, because it is directed at Arjuna's *Kshatriya* nature, which is akin to that of the Samurai warrior. For a righteous cause, the brave warrior does not hesitate or give way to this kind of petty faint-heartedness (*hridaya-daurbalyam*), which arises from a sense of weakness and self-pity, rather than genuine compassion. The courageous and compassionate warrior stands steadfastly supported by what is always right and true.

'Arise, awaken and stop not till the goal is reached!' is a message made popular by Swami Vivekananda that we need to invoke when we tend to get depressed and underestimate our own capabilities, besides getting confused about our dharma. In the following verse, the Divine Teacher reminds us that we need to lift ourselves up on our own. There is a True Self, the *Atman*, hidden in our innermost being — our true friend, that we need to awaken to and be inspired by. Yet, just as our true friend resides within us as our inner guru, so does an enemy lurk within us, in the form of our false ego-self (*ahankara*), living in fear and ignorance!

उद्धरेदात्मनात्मानं नात्मानमवसादयेत् ।
आत्मैव ह्यात्मनो बन्धुः आत्मैव रिपुरात्मनः ||6.5||

One should lift oneself up by one's Self,	उद्धरेत् आत्मना आत्मानं
And one should not degrade oneself,	न आत्मानम् अवसादयेत्
For the Self alone is one's true friend,	आत्मा एव हि आत्मनः बन्धुः
While the ego-self alone is one's foe!	आत्मा एव रिपुः आत्मनः

How do we recognise whether the inner voice that speaks to us comes from our friend or from our enemy? This is indeed our real challenge in inner transformation, helping us develop true discrimination. To be able to do this, in the first place, we need to be able to listen to both the voices! Unfortunately, the intuitive voice coming from our innermost being is very quiet, emerging from a peaceful silence, and it can get easily drowned by the loud cacophony of the agitated ego-self from the outer layers of our being.

The Gita describes all the movements in the lower nature, including those of the ego-self (*ahankara*), in terms of a combination of three qualities, called *gunas*. They are: *tamas* (ignorance, inertia, laziness, coarseness), *rajas* (lust-driven dynamism, excitation, struggle, restlessness) and *sattva* (harmony, illumination, lightness, equipoise, balance). Thus, the ego-self can assert itself typically in different ways: *tamasic*, *rajasic* or *sattvic*, or in some combination. Arjuna's trembling, confusion and ranting are clearly not reflective of his *sattvic ahankara*, although he is inclined to believe so in his confusion.

Sri Aurobindo comments insightfully on Arjuna's disposition: 'He advances to this gigantic struggle, to this Kurukshetra with the full acceptance of the joy of battle, as to 'a holiday of fight', but with a proud confidence in the righteousness of his cause... When this confidence is shattered within him, when he is smitten down from his customary attitude and mental basis of life, it is by the uprush of the tamasic quality into the rajasic man, inducing a recoil of astonishment, grief, horror, dismay, dejection, bewilderment of the mind and the war of reason against itself, a collapse towards the principle of ignorance and inertia. As a result he turns towards renunciation.'[2.1]

His decision to take the path of inaction in order to escape from his ethical dilemma and confusion, clearly points to a preponderance of *tamas*. Indeed, in some circumstances, it may well be that inaction is the wisest course of action. The decision to act or not to act must ideally emerge from our innermost being, our True Self. To use the language of the Gita, our intellect (*buddhi*) must be *yoked* (*buddhi-yukta*) to our True Self. Its command, issuing forth as *will*, must resonate in all the parts of our being (*physical*, *vital* and *mental*), which then act integrally and purposefully. On the contrary, if the physical being trembles, unable even to stand up, and the vital being finds itself drained of energy and the will to fight, with the heart rendered emotionally weak, and the mental being is subject to confusion and delusion (justifying and aggravating the paralysis), the situation is far removed from the *buddhi-yukta* condition. In such circumstances, it is also likely that the individual will invoke all possible arguments to justify his/her stance. It is not easy to get out of such a state of being, and the need for self-justification keeps asserting itself, as reflected in Arjuna's continued outpouring.

Arjuna Seeks Guidance

कार्पण्यदोषोपहतस्वभावः पृच्छामि त्वां धर्मसम्मूढचेताः |
यच्छ्रेयः स्यान्निश्चितं ब्रूहि तन्मे शिष्यस्तेऽहं शाधि मां त्वां प्रपन्नम्
||2.7||

Sentimental weakness has afflicted	कार्पण्य दोष उपहत
My warrior nature and confused me.	स्वभावः धर्म सम्मूढ चेताः
I ask you: what is my true dharma?	पृच्छामि त्वां
To fight or not, which is surely better?	यत् श्रेयः स्यात्
I pray to you to guide me decisively.	निश्चितं ब्रूहि तत् मे
I take refuge in You as your disciple!	शिष्यः ते अहं त्वां प्रपन्नम्

Even while being overwhelmed by *vishada*, Arjuna intuitively knows that he is in a confused state, and that any decision made from this confusion, would not be appropriate. This is his saving grace. Somewhere deep down, Arjuna knows that something is amiss, and he acknowledges Krishna's rebuke with regard to the apparent loss of his natural temperament of a brave *Kshatriya* warrior, and makes an honest admission of his confusion.

It is Arjuna's decision to submit himself humbly to the advice of Krishna that provides the basis for the main message of the Gita. It is noteworthy that Krishna does not venture to give any advice to Arjuna prior to this. Moreover, Krishna and Arjuna have been good friends for many years, and surely

Krishna would have had many opportunities to reveal to Arjuna the wisdom of the Gita, but he apparently needed to wait for this crucial moment to make this revelation. This is in keeping with the Indian wisdom tradition, where the spiritual teacher (*guru*) appears before and reveals wisdom to the student (*shishya*), only when the student is eager and ripe for such learning, and is found deserving (*adhikari*). Despite his sincere submission before Krishna, and his expressed intention of taking refuge as a disciple, he chooses to abide by his decision of not fighting in the war. This is made clear by Sanjaya, who reports about the scenes from the battlefield at Kurukshetra.

सञ्जय उवाच ।
एवमुक्त्वा हृषीकेशं गुडाकेशः परन्तपः ।
न योत्स्य इति गोविन्दम् उक्त्वा तूष्णीं बभूव ह ||2.9||

Sanjaya said:	सञ्जयः उवाच
Having thus spoken to Krishna,	एवम् उक्त्वा हृषीकेशं
Arjuna, the Scorcher of foes,	गुडाकेशः परन्तपः
Said: "I shall not fight",	न योत्स्ये इति गोविन्दम् उक्त्वा
And then he fell silent.	तूष्णीं बभूव ह

What is Krishna's response to Arjuna's *vishada*? This is described in the next chapter.

3

Death and Immortality, *Asat* and *Sat*, *Deha* and *Dehi*

श्रीभगवानुवाच ।
अशोच्यानन्वशोचस्त्वं प्रज्ञावादांश्च भाषसे ।
गतासूनगतासूंश्च नानुशोचन्ति पण्डिताः ॥2.11॥

The Blessed Lord said:	श्रीभगवान् उवाच
You grieve for the undeserved,	अशोच्यान् अन्वशोचः त्वं
Yet you speak like a learned man!	प्रज्ञा वादान् च भाषसे
But the truly learned never mourn,	न अनुशोचन्ति पण्डिताः
Either for the dead or for the living.	गतासून् अगतासून् च

The Divine Teacher's first response directly addresses Arjuna's primary concerns about the life and death of the human body. This is a key point for all of us, because like Arjuna, we too believe in the body's reality, and so we mourn when the body (of someone dear to us) dies.

Death is a topic that we are normally averse to discussing, as it is commonly perceived to be morbid and fear-inducing. Yet, we all know that death is an inevitable reality. Indeed, all forms, without exception, are subject to mutation in time, implying death of the original form. This may turn out to be a bitter truth, as it often does, when we shy away from exploring and understanding what it means to die, and what it is that dies. The Gita does not shrink from this topic of death. At the very outset itself, the Divine Teacher points out that death does not make wise people lose their calm and fall into grief, for they know the reality of form and essence, *asat* and *sat*. Spiritual essence (*sat*) is imperishable, and hence, Self-realised individuals have no fear of the occurrence of death, either to their bodies or to other bodies.

The body, *deha*, is a perishable entity and is thus naturally *asat* (subject to mutation). It is not the body that is immortal, but only the indwelling Spirit, *dehi*. It is that Divine Spirit that alone has the nature of *sat*; it does not die away. If this truth is deeply realised, it can be truly liberating. For then, knowing the truth about death, we would not thus lament or mourn. Krishna thus shows Arjuna that, for all his learned outpouring, Arjuna is only attempting to justify his inner revolt. He has missed out on this basic truth: that those enlightened never mourn for the living nor the dead.

Suffering: Mistaking *asat* for *sat*

नासतो विद्यते भावः नाभावो विद्यते सतः |
उभयोरपि दृष्टोऽन्तः त्वनयोस्तत्त्वदर्शिभिः ||2.16||

Mutable existence never exists by itself, — न असतः विद्यते भावः
The pure existent never ceases to be. — न अभावः विद्यते सतः
Seers of reality indeed perceive — तु दृष्टः तत्त्व दर्शिभिः
The basis of both, 'sat' and 'asat'. — अनयोः उभयोः अपि अन्तः

The clear distinction between unchangeable true existence, *sat*, and existence subject to birth and death and mutation, *asat*, is brought out in the above verse. The ancient sages (*rishis*) of India devoted much time and attention to a deep understanding of these truths: a study that seems noticeably absent in the West and our modern education. The great truth they discovered — something that is easy for any of us to testify — is that everything perceived, without exception, is subject to change. Everything belongs to the realm of *asat*. These could be physical objects, made of *matter* — accessible to our five senses of hearing, sight, touch, taste and smell, or vital objects, such as impulses, desires, feelings and emotions, or mental objects, like thoughts, judgements and visions. They do not endure in time; they come, stay for a while, mutate, and eventually they die. We experience grief when we tend to get attached to some objects and repulsed by others. We cling to objects of attachment, hoping and believing that they will somehow endure, will not degrade or decay or die. In short, we mistake *asat* for *sat*. We then find it difficult or even unbearable to discover our error of perception in failing to acknowledge nature's operating laws. For indeed, anything that is born, must also die.

If something is not to die, it must be unborn, prior to creation. This *sat* can be no object of consciousness. In other words, it cannot be a thing. What then is it, if at all it exists? In some Indian schools of wisdom, such as the older school of Buddhism, there is no notion of any such existence. However, they too recognised, following the Buddha's path, that all sorrow and suffering emerge from mistaking *asat* for *sat*, from clinging on to objects that are transient and have no ultimate reality. According to them, all objects of experience have emerged from and will eventually disappear into a mysterious *Emptiness* (*shunyata*).

In Upanishadic wisdom and the Gita, there is a fullness hidden in the Unmanifest, whose very nature is *sat* (existence), *chit* (consciousness) and *ananda* (bliss), and this fullness remains hidden even in manifest existence, which emerged from the Unmanifest. Collectively, all is spoken of as *Brahman*. This concept of an infinite fullness is reflected in these mystic lines from the *Shanti Mantra* of the *Ishavasya Upanishad*, which points to an organic wholeness inherent in all manifestation.

ॐ पूर्णमदः पूर्णमिदं पूर्णात् पूर्णमुदच्यते ।
पूर्णस्य पूर्णमादाय पूर्णमेवावशिष्यते ॥

That (unmanifest Brahman) is full, purnam;
This (manifest Brahman) is also full;
From That fullness, This fullness emerges.
Take away This fullness from That fullness,
And what remains is fullness!

In the Gita, there is a passage where the Divine Teacher tells Arjuna how *sat* gets embodied in the human form as the True Self, retaining its original qualities: indestructible, eternal, unborn and unchanging.

वेदाविनाशिनं नित्यं य एनमजमव्ययम् ।
कथं स पुरुषः पार्थ कं घातयति हन्ति कम् ||2.21||

The embodied Self is indestructible,	एनम् अविनाशिनं
Eternal, unborn and unchanging.	नित्यं अजम् अव्ययम्
How does one, knowing this truth,	वेद यः कथं सः पुरुषः
Kill anyone or cause killing, Arjuna?	पार्थ कं घातयति हन्ति कम्

Who are You?

If asked *Who are you?*, what would be the response? Typically, the reply would be to give one's personal name. However, such a name is just a collection of letters, written on a piece of paper. Surely, we are not that! The name here is just a label, not really who we are! We might then probably attempt to describe ourselves in terms of some aspect of status or profession — student at IIT Madras or doctor, engineer, etc. — or in terms of our family history — daughter of so-and-so, etc. But no matter how elaborate or detailed we make our story out to be, we still do not address the heart of the question. Shown pictures of ourselves taken over the years — as a baby, a child, a teenager, an adult, a senior citizen — we would agree that they all refer to the same individual. Though widely different outer forms of the same person, it is only that person who can feel a sense of indestructible continuity in them all.

What we see in the mirror is not who we really are. We are the ones who sees this self-image. The body (*deha*), which keeps changing in time, is but an outer form. We are not only not the body, but we are also not the sensations, desires, impulses, emotions and thoughts that keep changing relentlessly, making up our daily experience. All that is *asat*, not the True Self that we each individually are. Yet sadly, we lack clarity in this.

Typically, we all have a voice in the head, which keeps talking to us, trying to create our world of experience. We are not that voice, we are the one listening to that voice. The Self that knows is never any changing act. Its knowing and its being are identical. It knows by being only what it always is. No change applies to it at all. Unfortunately, we tend to get muddled and end up believing that we are that voice, thus paying undue attention to the make-believe world that it constructs for us. We mistake the object for the subject, and end up under the object's control.

Getting Lost in Object-centred Awareness

Our habitual experience is one of object-centred awareness, where the subject gets lost in objective experience. This happens, for example, when we go to a movie theatre: we forget that we are sitting in a cold dark air-conditioned room, seated next to strangers, looking at flickering projections of light and colour on a white screen. When we tend to identify with some of the characters in the movie, feeling their agony and ecstasy, we get completely lost, completely forgetting who and where we are. That is more-or-less what happens to us in our so-called 'real life'. We get lost in object-centred awareness, and sometimes never find our true selves, from birth to death.

Self awareness implies inwardly stepping back and objectively witnessing all the arising objects, without getting caught up and identifying with these passing or recurring vibrations. In ordinary 'introspection', we do not step back far enough into the pure witness consciousness, and so one part of our being ends up observing the other parts, constantly judging, approving, disapproving, etc. Self-realisation, according to ancient Indian wisdom, is all about finding our True Self. This requires us to awaken consciously to the reality of who we truly are, the true subject. It is possible to attain this awakening by simply refusing to get completely lost in object-centred awareness, in the drama of life, no matter how engaging it is. This calls for a calm, clear and sharply focussed, relaxed and non-judgemental attention.

This is what we need to do, whenever possible, and this is a conscious practice of sustained enquiry and lifelong meditation. We then discover that various kinds of objects come and go in our awareness, just as clouds of different changing shapes and sizes appear and disappear in the blue sky. The awareness, like the sky, remains pure and unchanged by the objects. Indeed, we will also experience blissful moments of pure awareness, devoid of objects, like a blue cloudless sky. We then make the huge discovery that our True Self is complete by itself, and does not really need objects to gain fulfilment.

Body and Indwelling Spirit, *Deha* and *Dehi*

The Divine Teacher points out to Arjuna, and to us, a great truth that we tend to remain blind to: the True Self in us is not the body or any other object in our object-centred consciousness that we habitually identify with. All these objects are indeed perishable, but the *sat* in our bodies, manifesting as the hidden indwelling Spirit (*dehi*) in the body (*deha*), is imperishable. Sri Aurobindo refers to the *dehi* as the 'conscious embodied soul', manifesting as a 'spark of the Divine Fire'.

Indeed, when someone known to us dies in front of us, our very attitude to the body changes. Looking at the dead body, we no longer refer to it by name, as him or her; instead we refer to it as a 'body', and we wish to get rid of it, before it starts decaying and decomposing. The same body, to which we may have had some attraction or attachment earlier, now becomes something repulsive and fearful, when life departs from the body.

The Sanskrit term *deha* ('body') is linked to the verb, *dahyati* ('to be burnt or consumed by fire'). Its very definition points to something that is going to perish. The *deha*, bereft of the indwelling *dehi*, is put away into the fire (in cremation): an act of purification.

One of the most graphic descriptions of the clear distinction between the *deha* and the *dehi* is given by Ramana Maharshi, in his narration of a 'near death experience' that he underwent as a sixteen-year old boy, as reported by Arthur Osborne: 'A sudden violent fear of death overtook me… The shock of the fear of death drove my mind inwards… Well then, I said to myself, this body is dead. It will be carried stiff to the burning ground and there burnt and reduced to ashes. But with the death of this body, am 'I' dead?… I am Spirit transcending the body. The body dies, but the Spirit that transcends it cannot be touched by death. That means I am the deathless Spirit!'[3.1]

Our experiences are usually limited to the world of the five senses and the psychological world of thoughts and emotions. Although Spirit is involved in all our experience, it is not something that can be grasped by the senses or inferred logically by reason. This is conveyed by the following verse in the Gita.

नैनं छिन्दन्ति शस्त्राणि नैनं दहति पावकः |
न चैनं क्लेदयन्त्यापः न शोषयति मारुतः ||2.23||

Weapons do not cut It,	न एनं छिन्दन्ति शस्त्राणि
Fire does not burn It,	न एनं दहति पावकः
Water does not drench It,	न च एनं क्लेदयन्ति आपः
Wind does not wither It!	न शोषयति मारुतः

These qualities point to the *sat* nature of the indwelling Spirit. The indwelling Spirit cannot be destroyed in any manner. It is greater than all manifestation and cannot be grasped by the limited mind. The Divine Teacher goes on to point out that all are that One Divine Self, taking on different forms and embodiments, 'eternally indestructible'. The truly wise know this, and hence, do not grieve on account of destruction of bodies and forms, which are by nature, subject to mutation.

देही नित्यमवध्योऽयं देहे सर्वस्य भारत |
तस्मात्सर्वाणि भूतानि न त्वं शोचितुमर्हसि ||2.30||

This One Self, eternally indestructible,	देही नित्यम् अवध्यः अयं
Is embodied in all bodies, O Arjuna.	देहे सर्वस्य भारत
Therefore, you have no cause	तस्मात् न त्वं अर्हसि
To grieve for all these beings.	शोचितुम् सर्वाणि भूतानि

What happens to the indweller after the death of the body is, of course, an open question, and we have different ideas about this, depending on our religious or other beliefs; these ideas are difficult to prove or disprove. There are some who choose to believe that the indweller also perishes along with the body. Many conventional religions give much importance to the after-life, which means either ascending to some heaven, or descending to some hell, depending on whether the karmic effects earned during this one lifetime turn out to be 'positive' or 'negative'.

The Evolving Soul

According to the ancient Indian wisdom tradition, all states of being and consciousness, including heaven and hell, belong to the realm of *asat*, and are temporary states. The only one eternal and timeless state is that of *sat*, and it is indeed to this state of *sat-chit-ananda* that every human being must eventually return to, through Self-realisation. Starting from a state of ignorance or *tamas*, it is entirely natural that one commits mistakes in one's ignorance, but one cannot be condemned to an eternal hell for this. Indeed, one lifetime is far too short to redeem oneself, and so a series of many, many reincarnations is inevitable to fulfil one's destiny. Moreover, karmic consequences need to be settled, according to the *law of karma*, and with every lifetime, one tends to add to one's stock of unsettled karmic effects. Evolution of consciousness is a slow process in nature, and can be speeded up only if one awakens and consciously participates in one's evolution.

In all instances, the *indweller* is none other than the One Divine Self in all, the *Atman,* the Godhead within. Sri Aurobindo refers to the Self presiding over an individual manifestation as the central being (*Jivatman*), and, although unborn, immortal and eternal, it manifests in creation, by taking on a body. Although originally initiated by the creative Divine energy, *chit-shakti*, for some Divine purpose, the true Divine qualities, *svabhava*, of the individual get contaminated with various karmic effects, arising from entrapment in the play of the *gunas* of *Prakriti*. Unaware and ignorant of its

Divine identity, it eventually evolves through the human form, going through many becomings, many lifetimes, performing many karmas, generating karmic forces, impressions (*samskaras*) and tendencies (*vasanas*) that sustain its continued separate existence. In the meantime, the original Divine spark in the individual, also develops as an evolving soul, as the Divine deputy of the presiding *Jivatman*.

The Divine Teacher points out that the embodied soul passes through childhood, youth and old age, and it continues its journey beyond after death, returning to the earth realm, to take on a fresh body — in a manner similar to discarding old and worn out clothes, in order to put on fresh ones.

वासांसि जीर्णानि यथा विहाय नवानि गृह्णाति नरोऽपराणि ।
तथा शरीराणि विहाय जीर्णानि अन्यानि संयाति नवानि देही
||2.22||

Just as worn-out clothes are discarded	वासांसि जीर्णानि यथा विहाय
So that a man can put on fresh ones,	नवानि गृह्णाति नरः अपराणि
In the same way, worn-out bodies	तथा शरीराणि जीर्णानि
Are discarded (when it is time),	विहाय
So that the embodied soul can	देही
Take on other bodies, new ones.	अन्यानि संयाति नवानि

Sri Aurobindo refers to this evolving soul, with its seat behind the heart chakra, as the psychic being, drawing from the Upanishads, where it is referred to as *Chaitya Purusha*, and elsewhere, more generically, as *Antaratman* (the innermost being and representative of the True Self, *Atman*). The basic nature of this evolving soul comprises truth, goodness and beauty (*satyam-shivam-sundaram*); it is our true Divine inner *guru*. With the evolutionary growth in consciousness through many lifetimes, involving development and purification, and eventually Self-realisation, this evolving soul breaks out of the veils of ignorance surrounding it, and comes forth to act

— as a true self-aware manifestation of the Divine, a *Vibhuti*, to serve some creative purpose that lay concealed in the original *svabhava*. It is then that the higher nature (*Para Prakriti* or *Shakti*) functions directly, operating appropriate 'Soul Forces' through the individual being, whose developed and purified parts of being serve as effective instruments. Once the mission is completed and its purpose is served, the individual being usually dissolves into the Divine Oneness, without any further reincarnation, but may also choose to get incarnated to take up a new Divine mission in the world.

Endurance (*Titiksha*) and Immortality (*Amritam*)

The fundamental question, *Who are you?*, is one that needs to be coupled with another, *Why are you?* What indeed is the purpose of human existence, of taking birth in this lifetime, in the circumstances that one finds oneself in? What is the highest aim?

In order to explore this, the Gita advises us to look beyond our apparent circumstances of body, life and mind, and to rise beyond the limited and unending desires of our lower nature. The human journey through multiple lives and deaths is a long journey, at the end of which one gains the *holy grail* of the *nectar of immortality* (*amritam*). It is something to be gained through self-effort, by meeting with all kinds of trials and tribulations, through development and purification.

Indeed, every difficult circumstance offers itself as an opportunity for us to grow and become fit. The adverse circumstance, in fact, is more valuable, than favourable ones, in this regard. We need not go out in search of such circumstances, for they will invariably come our way, often uninvited, dragging us out of our comfort zones. The more addicted we are to our comfort zones, the more reluctant we are to change and to render ourselves fit for immortality. Indeed, true freedom lies in being able to remain content under all circumstances, rather than insisting that the circumstances need to change to conform to our liking. The importance of meeting all the material and sensational touches of the world with acceptance, grace and equanimity is emphasised by the Divine Teacher in the verses to follow.

मात्रास्पर्शास्तु कौन्तेय शीतोष्णसुखदुःखदाः |
आगमापायिनोऽनित्याः तांस्तितिक्षस्व भारत ||2.14||

Sense contacts with objects, Arjuna,	मात्रा स्पर्शाः तु कौन्तेय
Cause cold and heat, pleasure and pain.	शीत उष्ण सुख दुःख दाः
They come and go, fleeting in nature.	आगम अपायिनः अनित्याः
Learn to endure them, O Bharata!	तान् तितिक्षस्व भारत

Indeed, it is the very nature of all contacts of our senses with various sense-objects to give rise to *dualities* such as cold and heat (*shita-ushnau*), as well as pleasure and pain (*sukha-duhkhau*). This includes contacts within our minds, manifesting through imagination and memory. The reactions generated seem to follow a kind of law, to which all beings are subject, be they saints or sinners. Our normal reaction is to seek and cling to the objects that give us pleasure and to resist or run away from objects that give us pain. This is so, because we stay identified with our physical and vital bodies — not aware of who we truly are in our innermost being.

All these experiences, belonging to the realm of *asat*, however, do not endure. They come and go. What we need to do is to stay centred in our innermost being, rather than in transient object-centred consciousness. The intensity with which we feel pain, while resisting extreme adverse circumstances, is similar in magnitude to the intensity with which we experience pleasure, while clinging to pleasant circumstances. The call of the Gita is for us to rise above these dualities. We need to develop tolerance, forbearance and endurance (*titiksha*) of discomforts that life inevitably brings to the outer parts of our being. It is a capacity that develops in us, in the same way as our muscles develop, with continued practice. This helps and serves to dis-identify with the *asat* in us, and to shift our identity inwards to our evolving soul and True Self.

It is especially important to appreciate the value of this teaching in our modern technological world, where so much emphasis is given to controlling artificially the outer environment, so that we can stay forever in an air-conditioned climate. By this, we not only lose contact with the natural world, but also render ourselves unfit for immortality. The practical significance of *titiksha*, of immediate and long-term benefit to all, is that by increasing our thresholds of tolerance, we can handle more stress with greater ease, without complaining, and being more accepting of external circumstances. Such acceptance does not imply meek submission to any wrong-doing or *adharma* or escapism from work that needs to be done; on the contrary, it enables us to fortify within us the patience, strength and clear thinking we need in order to fight successfully in the battlefield of life. Further, this also does not imply that we should deny ourselves comforts in life; it only implies that we need to strengthen our abilities to deal with discomforts.

This ability, gained through the practice of *titiksha*, invites us to learn to deny ourselves — occasionally, if not frequently — the temptation to reach out immediately for pain-killing medication whenever there is the hint of pain, or to turn on the air-conditioner whenever there is even a slight rise in the outside temperature. We can extend this practice to all domains where we experience discomfort — including the tendency to surf the internet or TV channels when there is a hint of boredom. This practice of self-denial is indeed a kind of de-addiction, and initially we are likely to be troubled by withdrawal symptoms. However, soon we discover the benefits and joy in self-mastery, and know for sure that conquering temptation is superior to yielding to it.

The practice of *titiksha* is made easier when it is combined with the *yogic* practice of withdrawing the senses from the sense-objects (*pratyahara*). This implies shifting our 'centre of gravity' from the outer parts of our being — which are always vulnerable to frequent disturbances (having the nature of *asat*) — to the quiet and powerful centre of our True Self (which has the nature of *sat*). This renders us fit for immortality, according to the Gita.

यं हि न व्यथयन्त्येते पुरुषं पुरुषर्षभ |
समदुःखसुखं धीरं सोऽमृतत्वाय कल्पते ||2.15||

The man who is no longer afflicted	यं हि न व्यथयन्ति पुरुषं
By these (sense contacts), Arjuna,	एते पुरुषर्षभ
The wise hero, equal to joy and sorrow,	सम दुःख सुखं धीरं
Becomes eligible to attain immortality!	सः अमृतत्वाय कल्पते

Sri Aurobindo explains, 'For by immortality is meant not the survival of death — that is already given to every creature born with a mind — but the transcendence of life and death... Whoever is subject to grief and sorrow, a slave to the sensations and emotions, occupied by the touches of things transient, cannot become fit for immortality.' [3.2]

This inspires Arjuna to raise questions on the nature of the one who is so fit for immortality. This is taken up in the next chapter.

4

The Calm and Wise Hero (*Sthitaprajna*)

अर्जुन उवाच ।
स्थितप्रज्ञस्य का भाषा समाधिस्थस्य केशव ।
स्थितधीः किं प्रभाषेत किमासीत व्रजेत किम् ।।2.54।।

Arjuna said:	अर्जुनः उवाच
What defines the man with steady insight,	स्थितप्रज्ञस्य का भाषा
Steadfast in meditative awareness, Krishna?	समाधिस्थस्य केशव
Steady in wisdom, how would he speak?	स्थितधीः किं प्रभाषेत
How would he sit? How would he move?	किम् आसीत व्रजेत किम्

Arjuna's curiosity has been aroused by Krishna's words of wisdom in the second chapter of the Gita. Although he remains afflicted by *vishada* (despair), he asks for more details about the nature of a man who has rendered himself 'fit for immortality'. In this verse, such a wise person has been referred to by Arjuna in three different ways: *sthita-prajna*, *sthita-dhih* and *samadhi-stha.* Common to all three is a steady state situation (*sthita*, *stha*). What is said to be steady here? It is *prajna* and *dhi*, both implying wisdom, insight or deep understanding. The term *samadhi* implies a state of *meditative absorption*, with the mind becoming unwaveringly calm and still or focussed one-pointedly. S*amadhi-stha* here means to have the mind firmly fixed in communion with the Divine Self. Arjuna's query is directed to the outward behaviour of such a calm and wise hero. How would such a person speak, sit and move about? Are there any special distinguishing features in outward actions that would set apart such an individual? This is a practical query from a practical man. It is rather ironic that Arjuna should pose such a query to Krishna, who is clearly a *sthitaprajna* himself — a living example standing right in front of Arjuna! Clearly, Arjuna does not recognise the *sthitaprajna* aspect of his charioteer, the Divine Teacher.

श्रीभगवानुवाच ।
प्रजहाति यदा कामान् सर्वान्पार्थ मनोगतान् ।
आत्मन्येवात्मना तुष्टः स्थितप्रज्ञस्तदोच्यते ||2.55||

The Blessed Lord said:	श्रीभगवान् उवाच
When one leaves behind all desires	प्रजहाति यदा कामान् सर्वान्
Arising from the ego-mind, Arjuna,	पार्थ मनः गतान्
And is content in the Self, by the Self,	आत्मनि एव आत्मना तुष्टः
Then he is said to have stable insight!	स्थितप्रज्ञः तदा उच्यते

The outward signs of a calm and wise hero are not that easy to discern. Perhaps, there are no such telling outward signs. Is it all internal? The Divine Teacher identifies two clear features of the *sthitaprajna*: freedom from desire and inner contentment (from abiding in the Self). Both of these features are clearly internal in nature, independent of the external mannerisms of the person (how he talks, walks, sits, etc.).

Freedom from Endless Thirst, *Thrishna*

Desires typically show entrapment in ego-driven acts. Behind these desires lurks the false self, the ego-self (*ahankara*), with which one habitually identifies. Lacking the true quality of *sat* (true being), it seeks happiness in various forms of *asat* (false becoming). Thus it remains confused, mistakenly entangled in a false show. Failing to find enduring fulfilment, it keeps oscillating in cycles of hope and fear.

Desires keep multiplying endlessly, acquiring new forms, but never satiating, as the Buddha pointed out. There is a perennial thirst, *thrishna*, for happiness. This usually takes the form of desiring sense-pleasures, wealth and power. So too with ideas and ideals, views, opinions, theories, conceptions and beliefs — collectively called *kama-thrishna*. The thirst can also take the form of a craving to become something or someone great, to gain a secure foothold, to establish and solidify one's self-image, to prevail and dominate — collectively called *bhava-thrishna*.

We suffer when we cannot quench our thirst. Even when we succeed, the pleasure and honour that we gain in quenching *kama-thrishna* and *bhava-thrishna* often turn out to be short-lived, as new kinds of thirsts spring up. Sometimes the very objects that had earlier given pleasure later bring us pain. So too, honour can turn into dishonour, revealing the precarious nature and character of the ego-self. When circumstances become extremely unfavourable (when things go badly 'wrong'), we tend to get fed up and wish to quit — like Arjuna who wished to quit the Kurukshetra battlefield. This condition of *vishada* commonly leads to depression. This is also a kind of *thrishna*. We wish to somehow dissociate from pain, anxiety, disappointment, despair or conflict. We may then seek to be nothing, we may even contemplate committing suicide. This kind of thirst, the opposite of *bhava-thrishna*, is called *vibhava-thrishna*.

Thus, for the normal unenlightened individual, there is an unending series of *kama-thrishna*, *bhava-thrishna* and *vibhava-thrishna* arising in our minds, as a play of the lower nature. The Divine Teacher points out that at a certain stage of spiritual development, one leaves behind and is no longer troubled by *thrishna*. Instead, one is filled with a supreme inner contentment — the second characteristic of the *sthitaprajna*.

The falling off of desires (arising in the mind) alone does not render one 'fit for immortality' (verse 2.15). Freedom from desire is a necessary, but not sufficient, condition. This must be accompanied by Self-realisation.

Inner Contentment (*Antahsukha*) and Radiance (*Antarjyoti*)

The arising of any kind of mental activity is referred to as *chitta-vritti*. Some vibration (*vritti*) or other invariably stirs up in our restless minds, with one thought or emotion linking up to another, often unconsciously. When this activity is motivated by *thrishna* — as it often is — we are led to doing some action (*karma*), engaging with the world outside, in some manner or other. This kind of outward movement is described as *pravritti*. The more we engage, the more we stir up the mental activity in us. The arising of *chitta-vritti* becomes ingrained in us as a strong habit — so much that even when there is no need to act or to think, it goes on relentlessly in our minds.

Its movement is outward, taking us away from the true centre of our being. If we wish to find our True Self, the *Atman*, and be centred there, we need to reverse this movement, through a process of withdrawal (going within, rather than outward), described as *nivritti*. Indeed, in meditative absorption, it is possible to remain free from *chitta-vritti*, and hence from *thrishna*, at least for some time, and certainly, this is bound to bring a happy relief from the tyranny of relentless thinking, and one may even experience a trance-like condition.

However, Self-realisation is all about finding the indwelling *dehi* in us, even amidst the rising of *chitta-vritti*. When this happens as a stable and enduring realisation, then one accesses a fountainhead of inner joy, inner contentment: 'in the Self, by the Self', *atmanyevatmana tushtah*. This is the condition of the *sthitaprajna*. We find another apt description of the nature of this inner contentment in the following verse.

योऽन्तःसुखोऽन्तरारामः तथान्तर्ज्योतिरेव यः |
स योगी ब्रह्मनिर्वाणं ब्रह्मभूतोऽधिगच्छति ||5.24||

He who finds delight and ease within, यः अन्तः सुखः अन्तः आरामः
And inner radiance, lit from within, तथा अन्तः ज्योतिः एव यः
That Yogin gets liberated in Brahman, सः योगी ब्रह्म निर्वाणं
Realising oneness with Brahman! ब्रह्म भूतः अधिगच्छति

The *sthitaprajna*, however, knowing the reality of *sat* and *dehi*, turns the awareness inwards to find the evolving soul, *Antaratman,* and its source, the True Self, *Atman*. This leads to the realisation that the true source of all happiness lies hidden, eternally, within one's innermost being. It is the *delight* of the Divine soul, *antahsukha*, which results in a constant sense of Divine ease of being, *antararama*. Further, *centred* in the Self, one also discovers an inner radiance, *antarjyoti*, from which one derives guidance on whatever is required to be done. This inner light, *jyoti*, is endlessly inspiring and uplifting, by which one experiences a lightness of being.

This is an enlightened state, by which one discovers the true source of all happiness and knowledge. This condition is described here in the Gita, and elsewhere, as *brahma-nirvana*. The concept of *Nirvana*, made popular by Buddhism, refers to an ultimate liberated state, a permanent dissolution and extinction of the ego-self. The Gita too invokes this concept, but with a distinct difference. It is not an extinction into nothingness, but a dissolution into the fullness of the All, known as *Brahman*. In this condition, inherent gladness comes forth spontaneously.

The mystic poet Kabir composed a beautiful couplet (*doha*), depicting the irony of searching for happiness in the outside world, not knowing that the true Divine Source of it is ever-present within us.

कस्तूरी कुंडल बसे मृग ढूंढे बन माहि |
ज्यो घट घट राम है दुनिया देखे नाही ||

The musk-deer carries its fragrance within itself,	कस्तूरी कुंडल बसे
But it runs all around the forest searching for it.	मृग ढूंढे बन माहि
Likewise, Divine bliss is within all,	ज्यो घट घट राम है
But the world fails to realise it!	दुनिया देखे नाही

Action, Free from Ego-based Desire

Traditionally the state of *brahma-nirvana* is associated with a transcendence of world-consciousness into the silent and static *Akshara Purusha*. Work then is done, not motivated by ego-based desire or for seeking happiness from outside, but as an expression of the inner happiness, of *Ananda*, without any feeling of 'doership'.

विहाय कामान्यः सर्वान् पुमांश्चरति निःस्पृहः |
निर्ममो निरहङ्कारः स शान्तिमधिगच्छति ||2.71||

Relinquishing all selfish cravings,	विहाय कामान् सर्वान्
The man who acts, free from lust,	यः पुमान् चरति निःस्पृहः
Free from notions of 'I' and 'mine',	निर्ममः निरहङ्कारः
Attains a state of deep inner peace.	सः शान्तिम् अधिगच्छति

Even if there is any trace of the ego-self, which is something very difficult to abolish completely, it is detected by means of self-awareness and relinquished. All desires are eventually traceable to the ego-self, which constantly seeks to assert and expand itself. Notions such as 'I am the doer', 'I deserve credit for what I do', 'What is gained belongs to me', etc., typically underlie its actions. The actions of the *sthitaprajna* are characterised by the absence of such notions of 'mine' and 'I' (*nirmama* and *nirahankara*, respectively). Such actions serve to deepen the state of inner peace.

Tranquillity, *prashanti*

A key aspect of the *sthitaprajna* is the attainment of a state of tranquillity (*prashanti*), which remains undisturbed even in the midst of all provocations and actions. This is described in the following verse.

जितात्मनः प्रशान्तस्य परमात्मा समाहितः ।
शीतोष्णसुखदुःखेषु तथा मानापमानयोः ।।6.7।।

In one who is self-controlled and serene,	जितात्मनः प्रशान्तस्य
The Supreme Self remains steadily poised,	परमात्मा समाहितः
In cold and heat, in pleasure and pain,	शीत उष्ण सुख दुःखेषु
As well as in honour and in ignominy!	तथा मान अपमानयोः

The steady serenity attained here is an outcome of the two characteristics mentioned earlier: self-mastery (associated with desires no longer causing agitation) and Self-realisation. This points to a very high level of attainment — conquest of the lower nature and attainment of the perfect calm that comes from realising one's identity with the One Supreme Self, the *Paramatma* in all. This is no passing state of *asat*. It is the enduring state of *sat*, where the realisation of the True Self, and the consequent insight (*prajna*) is steady and enduring (*sthita*).

The crucial characteristic of a *sthitaprajna* is the realisation of the True Self in that individual's inner being. This is implied by the term, *samahita* — a fixity in being to which the Gita also refers as *Samadhi*. According to Sri Aurobindo, 'He has conquered his lower self, reached the perfect calm in which his highest Self is manifest to him, that highest Self always concentrated in its own being, samahita, in Samadhi, not only in the trance of the inward-drawn consciousness, but always, in the waking state of the mind as well, in exposure to the causes of desire and of the disturbance of calm, to grief and pleasure, heat and cold, honour and disgrace, all the dualities.'[4.1]

It is this quality of tranquillity that gets reflected as a steady inner poise in the individual — an equipoise that sees the Divine essence, *sat*, in all beings, amidst all transient and varying appearances outside. The Gita gives much emphasis to attaining such equipoise or steady equilibrium, in the face of all kinds of provocation and dualities. Such equipoise, called *samatvam*, is discussed in detail in later chapters in this book.

Poise in the Supreme Spirit, *brahmi sthiti*

The quality of tranquillity is quite uncommon. However, when we look around, we may observe that a few people around do appear to maintain some degree of inner tranquillity and calm, even in adverse situations. We are of course not referring to those who show outward calmness, but get inwardly agitated and often vengeful — nursing grievances and looking to strike later (directly or indirectly) at some opportune time. Even inner calmness is not a condition that can be maintained permanently by most of us.

Indeed, we all tend to lose our poise, some time or another — often several times every day!

The Gita attributes such inner calmness, even if temporary, to a manifestation of the *guna* of *sattva*. This may indeed reflect an evolved and purified state of individual being. It may arise through adopting a philosophical or ascetic attitude to life, or through nurturing compassion, love and care for others. The Gita explains that even the *sattva-guna*, reflected by equilibrium and lucidity, belongs to the limited realm of the lower nature (*Apara Prakriti*). It is required to constantly battle against the other two *gunas* — the aggressive impulsiveness of *rajas* and the deluded blundering of *tamas*. While *sattva* may indeed predominate at times, there may be periods when *rajas* or *tamas* may override. Indeed, in most people, the behaviour is usually *rajasic* (prone to excitement and irritability) or *tamasic* (prone to dullness and insensitivity).

Helped by a daily practice (*sadhana*), our lower nature may be consciously purified, so as to abide in a predominantly *sattvic* mode of living. This may indeed bring tranquillity and equipoise in our lives, but this will still fall short of the *sthita* nature of the *sthitaprajna*. That would require shifting our identity inwards, from object-centred awareness to the True Self. The Gita suggests that this is the ideal condition of the accomplished *Karmayogin*, the Divine Worker, exemplified by the character of Krishna himself. Hence, the *sthitaprajna* is not to be construed as one who has withdrawn from the world, free from desire and lost in some 'other-worldly' trance. On the contrary, one is invited to remain in the firm poise of *sthitaprajna*, not only at times of rest and meditation, but also in the full flood of action.

The default condition of the *sthitaprajna* is Self-awareness. The tranquillity so attained is spiritual in essence, and not just a manifestation of the *sattvic guna* of *Prakriti*. So it has the nature of *sat* and is thus enduring in its essence. It is a supreme poise, stationed in the *sat-chit-ananda* of *Brahman*, and so is referred to here as *brahmi sthiti*. In the old Indian system, this is the ideal condition to remain stationed at the time of death — thus attaining self-extinction in *Brahman*, *brahma-nirvana*.

एषा ब्राह्मी स्थितिः पार्थ नैनां प्राप्य विमुह्यति ।
स्थित्वास्यामन्तकालेऽपि ब्रह्मनिर्वाणमृच्छति ।।2.72।।

Arjuna, such is the firm poise in Brahman, एषा ब्राह्मी स्थितिः पार्थ
Attaining which one is no longer deluded. न एनां प्राप्य विमुह्यति
Abiding in it even at the time of death, स्थित्वास्याम् अन्तकाले अपि
One attains self-extinction in Brahman! ब्रह्म निर्वाणम् ऋच्छति

At the time of the body's physical death, our attention tends naturally and automatically to focus on what we consider to be most important or valuable. When our lives are consumed in object-centred awareness, it will therefore be natural for us, at the time of parting, to be similarly concerned about some object or person 'outside', identified with our ego-self. It is only when the ego-self has dissolved and one has attained the blessed condition of *brahmi sthiti*, that we can remain blissfully centred in our True Self. We will then not be worried about what will happen to our near-and-dear ones or to the world, for all that remains a continuing Divine unfolding — the purpose for which this body (*deha*) has become fulfilled, and the *dehi* now happily returns to its Divine Source.

However, the Gita suggests that the attainment of *brahmi sthiti* is essential for a *Karmayogin*, not only at the time of death, but also while living in the world. It is then as though a *Divine rebirth* has occurred. In *brahmi sthiti*, the *sthitaprajna* discovers the One Divine — not only within oneself, but in all beings, and indeed it is this seeing of Divine oneness that lies at the heart of the tranquillity, *prashanti*, and equipoise, *samatvam*.

We need to have an abiding faith in the pure Divine consciousness (*sat-chit-ananda*), ever-present as the ultimate source and substance of all manifest reality, including our own selves. We need to dwell 'more and more within', as Sri Aurobindo puts it, 'looking from within outwards instead of living in the surface mind which is always at the mercy of the shocks and blows of life. It is only from that inner state that one can be stronger than life and its disturbing forces and hope to conquer.'[4.2]

If Self-realisation is our goal, if we need to truly know who we are and why we are here in this world, we must learn to go *inwards* and find our true centre there. Indeed, it is only by abiding in that centre of deep abiding peace that we can know how to deal effectively with all the 'shocks and blows of life'. That centre is like the eye of a storm, always still.

As Eckhart Tolle says, 'When you lose touch with inner stillness, you lose touch with yourself. When you lose touch with yourself, you lose yourself in the world. Your innermost sense of self, of who you are, is inseparable from stillness.'[4.3] This ability to stay centred and anchored in inner stillness (state of *sthitaprajna*), and thus to engage skilfully in work and life, is the inspiring message of the Gita.

Like Arjuna at the battlefield, we may be more concerned with the immediate challenges we face in our lives in the so-called 'outer world' than the noble ideal of Self-realisation. In such moments of crisis, our main concern is: *What to do? Or not do?* This is discussed in the next chapter.

5

Action and Inaction, Sin and *Svadharma*

अर्जुन उवाच ।
ज्यायसी चेत्कर्मणस्ते मता बुद्धिर्जनार्दन ।
तत्किं कर्मणि घोरे मां नियोजयसि केशव ।।3.1।।

Arjuna said:	अर्जुनः उवाच
Krishna, if you hold insight	चेत् ते मता बुद्धिः जनार्दन
To be superior to action,	ज्यायसी कर्मणः
Why then do you urge me	तत् किं मां नियोजयसि
To do this ghastly karma?	कर्मणि घोरे केशव

This query by Arjuna at the beginning of the Gita's third chapter reveals his state of mind. Unable to free himself from his *vishada* and reluctance to fight, he looks for some justifying position in Krishna's teachings.

He sees that on the one hand Krishna holds the path of wisdom and spirituality as supreme, culminating in the attainment of *brahmi sthiti*. Yet, on the other hand, Krishna also insists on Arjuna's engagement in work, *karma*. The *karma* here is not something noble, but instead ghastly and violent in nature (*karmani ghore*), resulting in much bloodshed. How then can Krishna urge him to this action, which seems thus unspiritual and inferior to the path of wisdom?

The Divine Teacher's reply is simple, yet profound, as indicated in the following verse.

न कर्मणामनारम्भात् नैष्कर्म्यं पुरुषोऽश्नुते ।
न च संन्यसनादेव सिद्धिं समधिगच्छति ।।3.4।।

By merely abstaining from initiating work,	कर्मणाम् अनारम्भात्
Man does not attain freedom from action,	नैष्कर्म्यं पुरुषः न अश्नुते
Nor by renouncing work initiated,	न च संन्यसनात् एव
Does one ever attain perfection.	सिद्धिं समधिगच्छति

Upholding the supremacy of insight and the state of *brahmi sthiti*, the Divine Teacher points out that this does not go against the need to act — to do what must be done. This poise of watching over *Prakriti's* operations, yet remaining unaffected, leads to freedom from getting bound to any acts. This freedom of the soul from action is *naishkarmyam*. This does not imply any ceasing of *Prakriti's* work. The Divine Teacher shows that it would be a mistake to believe that this freedom can be attained by abdicating work — either those yet to begin or those already initiated. Krishna makes it clear to Arjuna (and to us) that such outward renunciation does not lead to salvation. He even points out in the verses to follow, that complete cessation of work is in practice impossible for any being!

Action in Inaction

Man, as a being, is part of nature, thus existing as an organic part of a much larger whole. *Prakriti's* operations always function in terms of the three *gunas*. They happen naturally and relentlessly, according to their own laws. The very act of breathing is a clear and immediately obvious example of this. It happens on its own. The natural operation of these laws can also be clearly seen in plants and animals. Human beings are not different, though we seem to have the additional faculty to think and to apply some more wilful control on our activities.

न हि कश्चित्क्षणमपि जातु तिष्ठत्यकर्मकृत् ।
कार्यते ह्यवशः कर्म सर्वः प्रकृतिजैर्गुणैः ।।3.5।।

No one, for even a moment,	न हि कश्चित् क्षणम् अपि
Can ever exist, being inactive!	जातु तिष्ठति अकर्म कृत्
All are forced to act, helplessly,	कार्यते हि अवशः कर्म सर्वः
By the gunas, born of Prakriti.	प्रकृतिजैः गुणैः

Mostly we act helplessly (*avasha*), as though driven by some natural force. This is easily seen when we get angry (which is reflective of the play of the *guna* of *rajas* in us). The heat of anger felt inside spontaneously arouses in us the tendency to be aggressive and speak harshly! So also when we feel tired or lazy, a drowsiness tends to envelop our being, making us feel inert or fall asleep. This is the play of the *guna* of *tamas* in action. Hence, even seeming inaction is a sign of nature in action. Indeed, even in sleep, actions keep on taking place in our bodies — as they maintain the circulatory, digestive and other systems needed for human survival. Even as we sleep, our minds are often active in dreaming. So too in the waking state, even as our bodies appear to be physically inactive, our minds work relentlessly: thinking, desiring or daydreaming!

Appearances are often deceptive, and even matter that appears to be inert and inactive (reflecting *tamo-guna*) is subject to slow disintegration and dispersion, as established by the second law of thermodynamics. Furthermore, science has established the hidden presence of dynamism at the sub-atomic level. Electrons revolve around the nucleus of an atom at tremendous speeds, showing the kinesis of *rajas* within the outer appearance of *tamas*. The atom bomb exemplifies how this tremendous *rajasic* energy, hidden in the atomic core, can be unleashed. These are common examples of *action in inaction*.

According to the ancient Indian wisdom of *Sankhya* philosophy, an ever-changing dynamism in the relative proportions of these three *gunas* keeps sustaining the very functioning of *Prakriti*. Thus, as observed in the manifest universe, there is nothing that can rightly be called inactive. The very nature of *Prakriti* is to participate in actions that keep bringing change. The seeming inaction that we so often locally and fleetingly observe in any manifestation — especially matter — either reflects a very slow and barely perceptible movement at an outer level or a mere appearance that veils action within the entity.

'There is nothing permanent except change' is a famous statement attributed to the ancient Greek philosopher, Heraclitus, who also went on to proclaim famously, 'No man ever steps in the same river twice, and he is not the same man'! However, is there *inaction in action*?

Inaction in Action

कर्मण्यकर्म यः पश्येत् अकर्मणि च कर्म यः ।
स बुद्धिमान्मनुष्येषु स युक्तः कृत्स्नकर्मकृत् ।।4.18।।

He who sees inaction in action	कर्मणि अकर्म यः पश्येत्
And also action in inaction,	अकर्मणि च कर्म यः
He is truly wise among men,	सः बुद्धिमान् मनुष्येषु
Yoked, even amidst all actions.	सः युक्तः कृत्स्न कर्म कृत्

The above verse in the Gita shows clearly that there is also inaction hidden in action, but this is perceived only by wise men. While a scientist or philosopher can surely detect action in inaction, it takes spiritual wisdom to perceive inaction in action. This is so, because it is difficult to see anything permanent anywhere. Wherever we look, we see a flux of change. Whatever manifests is by nature *asat*, subject to change and destruction everywhere. Nature is ceaselessly at work.

Should there be anything immutable and imperishable, it must be by nature *sat*. Only pure Spirit, ever-present and boundless, has this nature. It can be realised by us in our own being, through self-enquiry and meditation, as the changeless essence of the indwelling *dehi* within the mutable *deha*. We gain a direct experiential insight of this truth of inaction in action whenever we step back in awareness inward — behind the ever-changing flux of our body sensations, behind our thoughts and emotions.

For this insight to stabilise, we need to remain centred in the stillness of the witnessing consciousness, the unchanging inner observer. Or else, there has to be a leap of faith — a supreme and unwavering devotion (*bhakti*) to the Divine, that eventually reveals the consciousness that lies unchanged within, as an act of Divine Grace. Being able to feel this imperishable Divine Presence of the *Purusha* amidst all the mutations in *Prakriti* is to find *sat* in *asat*, inaction in action!

According to ancient Indian wisdom, all that is manifested reveals a spectrum of consciousness, with movements continuously taking place. They may be *evolutionary* (from darkness to light and *asat* to *sat*), and also *involutionary* (from Spirit to Matter). Sri Aurobindo explains that during creation, an involution had at first taken place, with Spirit dwelling in the *Inconscient*. Subsequently, there has been an evolution over the aeons, through Matter, Life and Mind. It is continuing to evolve beyond, through what Sri Aurobindo referred to as *Supermind*, into the *Superconscient*, which is of the pure nature of *sat-chit-ananda*. Thus there exists, in manifestation, a profound spectrum of consciousness, with forms and beings at various stages of evolution — from the

Inconscient to the *Superconscient*, with the highest potentials yet to be fully revealed.

It is then that one ascends from the lower nature (*Apara Prakriti*), beyond the three *gunas*, into the higher nature (*Para Prakriti*), and begins to live in the freedom of the soul. Then one gets to contribute quite consciously to the Divine creative efforts by a *conscious involution* — bringing Spirit consciously down into the mental, vital and physical realms. In such creative endeavour, there is no feeling of 'doership' ('I am doing this'). Having transcended the ego-self, there is here no separate 'I', as all creation is perceived as an integral movement of the One Divine. The individual self-actualised and Self-realised instrument serves as one of the many channels of the Divine *Shakti* (or *Para Prakriti*), to manifest the Divine will.

The wise sage clearly sees that, in this perfect flow state, everything seems to manifest beautifully, synchronously and perfectly. In this condition, he remains centred and yoked (*yukta*) to the True Self, whereby the action done, *karma-krit*, is not something done in isolation by a separate ego-self. It is instead quite all-embracing and whole in its character, as implied by the term *kritsna*. Clearly, the accomplished *Karmayogin* is one who engages in work, not only as a means for attaining Self-realisation and abiding in *brahmi sthiti*, but also as a creative expression of its attainment.

In the words of Sri Aurobindo, 'The perfect *Yogin* is no solitary musing on the Self in his ivory tower of spiritual isolation, but *yuktah kritsna-karma-krit*, a many-sided universal worker for the good of the world, for God in the world.'[5.1]

Incidentally, the flow state is something that we all get to glimpse in any beautiful and perfect creative action — especially in the world of sport or the musical performance of an orchestra, where all goes right and nothing is perceived out of place. We get completely absorbed in the activity whose very nature is *Ananda*, and thus all participants enjoy a unified shared experience of creative fulfilment, without distinction between subject and object. We do not feel the passing of time. It is as though time stands still — a stillness of inaction amidst the full flood of action! While these experiences are rare — at best, few and far between — for the vast majority of us, they tend to occur very frequently in the daily life of the accomplished *Karmayogin*.

Work Inherent to One's Nature

If staying inactive is impossible, and nature compels us to act, what is the work we need to do? This is indeed a profound question, pointing to the very purpose of human existence. The Gita uses the term, *svabhava* — literally meaning 'own becoming', to point at some intrinsic nature that is unique to every being.

श्रेयान्स्वधर्मो विगुणः परधर्मात्स्वनुष्ठितात् |
स्वभावनियतं कर्म कुर्वन्नाप्नोति किल्बिषम् ||18.47||

Better is one's own dharma, imperfect,	श्रेयान् स्वधर्मः विगुणः
Than an alien dharma done perfectly.	पर धर्मात् सु अनुष्ठितात्
One never incurs sin while performing	कुर्वन् न आप्नोति किल्बिषम्
Work regulated by one's intrinsic nature.	स्वभाव नियतं कर्म

The term, *svabhava-niyatam karma*, refers to work that is regulated by one's intrinsic nature, i.e., *svabhava*. This intrinsic nature points to something that is inner and inborn. And associated with it, there is a unique law of being or *svadharma* — literally meaning "own *dharma*". Since this is inherent, when we follow this law, and act in a manner true to our *svabhava*, we live authentically.

The sense of 'intrinsic nature' is further emphasised in the next verse, where the term, *sahajam karma*, is introduced. It refers to work that one is born with, work that one is born to do. The emphasis here is primarily on an inner quality or spirit, expressing itself outwardly as karma. It does not necessarily imply work that is hereditary in nature.

सहजं कर्म कौन्तेय सदोषमपि न त्यजेत् |
सर्वारम्भा हि दोषेण धूमेनाग्निरिवावृताः ||18.48||

Work inherent to one's nature, Arjuna,	सहजं कर्म कौन्तेय
Even though defective, never abandon!	सदोषम् अपि न त्यजेत्
Defects, after all, are present in all work,	सर्व आरम्भाः हि दोषेण
As smoke is there, enveloping every fire.	धूमेन अग्निः इव आवृताः

The outer work or career we need to find is something that should conform to our inner nature, our *svabhava* — something that we *resonate* with naturally, and in which we can excel. For example, in Arjuna's case, it was obvious that his outer role as a *Kshatriya* warrior was in alignment with his inner nature and talent. So by developing his warrior skills to perfection, he came to be regarded as one of the greatest warriors of his time. Indeed, until the critical moment at Kurukshetra, he had always revelled in this role, and appeared to have no doubt about his *svadharma*.

Yet, there are times in all our lives, when we are filled with doubts about the nature of our outer engagement. In many cases, this doubting and questioning, induced by constant dissatisfaction with our work, may awaken us to a realisation of our true *svabhava*, and thereby to our *svadharma*. In such instances, when we discover that we have taken some vocation or career ill suited to our true nature and aptitude, it would be correct and proper to make a change. For many young people, lacking in self-awareness of their *svabhava*, much exploration through trial-and-error may be needed, to discover and settle into their true *svadharma*. This may happen, for example, in teaching: when one discovers a special aptitude for teaching and realises that one has been *born to teach*. Such a discovery can be extraordinarily revealing — like a fish taking to water!

Every *dharma* brings its own challenges — ethical and otherwise. It may also happen that, even after discovering and settling into a favoured *svadharma*, some other *dharma* may turn out to be more appealing and glamorous. On the other side of the hill, the grass may appear greener, as the saying goes, and that may persuade us to cross over. We may even adopt the alien *dharma* (*paradharma*), and for a while succeed in it, but find it to be not something we are meant to do. Hence, even if at times our own work and duty may appear to look defective — as with Arjuna at Kurukshetra — it is still best to carry on our inborn *karma*, ideally as a *Karmayogin*. There will always be aspects in every *dharma* that appear defective. However, such defects are 'present in all work, as smoke enveloping every fire'. Even the most beautiful vase will be seen filled with hundreds of cracks, when viewed under a magnifying lens — but this should not deter the potter from creating the best vase he can!

स्वधर्ममपि चावेक्ष्य न विकम्पितुमर्हसि |
धर्म्याद्धि युद्धाच्छ्रेयोऽन्यत् क्षत्रियस्य न विद्यते ||2.31||

Seeing clearly your unique dharma,	स्वधर्मम् अपि च अवेक्ष्य
You should not waver (in its action).	न विकम्पितुम् अर्हसि
Nothing's nobler for a Kshatriya	श्रेयः अन्यत् क्षत्रियस्य न विद्यते
Than to fight in a righteous war!	धर्म्यात् हि युद्धात्

It is natural for the evolving soul in anyone to struggle and be subject to self-doubt and troubled by defects, while operating in the lower nature, subject to the play of the three *gunas*. Only after self-actualisation, ego-transcendence and Self-realisation, can anyone feel true completion and fulfilment in life's journey. Till then, the journey must continue on the path of *Karmayoga*, without wavering from one's *svadharma*.

What is the consequence of abandoning one's *svadharma*?

Sin, *papam*

Arjuna had raised the issue of *sin* in his initial query, as it was a perception of a sense of sinfulness in killing his own people in battle that had triggered his ethical dilemma and *vishada* in the first place. The Divine Teacher points out in the following verse that 'sin' in this case would arise when one who, having perceived his *svabhava* and *svadharma*, chooses to *abstain* from taking the action demanded.

सुखदुःखे समे कृत्वा लाभालाभौ जयाजयौ |
ततो युद्धाय युज्यस्व नैवं पापमवाप्स्यसि ||2.38||

Treating alike pleasure and pain,	सुख दुःखे समे कृत्वा
Gain and loss, victory and defeat,	लाभ अलाभौ जय अजयौ
Get set to engage in the battle!	ततः युद्धाय युज्यस्व
In this way, you will incur no sin.	न एवं पापम् अवाप्स्यसि

For a warrior, the action demanded must involve doing battle and thus killing, for a righteous cause. Arjuna, as an accomplished warrior, knows this only too well. As corrective action must be taken, there should not be double standards —bestowing lenience on one's near and dear. There must be impartiality in the execution of one's duty. Thus, it would be sinful for judges not to pass deservedly harsh sentences, or for teachers to pass students performing miserably, merely because the persons involved are near and dear. For the ultimate truth is that indeed we are all intimately connected to one another. All are our own people, without exception. So we must put aside our partiality and sentimental weakness in such matters, and do what needs to be done. This doing what is right must be the very essence of all *dharma*. Acting with partiality, or weakly abstaining from the right duty, constitutes *adharma*.

However, in the Indian tradition, *sin* (*papam*) is not viewed with the harshness that is perceived in traditional religions. It is perceived more in the context of ignorance (*avidya*). So-called *sin* comes out of ignorance, when the *gunas* of *tamas* and *rajas* predominate in one's truth of being. The wise know this to be an action of *Prakriti*. So they are not inclined to judge harshly, in blaming and condemning unenlightened individuals entrapped by the lower nature. Inwardly, they are inclined to take the position of Jesus Christ: 'Forgive them, for they know not what they do'. Yet, they will take appropriate steps to bring in correction.

In the Indian tradition, therefore, it is well recognised that an evolution in consciousness keeps taking place. One who awakens to this reality seeks to evolve consciously, rather than unconsciously. In the ancient Vedic prayer referred to in the first chapter, we remind ourselves daily to value this waking journey in consciousness, as an ascent from *asat* to *sat*, from *tamas* to *jyoti*, and from *mrityu* to *amritam*.

When, instead of ascending to the truth, we descend into ignorance, then that movement could be described as sin. Spirituality at work implies that we do not make this slide downwards, but instead keep moving upwards, through development and purification of the various parts of our being, and awakening the realisation of the True Self. While development leads to self-actualisation, purification implies an inner transformation, whereby the *gunas* of *tamas* and *rajas* are increasingly replaced by *sattva-guna* (to the extent possible) and the entire *guna* nature is also transformed, leading to self-discipline and a shift from the lower nature to the higher. Thus, the developed and purified individual can serve as a perfect instrument of the Divine for the flow of *Shakti* in the higher nature.

The shift upward in consciousness is to be accompanied by a shift inward: from object-centred consciousness, driven by identification with the false ego-self, to the reality of the True Self hidden in our innermost being. This implies a conscious awakening and faith in the ultimate truth that all the happiness, ease and illumination we seek is already present, although hidden, in our *Antaratman*, in the form of *antahsukha*, *antararama* and *antarjyoti*, as discussed earlier (verse 5.24).

Guided by that alone, we should do our work, based on our inner calling and true consciousness. Thus centred in pure knowing, we always stay rightly true at the purely subjective core of our outgoing personality. It is only there that we stay rightly unperturbed by external circumstances and the outcome of our work. This gives us an essential sense of equipoise, enabling us to treat equally (*sama*) the reactions that are naturally aroused in us by the contact of the senses with sense-objects, be it pleasure or pain (*sukha-duhkhau*). Or, it could be an outcome of our work, be it gain or loss (*labha-alabhau*) or be it victory or defeat (*jaya-ajayau*). We will explore this theme in greater detail in the chapters to come.

But before concluding this chapter, let us take one more look at the issue of sin that has been bothering Arjuna. When (in verse 1.45), he refers to slaughter as a heinous sin or evil crime (*mahat papam*), it does ring a sympathetic chord in us all. For when incidents of genocide or terrorist attacks on innocent victims are brought to our notice, we do (and should) feel that some terrible evil is taking place. Yet, the scenario is different in Arjuna's case at Kurukshetra, where the enemies that he must kill are not innocent victims, but perpetrators or supporters of great evil in society. Thus it is his duty and responsibility to engage them in battle.

However, sometimes, even when we know what is right and wrong, we get somehow led to taking the path of *adharma*, and engaging in wrong-doing (either to others or to ourselves), as if by some force. Such evils could be something obviously extreme and wrong, such as rape, or could be less obvious — as in the case of harmful addictions, varying from substance abuse to cheating and copying.

Arjuna poses this question to Krishna in the following verse.

अर्जुन उवाच ।
अथ केन प्रयुक्तोऽयं पापं चरति पूरुषः ।
अनिच्छन्नपि वार्ष्णेय बलादिव नियोजितः ॥3.36॥

Arjuna said:	अर्जुनः उवाच
What is it that compels	अथ केन प्रयुक्तः
A man to commit evil,	अयं पापं चरति पूरुषः
Even against his will, Krishna,	अनिच्छन् अपि वार्ष्णेय
As if driven by some force?	बलात् इव नियोजितः

Here, the sin referred to is not caused by abstention or inaction, but by deliberate action, not caring for the harm that such action causes. The predominant *guna* that operates here is *rajas,* not *tamas.* In both cases, however, the sin occurs due to a lack of wisdom, a sense of irresponsibility, and lack of care and concern for the negative consequences — reflective of an absence of *sattva-guna*. Arjuna refers to a forceful impulsion acting from within, against which one feels helpless.

The reply of the Divine Teacher to Arjuna's query, as well as his explanations on how we tend to get trapped into wrong-doing by uncontrolled *rajas*, are discussed in the next chapter.

6

Desire and Indiscrimination

श्रीभगवानुवाच ।
काम एष क्रोध एष रजोगुणसमुद्भवः ।
महाशनो महापाप्मा विद्ध्येनमिह वैरिणम् ।।3.37।।

The Blessed Lord said:	श्रीभगवान् उवाच
It is desire, which can turn into wrath,	कामः एषः क्रोधः एषः
Arising from the guna of rajas in nature.	रजः गुण समुद्भवः
It is all-devouring and all-corrupting.	महा अशनः महा पाप्मा
Beware here of this enemy (of the soul)!	विद्धि एनम् इह वैरिणम्

This is the direct response given by the Divine Teacher to Arjuna's query, 'What compels a man to commit evil, even against his will, as if driven by some force?'

Desire is invariably the root cause of all wrong-doing — perpetrated either on oneself (as with substance abuse) or on others (as with rape and mindless slaughter of innocent people). Desire in the form of *kama-thrishna* arises in our being naturally, when the *guna* of *rajas* (*rajo-guna*) in lower nature takes possession of our being, manifesting as *lust* and *greed*. Unless controlled in some way, it can turn into a raging fire, often demanding immediate gratification. This is sometimes referred to as the animal nature in us. Yet, when animals act with aggression and violence, we do not find fault with them, for we know that they are not responsible for their actions. This is simply a case of nature acting through their being.

However, we do find fault with human beings when they indulge in such acts, because we expect them to show care and concern for other beings. This implies invoking the *sattva-guna* — manifesting as the discriminating intellect (*buddhi*) and resolute will (*dhriti*), thus making the human *svadharma* different from that of animals. According to the Gita, this humanly intelligent discernment arises from the light of the indwelling soul, which, when awakened, is always able to witness, understand, approve or disapprove, and give or withhold sanction, thus asserting its lordship over the mechanical movements of the lower nature.

In the absence of such control, the *rajasic guna* can wreak havoc. Thus acting 'freely' on its impulsions, it tends to be all-devouring and all-corrupting (*mahashano mahapapma*). This, of course, is no freedom! True freedom arises where there is control, to act one way or another, when there is free will to choose. Animal nature has no such free will. Human indulgence in this nature can cause great harm to oneself and the environment, as it reflects a downward movement in the evolution of consciousness. Thus, uncontrolled desire is described here as the enemy of the soul.

Wrath (*krodha*) is described here as the companion of desire, also reflecting *rajo-guna*. When desires are obstructed — as they often are — we feel frustrated, with anger rising naturally in us. What starts as a mild irritation can flare up into a raging fire. In the resulting heat, we often lose discrimination, acting thus in destructive ways. Anger arises not just when we do not get what we want, but also when we get what is unwanted: desire manifesting in a negative form.

The Seat of Desire

The True Self (*Atman*) is considered to be veiled by five sheaths (*panchakosha*) of ignorance. Outermost is the physical sheath, called *anna-maya kosha*: covering the physical body, which is predominated by *tamo-guna*. The next sheath inside the physical is the vital sheath, called *prana-maya kosha*: covering the subtle-energy body, which is predominated by *rajo-guna*. The energy here is the vitality of the life-force in the body. The next inner sheath is the mental sheath, called *mano-maya kosha*: covering the mental body, which, when fully developed, has the potential to be predominated by *sattva-guna*. However, in the undeveloped and unpurified condition, the mind tends to be driven by the *gunas* of *rajas* and *tamas*. Of course, all the three *gunas* of *Prakriti* tend to inter-mix and have a dynamic and often conflict-ridden interaction in Mind, Life and Matter.

Through spiritual development, it is however possible for *sattva* to predominate and assert itself. Then it is possible to go beyond the play of the *gunas*, and thus penetrate inwards beyond the outer three veils into the next inner sheath, called *vijnana-maya kosha*, which is *intuitive* in nature. Finally, one is able to penetrate the innermost sheath, called *ananda-maya kosha*, which points to the blissful realm of the *Antaratman*, the evolving soul or psychic being. According to Sri Aurobindo, spiritual evolution implies not only this journey *inwards* into our innermost being, but also a journey in consciousness *upwards*, beyond the limitations of the physical-vital-mental planes (*annamaya*, *pranamaya* and *manomaya* respectively), to supra-mental (*vijnana*) levels above the mind, culminating in the *Supermind*, and connecting to *sat-chit-ananda*.

In this evolutionary process, the seat of desire (where *rajas* abides) appears primarily to be in the *prana-maya kosha*. The natural seat of vital desire is in the *senses*, *indriyas*. It is through the five *cognitive senses* — of *hearing, touching, seeing, tasting and smelling* (associated with the five sense organs — ear, skin, eye, tongue, nose respectively) — collectively called *jnanendriyas* — that we apprehend the outer world. It is through their contact with various *sense-objects*, *vishayas*, that desire is aroused in us: to acquire, to consume or to possess them — reflective of *kama-thrishna*.

The impulsions seeking gratification in us are primarily vital forces. They end up exerting their influence in all parts of our being, as described in the following verse.

इन्द्रियाणि मनो बुद्धिः अस्याधिष्ठानमुच्यते ।
एतैर्विमोहयत्येषः ज्ञानमावृत्य देहिनम् ।।3.40।।

In the senses, mind and intellect,	इन्द्रियाणि मनः बुद्धिः
It finds its dwelling place, its seat.	अस्य अधिष्ठानम् उच्यते
By these, clouding knowledge,	एतैः ज्ञानम् आवृत्य
It bewilders the embodied soul.	विमोहयति एषः देहिनम्

The cognitive senses provide a basis for the vital forces to emerge. As these urges are primarily sensory in nature, they may be called lower vital impulses. Their seat in the body is traditionally linked to the first and second *chakras* (*muladhara* and *svadhishthana*), whose seats in the physical body are at the bottom of the spine and near the genital organs respectively. These *chakras* represent subtle energy centres in the subtle body, with their seats in the central spine in the body, where subtle energy vortices are believed to form.

But, for action, *karma*, to take place, there needs to be an exercise of volition, of will. The physical instruments through which actions take place are also perceived to be a kind of *indriya*, which broadly means capacity. In the Indian tradition, they are called *karmendriyas*, which are also five in number: speaking, grasping, moving, sexual activity and excretion (associated with corresponding organs of action — mouth, hand, feet, genitals and anus).

In animals, the use of *karmendriyas* seems spontaneous (by means of animal instinct). However, in humans, endowed with mental faculties, the sense-mind (*manas*) intervenes, using information meaningfully to direct and command the sense organs as desired. That sense-mind, or mind in short, can also use the added resource of discrimination, which is the domain of the intellect, *buddhi*. Indeed, this is needed for man's *svadharma*. The wise use of *buddhi* must depend on the degree of its development and purity. When *rajasic* desire is too strong and uncontrollable, use can turn into misuse, and sometimes abuse.

For this reason, the Divine Teacher includes the *manas* and the *buddhi* also as seats of desire in the human being, in addition to the primary seat of the senses, *indriyas*. The impulsive and restless energy of *rajasic* desire, originating in the *indriyas*, can overwhelm and overpower the *manas* and the *buddhi* into relenting to its power, thereby according sanction to the desired action. The judgement of the intellect gets clouded in this process, and the embodied soul in turn gets bewildered.

Behind the scenes, there is of course the actor, in the form of the ego-self (*ahankara*), which imparts a sense of doership to the action. It is the *rajasic ahankara* that manifests, whenever desire rages and overpowers the individual being. *Rajasic ahankara* is also linked to the desire to become someone great — reflective of *bhava-thrishna*. This develops the will and the ability to work hard and to succeed. The nature of desire here is more enduring, and not transient as in the case of lower vital sensory impulses. Such desires of ambition (for achievement and success) may be referred to as central vital desires, and their centre in the body is traditionally linked to the third *chakra* (*manipura*) located behind the navel. A healthy development of the central vital being is needed to achieve success and thereby the ability to do whatever one wishes. The ultimate conquest is, of course, self-conquest!

It may be noted that the Gita's message is not limited to the purification of the *gunas*, leading to a predominance of *sattvic ahankara*, which is still binding in nature. The Gita is not just about developing the best in the human; its main objective is to bring the Divine in the human. This implies Self-realisation through ego-transcendence and the flow of higher nature in the individual being. In terms of *chakras*, this implies free functioning of the higher energy centres — located at the heart region (*anahata*), throat (*vishuddha*), between the eyebrows (*ajna*) and above the crown of the head (*sahasrara*).

The desires predominating in our lower nature (typically, for wealth, *artha*, and sensual pleasures, *kama*) are not forbidden in the Indian tradition. They have a rightful place as human objectives, called *purusharthas*, but they need to be subservient to the other great human objective of *dharma*. Furthermore, *artha* and *kama* need eventually to be transcended in order to realise the ultimate human objective of *moksha*, which implies complete liberation from the entrapment of the lower nature through Self-realisation and ego-transcendence. The Divine Teacher refers to desire as the enemy of the soul, because the insistent pull it exerts in our being is downward in nature — opposite to the spiritual pull upwards.

The *sattva-guna* needs invoking, so that *rajasic* desire is regulated and made to conform with *dharma*. If such self-control is missing — as is often the case — one is tempted to use all kinds of *adharmic* means, including force, deception, fraud and manipulation, in order to gratify the insistent desires. Indeed, modern education has done little to bring in the required correction. The discriminating intellect, instead of exercising a moral control, is then made to serve as an instrument of cunning, rationalisation and self-justification.

Moreover, in modern times, we witness a growing globalised culture promoting high consumption and sensual gratification, with easy access to diverse sources of supernormal stimuli. In today's world, young people are so vulnerable to getting hooked to excessive consumption of junk food, alcohol, drugs, as well as social media and pornography. Once hooked, they find it extremely difficult to free themselves from addictive over-indulgence.

So it is not without good reason that the Divine Teacher warns: desire is all-devouring and all-corrupting. We may like to believe that we are the masters and possessors of various objects of desires, but the bitter truth is quite the opposite. We are slaves — not masters. We are the possessed —not the possessors. The pleasures gained in this process are invariably short-lived, often harming others and the environment. So the price we end up paying is often heavy, causing us much pain and suffering.

From Desire to Indiscrimination

As discussed earlier, the basic shift needed on the spiritual path is from habitual object-centred awareness to our innermost being or soul-centred awareness. We need to retain this Self-awareness of the indwelling *dehi*, while squarely engaging with the outside world.

In Sri Aurobindo's words, 'We must enter into these inner and higher parts of ourselves by an inward plunge or disciplined penetration and bring back with us to the surface their secrets... We must learn to live within and no longer on the surface, and be and act from the inner depths and from a soul that has become sovereign over the nature.'[6.1]

Sadly, at present, it is the lower nature that holds sovereignty over us: a condition that will persist until we make the inner transformation. To make the inward shift, we must realise how unconsciously we get obsessed with the outer world and get lost in it, losing our discrimination. Unless we train ourselves in self-control, the senses tend to get excited by their objects, creating an agitation. The lesser trained minds are easily driven by a strong outward movement towards acquiring or grasping the objects of desire. This is pithily described in the following verse.

इन्द्रियाणां हि चरतां यन्मनोऽनुविधीयते |
तदस्य हरति प्रज्ञां वायुर्नावमिवाम्भसि ||2.67||

By the roving of the senses	इन्द्रियाणां हि चरतां
The mind is led to follow,	यत् मनः अनुविधीयते
Carrying away one's discrimination,	तत् अस्य हरति प्रज्ञां
As wind drags away a ship on water.	वायुः नावम् इव अम्भसि

The metaphor used here is that of a ship on water, driven by the action of strong winds (*vayurnavam-ivambhasi*). In a similar way, the discriminating intellect can get carried away by the sense-mind, excited by the longings and impulsions aroused by various sensory inputs — especially when the senses are, by force of habit, scanning the environment for such inputs. How desire turns into indiscrimination is depicted beautifully in the following two verses.

ध्यायतो विषयान्पुंसः सङ्गस्तेषूपजायते |
सङ्गात्सञ्जायते कामः कामात्क्रोधोऽभिजायते ||2.62||

Thinking about sense-objects	ध्यायतः विषयान् पुंसः
Evokes attachment to them.	सङ्गः तेषु उपजायते
Such attachment leads to desire,	सङ्गात् सञ्जायते कामः
And desire (frustrated) causes anger.	कामात् क्रोधः अभिजायते

क्रोधाद्भवति सम्मोहः सम्मोहात्स्मृतिविभ्रमः |
स्मृतिभ्रंशाद् बुद्धिनाशः बुद्धिनाशात्प्रणश्यति ||2.63||

Anger leads one to bewilderment,	क्रोधात् भवति सम्मोहः
Bewilderment leads to confused memory,	सम्मोहात् स्मृति विभ्रमः
Confused memory to indiscrimination,	स्मृति भ्रंशात् बुद्धिनाशः
Indiscriminate action leads to one's ruin.	बुद्धि नाशात् प्रणश्यति

The very nature of the sense-mind, *manas*, is to observe the sense-objects, *vishayas*, with interest. This naturally triggers thoughts about them — one thought leading into another. If this thinking process is not nipped in the bud, the thinking gathers momentum. Then one develops an attachment, *sanga*, to the sense-object that has captured one's attention. This naturally creates a longing, *kama*, to acquire or possess the sense-object. So, one tends to indulge in fantasy, further strengthening the longing and attachment. Sometimes, the urge is not driven by attraction, but by repulsion. When the sense-object induces in us a sense of revulsion or hatred, we still dwell mentally on the object, thereby developing a kind of negative attachment, desiring to push away or destroy the object.

As seen earlier, the natural companion of desire is wrath, and so, when the desire (positive or negative) is not satisfied immediately or is thwarted or opposed, anger (*krodha*) starts building up. Anger is something that we all feel in our bodies — a discomfort that we experience as a kind of energetic heat welling up within us, prompting us to lash out, with words or action. However, before our *karmendriyas* get into action, some activity is triggered by the heat of anger in our brains.

Anger (*krodha*) causes bewilderment (*sammoha*) in our minds. We tend to get confused in this process, and this causes things to get mixed up in our memory, *smrti-vibhrama*. In extreme anger, we tend to forget norms and relationships. We may claim to love our spouse or parent, but in the heat of anger, all that love is lost (at least temporarily) and we treat the other person as an adversary. Forgetting the relationship, love turns to hatred. We may even feel a sense of power during these moments, but the truth is that we are helplessly rendering ourselves vulnerable to the *rajasic* force of the lower nature.

The *sattvic guna*, which alone can give us clarity and discrimination in such crucial moments, is rendered powerless. Thus, we lose all sense of discrimination. It is then that we may be led to act indiscriminately, and this can sometimes lead us to complete ruin (*buddhinashatpranashyati*). Thus, we may lose friendships and other relationships; we may also lose our jobs; we may get convicted; we may lose our very lives! Sometimes, we may choose to suppress the turmoil, instead of releasing it externally. However, such suppression, especially done in excess, can also lead to ruinous situations, such as nervous breakdowns and mental illnesses. It is indeed the *sattvic guna* that makes us aware of our indiscrimination at a later point in time. It may be too late, and the damage done may be irredeemable.

Attraction and Aversion, *ragadveshau*

Prevention is always better than cure! To do this, it is helpful to trace the chain of events that led to our indiscriminate action. We find that the chain begins with the sense-object, followed by mental dwelling on the object, leading to attachment, further strengthening into desire, which later develops into anger and bewilderment. Experience shows that it becomes more and more difficult to check the flow of such events, and to take corrective action as we move down the chain. It is easier to do so at the early stages — nipping the growth in the bud itself. Otherwise, it can sometimes get to be impossible.

इन्द्रियस्येन्द्रियस्यार्थे रागद्वेषौ व्यवस्थितौ |
तयोर्न वशमागच्छेत् तौ ह्यस्य परिपन्थिनौ ||3.34||

In the object of a sense experience	इन्द्रियस्य इन्द्रियस्य अर्थे
Attraction and aversion lie in ambush.	राग द्वेषौ व्यवस्थितौ
One should not fall prey to these two;	तयोः न वशम् आगच्छेत्
They are major obstacles on one's path.	तौ हि अस्य परिपन्थिनौ

Both possibilities, attraction (*raga*) and aversion (*dvesha*), potentially lurk in every sense-object. It is possible that what may attract one person may repulse another. Both *raga* and *dvesha* are seen here as obstacles on the spiritual path. They both cause the same chain of events, leading from uncontrolled desire to indiscriminate action. It is as though they are lying in ambush to capture us. Until we gain the equipoise to deal effectively with them, it would be wise to guard ourselves against them.

The easiest course of action is to stay away from such sense-objects. Of course, that is easier said than done! The antidote to the pull of external objects is the attraction to the inner spiritual soul. It is this inner contact that alone can deliver on the promise of enduring happiness and fulfilment. The more we discover this, the more external attractions tend to fall away on their own. The conscious cultivation of dispassion or detachment to external sense-objects is recommended on the spiritual path, and it is called *vairagya*. It liberates us from the snare of *ragadveshau*, and also from fear (*bhaya*). After acquiring and possessing sense-objects, we have to deal invariably with the fear of losing them. Similarly, after successfully attacking or repulsing sense-objects, we tend to keep thinking of them, afraid of their return to torment us. Thus, *ragadveshau* turns into *bhaya*! While the trigger for *ragadveshau* lies hidden in the external sense-object, *bhaya* lurks in our own minds.

The following verse, composed by the fifth-century Indian poet, *Bhartrhari*, in his *Vairagya shatakam* (verse 31)[6.2], expresses this beautifully. It covers a wide spectrum of sense-objects that induce fear in us; these are mere examples; the list is, of course, inexhaustible!

भोगे रोगभयं कुले च्युतिभयं वित्ते नृपालाद्भयं।
माने दैन्यभयं बले रिपुभयं रूपे जराया भयम् ।।
शास्त्रे वादिभयं गुणे खलभयं काये कृतान्ताद्भयं।
सर्वं वस्तु भयान्वितं भुवि नृणां वैराग्यमेवाभयम् ।।

In enjoyment is fear of disease,
In reputation is fear of disgrace,
In wealth is fear of rulers (taxes)!

In honour is fear of humiliation,
In power is fear of adversaries,
In beauty is fear of ageing!

In knowledge is fear of opponents,
In virtue is fear of slander,
In the body is fear of death!

All things are fraught with fear!
Vairagya alone brings fearlessness in men!

The insight that emerges from the above verse is that fear lurks in the desire itself, like a shadow — rather than in the sense-object. When we desire something, the enjoyment in what we desire is invariably marred by the fear of encountering the opposite of what we desire!

What we desire and its exact opposite form a duality, referred to as *dvandva* in the Gita. Thus, pleasure and pain, attraction and repulsion, honour and dishonour form natural pairs of opposites — like two sides of one coin. We cannot get rid of one, without getting rid of the other. If we seek freedom from one end of a polarity, it follows that we must no longer be attracted to the other end. In other words, fearlessness comes with *vairagya*. Indeed, it is then, in a state of fearlessness in the presence of any external circumstance, that one qualifies to be a *sthitaprajna*. By letting go of *raga*, we also let go of *dvesha*, and we become free of *bhaya*. In this process, we also become free of the enemy of the soul, *kama*, along with its companion, *krodha*.

This total release from the entrapment of the lower nature is captured in the Gita by the term, *vita-raga-bhaya-krodha*, as described in the following verse in the Gita. Then, there is no longer any psychological agitation caused by hankering for pleasure, or by suffering induced by thwarted desires.

दुःखेष्वनुद्विग्नमनाः सुखेषु विगतस्पृहः |
वीतरागभयक्रोधः स्थितधीर्मुनिरुच्यते ||2.56||

One whose mind is unperturbed by sorrow,	दुःखेषु अनुद्विग्न मनाः
Who does not crave for sensual pleasures,	सुखेषु विगत स्पृहः
Who is free from attraction, fear and wrath,	वीत राग भय क्रोधः
Such a one is called a sage of steady wisdom.	स्थितधीः मुनिः उच्यते

In the next chapter, we will explore how through wise self-regulation and the practice of meditation, equipoise can be attained.

7

Self-control, Meditation and Regulated Action

इन्द्रियाणि पराण्याहुः इन्द्रियेभ्यः परं मनः |
मनसस्तु परा बुद्धिः यो बुद्धेः परतस्तु सः ||3.42||

Superior to objects are the senses,	इन्द्रियाणि पराणि आहुः
Superior to the senses is the mind,	इन्द्रियेभ्यः परं मनः
Superior to the mind is the intellect,	मनसः तु परा बुद्धिः
Superior to the intellect is the Self!	यः बुद्धेः परतः तु सः

On the spiritual path, it is always necessary to keep in mind the main objective — *Self-realisation* and *union with the Divine*. At least, the aim should be *fulfilment in life* — by nurturing knowledge, skills and a positive attitude, and also by rejecting or changing habits found to be unhealthy and dysfunctional. We need a deep aspiration to evolve consciously — from *asat* to *sat*, from *tamas* to *jyoti*, and from *mrityu* to *amritam*.

The more this aspiration seeps into all parts of our being, the easier and fuller will be this adventure of life. Mere theory on this path is clearly not enough. As Arjuna points out, even knowing right from wrong, we may get driven helplessly to wrongdoing. For example, even shown the ills of cigarette addiction, one may yield to the habit of smoking. Similarly, knowing that cheating and copying are wrong does not prevent some students from carrying on with these habits. Here we find that the human will may fail, through weakness, to execute acts known to be right and true.

Every individual (*jiva*) is like a complex organisation, with the different parts of being working like different employees. For this system to function successfully, the employees need a common vision and mission. Ideally, all need to act in synergy, fully cooperating with one another. To resolve their differences, a proper chain of command is needed under a CEO, established in a position to assert authority. The CEO of this company should doubtless be the True Self, the *Atman* (more appropriately referred to here as *Jivatman*, the central being presiding over the individual *jiva*). It should stay in command above the intellect (*buddhi*), which is superior to the sense-mind (*manas*). This in turn is superior to the senses (*indriya*). It is these senses that interact with objects (*vishayas*) of the outside world, receiving inputs through the cognitive senses (*jnanendriyas*), and acting on them through the *karmendriyas*.

In the case of the evolving individual (not yet fully Self-realised), it would be more correct to assign the CEO's role to the evolving soul, called *Chaitya Purusha* or *Antaratman*, who is the deputy of the presiding *Jivatman*. It is from the guidance of this indwelling soul that ideally all other parts of the being should act. The functioning would then be integral, harmonious and complete. Unfortunately, for most of us, this is presently far from true.

The Chariot Allegory

Sense-objects may be so bewitching that we lose all sense of self-control and discrimination. This is depicted in the *Kathopanishad's chariot allegory*, also symbolised by Arjuna's chariot in the Gita.

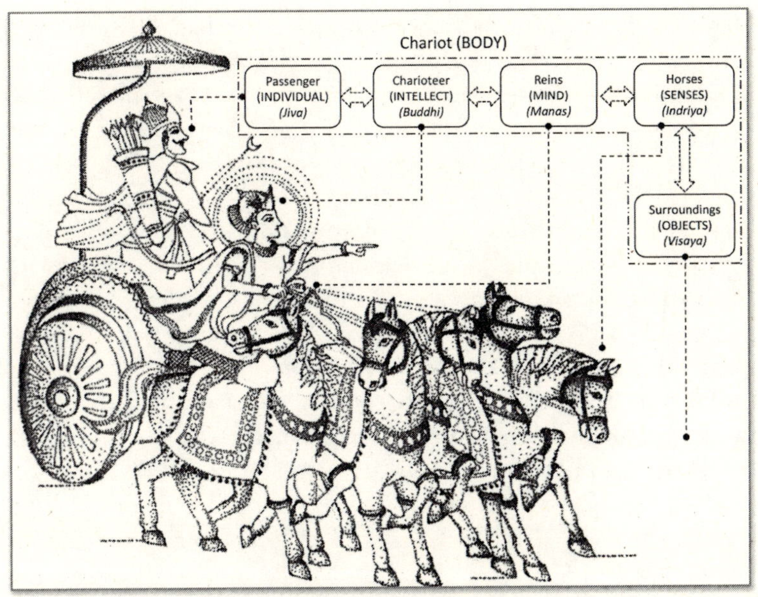

Chariot Allegory
(Illustration by Swati Bali)

In the presence of *ragadveshau* entangled in the sense-objects, the five senses (represented by the horses in the above allegory) tend to go wild. In wanting to contact the objects, each of the five horses may pull in a different direction, making it very difficult to control and direct the chariot's movement. Without a skilled and wise charioteer (representing *buddhi,* the intelligent will), the objective of riding the chariot (living the adventure of life meaningfully) cannot be rightly achieved. So the charioteer holds the key to the chariot's performance. That charioteer, for Arjuna, was none other than Krishna, the Divine *Avatar.* According to the Gita, the same Supreme Divine Being lives hidden alike in the hearts of each one of us. Though hidden thus within, we need to awaken to its reality, so that our *buddhi* abides by its light.

The charioteer operates the reins (representing the mind, *manas*), which in turn controls the horses. Such is the ideal chain of command. Sadly, in our case, the *buddhi* is not yet awakened and assertive. Instead of it controlling the mind, it is *manas* that gets the *buddhi* to sanction what it wants. What it wants, of course, is dictated by the insistent pull of the senses, which are enslaved, through *ragadveshau*, by the sense-objects. So, for an ordinary person led by the false *ego-self* or *ahankara*, the entire chain of command gets reversed! The locus of control does not even seem to be in the individual, but rather outside — in the world of sense-objects. We get to see an interesting analogy of such reversal in the chain of command in some of our most popular schools for rich children. Parents with money power exert control over the school management, who in turn control the teachers and make them fall in line with the demands of their kids!

Withdrawal of the Senses, *pratyahara*

The chariot allegory shows clearly the need to wrest control over the wild horses. Taming them is not easy. So we need a training programme or a practice by which we can gain mastery. However, in the present instance, we need to recognise that we alone can help ourselves; there is no other. As discussed earlier in the second chapter (verse 6.5), you are your best friend, but can also be your worst enemy! To lift oneself up, an inner discipline is needed, keeping goal and aspiration always at heart.

There are many suggestions for self-regulation in the verses of the Gita. Some are touched upon in this chapter. In the sixth chapter of the Gita in particular, there are broad references made to the traditional practice of *Rajayoga* — made popular in the Indian tradition by the *Yoga Sutras of Patanjali*. According to this system of practice, called *yogabhyasa*, there are typically eight stages of practice. We begin with the practice of *yama* (absentions such as non-violence, non-stealing, speaking truth and sexual purity) and *niyama* (observances like cleanliness, scriptural study and various austerities) — which are a set of dos and don'ts, the practice of which has a purifying effect on our being. Along with this, we practice the physical *yogic* exercises of *asana* (nurturing stillness, strength and flexibility in the body and correcting our posture) and *pranayama* (related to breath control) — practices that are increasingly gaining popularity all over the world, commonly called *yoga*.

The true purpose of *yoga* is not to master the physical body, but to attain union with the Divine. In this context, the next four stages of *Rajayoga* gain importance, although they are often overlooked in the popular understanding and practice of *yoga*. The fifth stage of *Rajayoga* practice is of relevance here — in the context of the senses getting entrapped by various sense-objects. This practice is called *pratyahara*, literally meaning weaning away from food. In this practice, we deliberately stay away from the food offered by the sense-objects, consciously withdrawing our senses, with the aim of bringing our awareness deep within ourselves. This is reflected in the following Gita verse, using the analogy of a tortoise (*kurma*) retracting its limbs inside its shell on sensing danger.

यदा संहरते चायं   कूर्मोऽङ्गानीव सर्वशः |
इन्द्रियाणीन्द्रियार्थेभ्यः   तस्य प्रज्ञा प्रतिष्ठिता ||2.58||

When one is able to withdraw fully	यदा संहरते च अयं
His senses from entangling objects,	इन्द्रियाणि इन्द्रय अर्थेभ्यः
As a tortoise draws in all its limbs,	कूर्मः अङ्गानि इव सर्वशः
Then he is said to have stable insight.	तस्य प्रज्ञा प्रतिष्ठिता

In Sri Aurobindo's words, 'We must put an end to the cause of desire, the rushing out of the senses to seize and enjoy their objects. We must draw them back when they are inclined thus to rush out, draw them away from their objects,

— as the tortoise draws in his limbs into the shell, so these into their source, quiescent in the mind, the mind quiescent in intelligence, the intelligence quiescent in the soul…'[7.1]

The *yoga* of the Gita, unlike traditional ascetic practices, emphasises the need for and importance of living in the world, rather than permanently withdrawing. The physical withdrawal may be done every now and then, for the purpose of practice of self-mastery. The focus of the Gita is thus on inner renunciation, not outer. It should be ultimately possible to practice *pratyahara* in the hustle and bustle of the marketplace.

One-pointed concentration, *dharana*

In order to achieve the objective of making the 'mind quiescent in intelligence, the intelligence quiescent in the soul', it is necessary to engage in daily practice. Such meditative practices should ideally be done in isolation. It is extremely beneficial to find for oneself a quiet place to sit comfortably, undisturbed in meditation for a prolonged period, not less than about twenty minutes at a stretch. The objective of this practice is a progressive stilling of body and mind, so that attention can be exclusively and wholly directed to the True Self.

योगी युञ्जीत सततम् आत्मानं रहसि स्थितः ।
एकाकी यतचित्तात्मा निराशीरपरिग्रहः ।।6.10।।

The Yogin should always strive to be yoked,	योगी युञ्जीत सततम्
To the Self, by choosing to be in seclusion,	आत्मानं रहसि स्थितः
Alone, with thought and being under control,	एकाकी यत चित्त आत्मा
Free from the pull of desires and possessions.	निराशीः अपरिग्रहः

The basic abstentions and observances of *yama* and *niyama* of *Rajayoga* will prove to be helpful here, because they introduce a moral purification that is conducive to enabling psychological stillness. It is then relatively easier to be free from the pull of desires and possessions.

The other two basic practices of *asana* and *pranayama* contribute greatly to the ability of sitting still, with ease, for a prolonged period. Indeed, only after the body finds integrity in a still posture (without any twitches, aches and pains troubling the mind), can there be a possibility of stilling the mind of other disturbances. The vertical and erect posture of the spine is also known to be highly conducive for meditation, and for staying alert and still. One is awake and alert, but calm and at ease, not tensed. Regulating one's breath gently (making it take a comfortably slow rhythm) serves to be very helpful in staying calm throughout the meditation.

It is not enough to control the body and make it still, if the mind remains active in its usual habit of object-centred awareness. The following Gita verse warns against this and refers to such practices as self-deluding and deceiving (*mithyachara*), not achieving the desired purpose of meditation. The deluded person indulging in such practices is described as a *vimudhatma*.

कर्मेन्द्रियाणि संयम्य य आस्ते मनसा स्मरन् ।
इन्द्रियार्थान्विमूढात्मा मिथ्याचारः स उच्यते ||3.6||

He who sits, with his organs of action	कर्मेन्द्रियाणि यः आस्ते
Under control, yet mentally recalling	संयम्य मनसा स्मरन्
Objects of the senses, is self-deluded,	इन्द्रिय अर्थान् विमूढात्मा
Having false notions of self-discipline.	मिथ्या आचारः सः उच्यते

One can choose any object of meditation that is conducive to stilling the mind and releasing it from its natural habit of rushing out towards sense-objects (existing outside, or imagined or remembered). It is helpful to make use of objects that are readily accessible at all times and all places: such as one's breath or heart-beat. In breath meditation (a practice recommended by the Buddha), the objective is simply to pay attention to the breath, to observe and feel the passage of cool air through the nostrils (or the gentle expansion of the abdomen) during the in-breath, and the passage of warm air through the nostrils (or the gentle falling of the abdomen) during the out-breath. We simply stay focussed on the breath throughout the practice. The breath is also an expression of life-energy (*prana*), and it is found helpful to not only be simply conscious of the breath, but to control it gently (as in the practice of *pranayama*) so as to make it deep, regular and rhythmic, typically making the in-breath and out-breath equal in duration.

In Sufi heart rhythm meditation, the breath movement is synchronised with the heart-beat (around eight beats per in-breath or out-breath), and one feels the natural beat of life-energy pulsating throughout one's being. Done regularly, this practice is found to stabilise and calm one's metabolism, improving one's heart rate variability, and enhancing one's ability to tolerate stressful situations with ease.[7.2]

It helps to choose the object of our meditation such that we naturally associate a sense of sacredness with it. The key is to hold our attention steadily there. 'Unwavering like a lamp in a windless place' is the metaphor used in the Gita (verse 6.19) to describe this condition of perfect concentration. One needs to develop the ability to focus on a single object with mind and heart, for a prolonged period, without getting distracted. Such *one*-pointed concentration is called *dharana*: the fifth stage of traditional *Rajayoga* practice. For this, not only must the body be still, but the entire being must enter into stillness, with a single focus — as described in the following verse.

व्यवसायात्मिका बुद्धिः एकेह कुरुनन्दन ।
बहुशाखा ह्यनन्ताश्च बुद्धयोऽव्यवसायिनाम् ।।2.41।।

The intellect, resolute at its core,	व्यवसाय अत्मिका बुद्धिः
Is one-pointed here in its will, Arjuna!	एका इह कुरुनन्दन
Multi-branched, endlessly distracted	बहु शाखाः हि अनन्ताः च
Is the nature of the unresolved intellect.	बुद्धयः अव्यवसायिनाम्

Developing such powers of concentration is not only helpful in meditation, but also achieving success in any endeavour. For it reflects the ability in paying attention exclusively to anything that one chooses. In the words of the Mother (the spiritual collaborator of Sri Aurobindo), 'If you are able to gather together the rays of attention and consciousness on one point and can maintain this concentration with a persistent will, nothing can resist it — whatever it may be, from the most material physical development to the highest spiritual one.'[7.3]

'To attend' also has the meaning 'to care for' — suggesting that both heart and mind are involved. In communication, we feel pleased whenever other persons take care to listen to us whole-heartedly. We hate to discover that they are hardly listening to us because they are distracted. The intellect (*buddhi*) must be resolute at its core (*vyavasayatmika*) and one-pointed (*ekeha*) for the power of *dharana* to develop. Sadly, many of us suffer from *attention deficit disorder*, and it is as though our minds are waiting to be distracted! The term *bahushakha* is used here to describe an intellect that is easily distracted by a hundred other things, and that too endlessly (*anantashca*).

Developing one-pointed concentration is particularly useful in learning and research. One can then generate a laser-like penetration into knowledge that needs to be acquired, undistracted. It is especially effortless when one loves and enjoys whatever one is doing. As a Sufi saying goes,

'One does not have to struggle at all to recall the face of one's beloved: it is always there'! That is how one can be yoked to the Divine.

Meditation, *dhyana*

The ability to enter into and hold one-pointed concentration, *dharana*, leads naturally to the practice of meditation, *dhyana*. There are many methods of practice. The Gita provides simple and broad instructions to enter a calm state of inner stillness, and thereby be yoked (*yukta*) — not only while sitting in meditation, but staying yoked as often as possible. One has to learn to develop and inculcate a meditative poise at all times.

यदा विनियतं चित्तम् आत्मन्येवावतिष्ठते ।
निःस्पृहः सर्वकामेभ्यः युक्त इत्युच्यते तदा ।।6.18।।

When his mental activity is under control,	यदा विनियतं चित्तम्
And he stays anchored in Self-awareness,	आत्मनि एव अवतिष्ठते
Free from craving for all objects of desire,	निःस्पृहः सर्व कामेभ्यः
Then he is said to be established in Yoga.	युक्तः इति उच्यते तदा

The object of meditation here is the Divine — in its many forms: individual, universal or transcendental. The form or level so conceived to be Divine depends on the stage of the evolving spirit in the one who meditates. The purpose here is not seeking fulfilment of some desire or wish to be fulfilled. This is what makes meditation different from prayer, which is often a petition of some kind.

The aim of meditation is simply to commune with the Divine, to be thus spiritually yoked (*yukta*). In this condition, the separate ego-self gets dissolved in a state of pure awareness — found essentially free of all kinds of outside objects (seen or thought or felt to be involved). While prayer calls for the Divine to listen to one's prayer, meditation calls for one to listen to the Divine.

In *dharana*, one concentrates upon a specific object of meditation, undistracted otherwise by other objects and all the relentless *chattering of mind*. As concentration deepens, a stage comes where there is no longer any separation distancing the subject from its seeming object. What remains is One, and that alone. This resonant condition of *perfect yoking* is implied by *dhyana* in *Rajayoga* practice. It is as though the subject dissolves into the object, which could be either internal or external. Here is a poetic description of separated ego-self dissolving into an external object (a distant mountain) by the Chinese poet *Li Po*[7.4].

The birds have vanished into the sky,
And now the last clouds fade away.
We sit together, the mountain and I,
Until only the mountain remains.

The mountain here symbolises the Impersonal Universal Divine. It is no object, but instead, a state of open and wide consciousness, capable of extending through and thus embracing the entire universe. Entering into such wideness is also possible in meditations that do not necessarily call for one-pointed concentration on a single object.

The aim here is an objectless meditation — by simply allowing everything to be just the way it is, not paying any exclusive attention to some particular thing or wanting the current experience (whatever it may be) to be different. One could begin with the sense of hearing, listening in general to all sounds that arise in current awareness, as they eventually fade away. The key here is to pay attention, not to any particular sound, but to the vast background from which all sounds emerge and into which they recede. One then pays attention essentially to Silence. In so doing, one discovers that this Silence, simple yet profound, is quietly present always — of which one had been completely unaware earlier! That Silence is like the mountain in the poem: vast and still, unaffected by the various sounds that come and go, no matter whether one pays any attention or not. That Silence is a pure expression of the Impersonal and Immutable Divine, described as *Akshara Purusha* in the Gita.

In this attempt to stay yoked to that Silence, one is likely to be disturbed by mental chatter that mind keeps on habitually generating. These thoughts can now be treated in the same way as one had previously treated the sounds. One discovers that thoughts and images arise on their own and — if not engaged with and so given continuity — also tend to disappear on their own. The commentator in the head that keeps generating mental noise out of habit, gets tired and becomes subdued, when there is no engaged response!

Let go of the habit of following perceptions, thoughts and feelings, and thereby getting engaged and lost in thought! Just be aware of unending background space, and of its infinite powerful Silence. In that, all this arising and falling keeps taking place. Objects that arise in awareness most commonly are sense perceptions from the outer world (perceived by the cognitive senses, *jnanendriyas*) as sights, sounds, odours, flavours and sensations of touch. Similarly, other subtle objects such as impulses, feelings, emotions, thoughts and images, are constantly generated by our inner world. All these seem to arise in awareness, on their own. On their own, they must invariably disappear, should one simply disregard them, and instead stay with the common background. It is a vastly spacious, silent, boundary-less Awareness, in which all movements and changes occur.

This Awareness is pervaded by a mysterious Divine Presence, described succinctly in the *Ishavasya Upanishad* as '*Om ishavasyam-idam sarvam*'. Simply translated, it means that all This (universe) is pervaded by *Ishvara*. The *Upanishad* verse goes on to conclude: Let go and rejoice! This letting go of all transient objects is nothing less than an act of conscious surrender. In Patanjali's system of *Rajayoga*, success in *dhyana* ends in a state of blissful trance and complete absorption, called *samadhi*. Following this, all action and work fall off and lose importance. It is here that the *yoga of the* Gita differs significantly in the meaning and purpose of *samadhi*.

As explained by Sri Aurobindo, 'Its idea of *samadhi* is quite different from the ordinary notion of the *Yogic* trance; and while Patanjali gives to works only an initial importance for moral purification and religious concentration, the Gita goes so far as to make works the distinctive characteristic of *Yoga*'[7.5]. Work, according to the Gita, continues even after Self-realisation — but performed by higher nature (*Para Prakriti* or *Shakti*) working through one's instrumentation, not by the ego-self of lower nature. It is then that spirituality at work attains its pristine form.

Lingering Taste of the Senses

The grip of the lower nature is not to be underestimated. Practices of *pratyahara*, *dharana* and *dhyana* are very useful and necessary to gain self-control, but until there is a stable Self-realisation and one attains the state of a *sthitaprajna*, one remains vulnerable to the pull of the senses.

विषया विनिवर्तन्ते निराहारस्य देहिनः ।
रसवर्जं रसोऽप्यस्य परं दृष्ट्वा निवर्तते ।।2.59।।

Sense-objects turn away, ceasing to affect,	विषयाः विनिवर्तन्ते
When the embodied self abstains from food.	निराहारस्य देहिनः
But the taste for them continues to linger,	रस वर्जं रसः अपि अस्य
Disappearing only on seeing the Supreme.	परं दृष्ट्वा निवर्तते

As the above verse suggests, the taste (*rasa*) for various sensory pleasures is likely to continue to linger. This is generally harmless; but if it is a case of addiction to harmful indulgences, and one suffers from *withdrawal symptoms*, it is imperative that one should continue to abstain from such 'food'. The instrumental cause of bondage is the mind's habit of continually remembering and dwelling on the sense-objects. Absolute freedom from the pull of the senses can manifest only upon seeing the Supreme (*param drshtva*). Till then, it would be wise to stay vigilant.

In the next verse, the Divine Teacher points out that even wise persons who strive for perfection stay vulnerable to the violent insistence of the senses (*indriyani pramathini*).

यततो ह्यपि कौन्तेय पुरुषस्य विपश्चितः ।
इन्द्रियाणि प्रमाथीनि हरन्ति प्रसभं मनः ।।2.60।।

Arjuna, even for a wise person,	कौन्तेय पुरुषस्य विपश्चितः
Who tries earnestly for perfection,	यततः हि अपि
The mind can get carried away forcibly	हरन्ति प्रसभं मनः
By the violent insistence of the senses.	इन्द्रियाणि प्रमाथीनि

Although, by earnest striving, a predominance of the *sattvic guna* may be attained, there is always a vulnerability to the sudden emergence of *rajas* and *tamas*. When they do so erupt, after being suppressed for long, they can wreck havoc — in the way an overstressed dam can suddenly crack up and collapse, causing extensive damage through flooding.

Mastering Control of the Senses

Clearly, control of the senses cannot be perfectly achieved by mere mental discipline, no matter how well done. One must access something higher than the intellect, some entity whose very nature is calmness and self-mastery.

This is the Supreme Divine, which the Divine Teacher refers to as 'Me' in the following verse. The phrase, *yukta asita matparah* (meaning: sitting, firmly intent on Me), used here (and in verse 6.14), contains the supreme secret of the Gita's *yoga*.

तानि सर्वाणि संयम्य युक्त आसीत मत्परः ।
वशे हि यस्येन्द्रियाणि तस्य प्रज्ञा प्रतिष्ठिता ||2.61||

While restraining all his senses,	तानि सर्वाणि संयम्य
He should sit, firmly intent on Me.	युक्तः आसीत मत्परः
Thus, mastering control of senses,	वशे हि यस्य इन्द्रियाणि
His insight gets firmly established.	तस्य प्रज्ञा प्रतिष्ठिता

It is only through the Divine Grace of the *Purushottama* (the Supreme Divine, having aspects of both the Personal and the Impersonal Divine) that a stable Self-realisation is possible. There is an element of devotion (*bhakti*) that is implied here, and expanded upon later in the Gita. The term 'Me' used here, instead of the Impersonal *Paramatman*, also points to the Divine Teacher's additional role as an *Avatar*, the *Purushottama* descended in human form as the Divine Teacher of the Gita.

Staying yoked to the Divine, it is possible to move among various sense-objects (and even interact with them) but remain in perfect control, as suggested in the following verse. This is the state of liberation of the *sthitaprajna*. While withdrawal from the world of senses and temporary renunciation are helpful in attaining self-control, the final objective is to realise the *Purushottama* dwelling in our hearts and abiding by it. Self-mastery is meant to be proven, not when one stays in hiding, but in the very circumstances (the Kurukshetra) that are uniquely presented to each one of us in our lives. The challenge is to stay unmoved, living amidst inrushing desires, and yet, always doing the right thing to perfection. This is the essence of the *Karmayoga* of the Gita.

आपूर्यमाणमचलप्रतिष्ठं समुद्रमापः प्रविशन्ति यद्वत् ।
तद्वत्कामा यं प्रविशन्ति सर्वे स शान्तिमाप्नोति न कामकामी ।।2.70।।

Always getting filled is the vast ocean, आपूर्यमाणम् समुद्रम् यद्वत्
Staying unmoved by inrushing waters. अचल प्रतिष्ठं आपः प्रविशन्ति
Likewise, living amidst inrushing desires, तद्वत् कामाः यं प्रविशन्ति सर्वे
He who can stay unperturbed, attains सः आप्नोति
Deep inner peace, not he who gets शान्तिम् न
Agitated into fulfilling all his desires. कामकामी

Keeping this in mind, we must perceive all practices of self-control and meditation as not ends in themselves — but also to serve a Divine purpose in terms of implementation in practice. Thus, for example, sitting daily for meditation should not be reduced to a ritual — as it often happens in practice. The objective is to awaken and abide in the Self, and be *yukta* and accordingly remembering to retain this connection and sense of *sat*, while engaging in the world of *asat*. Life then becomes a field (*kshetra*) for living meditation all the time. Accomplishment here is measured, not in terms of outer success or failure, but in staying *yukta*. The intensity of staying yoked and being in communion can be visualised as being measurable in terms of *signal strength* — as in wireless connectivity. We need to take responsibility, so as to realise that we alone can increase the signal strength, through conscious and sustained effort.

Self-regulated Action, *niyatam karma*

In the following two verses, the Divine Teacher begins to outline the foundation of *Karmayoga*. First, we must exercise mental control over the senses, as we engage in the world of sense-objects (using the *karmendriyas*), ideally staying *yukta*. In the previous chariot allegory, this implies that the wild horses of our wilful senses need to be reined in and regulated (*niyamya*) by mind and intellect, anchored in the Self.

यस्त्विन्द्रियाणि मनसा नियम्यारभतेऽर्जुन ।
कर्मेन्द्रियैः कर्मयोगम् असक्तः स विशिष्यते ।।3.7।।

He who, controlling his senses	यः तु इन्द्रयाणि नियम्य
By his mind, yet engages, Arjuna,	मनसा आरभते अर्जुन
His organs of action in karmayoga,	कर्मेन्द्रियैः कर्मयोगम्
Without attachment, he stands out!	असक्तः सः विशिष्यते

Secondly, the action must be done freely, quite unattached (*asakta*). It is possible to act with discernment and integrity only to the extent one is free from attraction or aversion posed by the sense-object, as desire for sense-objects tends to cloud the *buddhi* and corrupt the *manas*.

नियतं कुरु कर्म त्वं कर्म ज्यायो ह्यकर्मणः ।
शरीरयात्रापि च ते न प्रसिद्ध्येदकर्मणः ।।3.8।।

Perform such self-regulated actions!	नियतं कुरु कर्म त्वं
This is indeed superior to 'inaction'.	कर्म ज्यायः हि अकर्मणः
Even your body's maintenance	शरीर यात्रा अपि च ते
Is impossible without action!	न प्रसिद्ध्येत् अकर्मणः

Detachment here does not mean indifference, resulting in inaction (*akarma*). The action must be purposeful (conforming to one's *svadharma*), and done in a self-regulated way (*svabhava-niyatam karma*) — as part of the evolutionary journey (*sharira-yatra*) of the embodied soul. The next chapter describes the essential details of the Gita's *Karmayoga*.

8

Desireless Action (*Nishkama Karma*) — with Equipoise and Skill

कर्मण्येवाधिकारस्ते मा फलेषु कदाचन ।
मा कर्मफलहेतुर्भूः मा ते सङ्गोऽस्त्वकर्मणि ||2.47||

Your right is to action alone,	कर्मणि एव अधिकारः ते
Never to the fruits of action!	मा फलेषु कदाचन
Never let the fruits be the motive,	मा कर्म फल हेतुः भूः
Nor ever be attached to inaction.	मा ते सङ्गः अस्तु अकर्मणि

This is often quoted as the most celebrated verse of the Gita's *Karmayoga*. However, it needs to be read in conjunction with many other verses, in order to be fully understood. Otherwise, it may be viewed as too idealistic and impractical. Indeed, for most of us, the very concept of doing work without the motivation of the fruits of action (*ma karmaphalahetuh*) would seem to be too challenging. What is the basic motive of action for most beings? It would clearly be the desire for an expected result. 'What's in it for me?' seems to be the obvious question one normally asks before thinking of doing any work! If there is no fruit to be desired, why choose to act at all? If this is deemed as attachment to inaction (*sango'stvakarmani*), what is wrong with it?

This needs to be explored further. However, we need a better comprehensive understanding of the need to do anything. There are different types of need, and there is a difference between 'need' and 'greed'.

'Deficiency' Needs and 'Being' Needs

Why do we work, in the first place? We do so, because we are driven by a sense of 'need'. As psychologist Abraham Maslow[8.1] says, needs follow a certain hierarchy — with the 'lower' deficiency needs providing the basic motivation for the vast majority. Yet, there are also 'higher' or self-actualisation or 'being' needs providing the motivation for those who have more or less transcended the deficiency needs. This is often represented schematically by a pyramidal structure.

The deficiency needs themselves form a hierarchy, starting with physiological needs (for the body's survival and healthy functioning). We share such needs with animals. On finding them satisfied, the focus shifts to safety and security — in our jobs, careers, savings and other wealth-related aspects, life and medical insurance, pension and so on. All of these aim to secure one's future well-being against perceived uncertainties. It is interesting to note that other sentient beings (other than humans) are not motivated by such needs pertaining to the future — primarily because they live in the present.

Along with safety needs, human beings have the interpersonal need for a sense of belongingness — to some family or clan or social or religious group or profession. There is a need to love and be loved, and get to be accepted by others. A fourth level of need is that related to esteem and respect. Maslow distinguished between the 'lower' esteem need of needing recognition from others (manifesting as seeking attention, status, honour and fame) and the 'higher' esteem need of self-confidence, self-mastery, strength, independence and freedom.

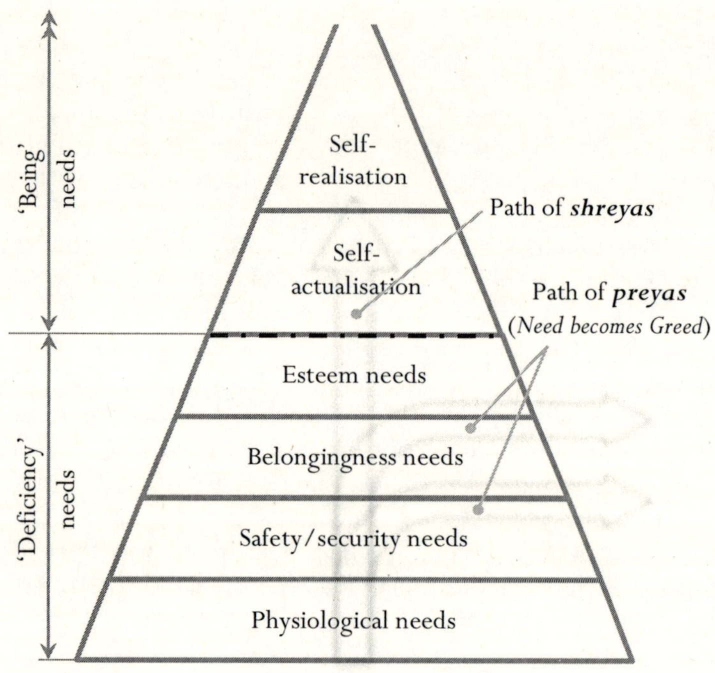

Hierarchy of needs
(adapted from Abraham Maslow)

When the basic deficiency needs (especially the higher esteem need) are reasonably satisfied, a person can enter into and abide in a stage of self-actualisation, without being troubled by the deficiencies. In Maslow's own words, 'What a man can be, he must be'. It is then that a man acts, not to fill a deficiency, but to express a sense of fullness — creatively, through some well-honed talent or skill, through art or knowledge. For example, here the pursuit of knowledge is done for the sake of knowledge, and not to fill some deficiency (to get a good grade or gain recognition). Likewise, one engages in creative arts for the sake of art, and not to satisfy the deficiency need to gain recognition or to make money. In his later years, Maslow proposed a meta-need, beyond self-actualisation, in response to a higher spiritual need, including altruism.

What is the Gita's take on all this? It would hold supreme the highest human need (to which Maslow referred as meta-need) as Self-realisation, by which the Self's true Divine identity and the unified consciousness of *Brahman* are fully realised. The Gita also upholds the importance of self-actualisation, for indeed this is what is expected of the *Karmayogin*'s *svadharma*, based on the individual's unique *svabhava*. This corresponds to the concept of *being needs*, implying the performance of work without concern for the fruit of actions. However, there is much emphasis in the Gita with regard to purification of the *gunas* (becoming more *sattvic*), and this needs to be coupled with the development of individual faculties.

The self-actualised individual stands out, not just in unusual excellence of work performed, but also through inner development, implying a shift from identification with the ego-self to the evolving soul. Only then can true individuation take place. Since the soul, in its Divine essence, is connected with the whole cosmos, the individual's development is then in sync with that of the collective — truly, a manifestation of Divine will.

In traditional Indian spirituality, the emphasis has been on Self-realisation, often at the cost of self-actualisation. However, the *Integral Karmayoga* of the Gita is in line with Maslow's model of development, laying emphasis on individuation along with unification. It is not enough for the ego-self to dissolve into the supreme state of *brahma-nirvana*; it is also desirable to become a perfect instrument of the Divine to carry forward Divine creation.

Arjuna was no ordinary person, but one who was fairly self-actualised himself! So the Gita's teachings would appeal more directly to individuals like Arjuna, who are accomplished and skilled at their work, and have achieved considerable mastery over all their deficiency needs: physiological, safety, belongingness and esteem. For others, these teachings reveal a direction, a pathway to explore. This is the path of *shreyas* — the path of authentic individuation and unification. Although initially pressed by deficiency needs, sooner or later, we need to recognise and align ourselves to this path of *shreyas*.

The problem with deficiency needs is that, in the absence of discrimination, they tend to scale up. In the path of *preyas*, we believe that the source of all our happiness lies in the external world. Need turns into greed, and thus ensnared by *kama-thrishna* and *bhava-thrishna*, our cravings tend to get inexhaustible. For one seeking to walk on the path of *shreyas*, discrimination must be nurtured, by giving importance to mastering and transcending deficiency needs, without getting lost in greed. Beyond a point, increasing wealth, sensual pleasures, projects and fame do not bring proportionate happiness. It is like a caterpillar getting bigger and bigger in size — not realising that its evolution and freedom lie in its transformation into a butterfly. For the human being, the key to such evolution lies in awakening the inner resources and thus finding the truth of Self that is completely free.

Motivation and the *Gunas*

Traditional Indian wisdom, including the Gita, recognises the validity of the need to satisfy deficiency needs. These are humanly legitimate and are included among the four *purusharthas* (objects of human pursuit). Strictly following *dharma*, while pursuing *artha* and *kama*, and eventually aspiring for *moksha* serve to bring self-regulation in our actions, and to bring a shift from the path of *preyas* to that of *shreyas*. In terms of the three *gunas*, this usually implies a progressive shift in our character: from *tamasic-rajasic* to *rajasic-sattvic* and thence *sattvic* predominantly.

The Gita's emphasis on doing work that needs to be done in a self-regulated manner (*niyatam karma*) and without the motivation of the action's fruits is an invitation to shift our character from *rajas* to *sattva* and beyond. Work then becomes the very means to enable such a shift: from desire-motivated action (*sakama karma*) to desireless action (*nishkama karma*). Thus we eventually go beyond all three *gunas* so as to realise our higher Divine nature. Indeed, this is what is implied by progression from *asat* to *sat*, from *tamas* to *jyoti*, and from *mrityu* to *amritam*.

Deprived of desire-based motivation towards objective result, the *guna* of *rajas* is bound to fall. However, in its place, for the unevolved human being, it is *tamas* that is likely to rise up, not *sattva*! So there is a tendency to slide either into dull inertia or a half-hearted mechanical action. The Gita clearly warns us against this danger, and makes it clear that the practice of *Karmayoga* calls for freedom from attachment (*sanga*) not only to the fruits of action but also to inaction.

The Role of Devotion

Deficiency needs are certainly not to be ignored. Those who do so, in the name of spirituality, often end up needing to satisfy basic needs in covert or perverted ways. In the ancient *chakra* theory, it is well recognised that the lower three *chakras* (corresponding to the domain of Maslow's deficiency needs) need to be first mastered adequately before the higher *chakras* (the domain of spirituality at work) can be easily accessed. A strong aspiration to go beyond the lower nature's entrapment can surely provide much motivation to enable this. Yet, this needs to be combined with a growing ability to *reject* unnecessary desires. For this, nurturing a clear discrimination between *need* and *greed* is very helpful. The ability to sit, firmly intent on the Supreme Divine (*yukta asita matparah*), is a powerful means not only as meditative practice to get into the *yukta* condition, but also for crossing over one's deficiency needs. This is made clear in the following Gita verse.

अनन्याश्चिन्तयन्तो मां ये जनाः पर्युपासते ।
तेषां नित्याभियुक्तानां योगक्षेमं वहाम्यहम् ।।9.22।।

For those persons who worship Me,	मां ये जनाः पर्युपासते
With no other object in their thoughts,	अनन्याः चिन्तयन्तः
For them, who are steadfast in devotion,	तेषां नित्य अभियुक्तानां
I provide for their security and welfare.	योग क्षेमं वहामि अहम्

Here is a wonderful assurance, a guarantee, given by the *Purushottama* to the sincere devotee. This does not absolve us from doing out bit to take care of our deficiency needs, but we need not be obsessed and worried about them. If our aspiration and faith are very strong, we can be certain that our deficiency needs will be adequately met with. The words, *yogakshemam vahamyaham*, convey unequivocally this assurance. It covers not only the acquisition of whatever is required for basic needs, but also their maintenance and safety. With such faith, we get liberated from our obsession for the fruit of our actions — for we are no longer worried about the outcome. We leave the fruit to the Divine.

The Need to Win and Its Fallout

The outcome of any human action is a resultant that depends on a large number of inputs. Sadly, we often tend to disregard the fact that there are indeed a large number of factors involved, many of which we are unaware. In Gita verses 18.13-18.15, the Divine Teacher spells out various *causes* that decide the outcome of any action. The individual has a primary role in contributing to the outcome, but the result also depends on several other factors that lie beyond the individual's control and knowledge. Moreover, it is ignorance that leads us to a notion of doership of action (*kartrtva-bhava*).

In Sri Aurobindo's words, 'The ego is the ostensible doer, but the ego and its will are creations and instruments of nature with which the ignorant understanding wrongly identifies our self and they are not the only determinants even of human action, much less of its turn and consequence.'[8.2]

When we are able to rise above this ignorant way of living, we observe that no action is governed by anything, or any person, operating in isolation. As verse 2.47 of the Gita suggests, our right is limited to the performance of the action entrusted to us, and our duty lies in performing it to the best of our ability. The fruit is not in our hands, and does not belong to us. It is for this reason that we do not have a right to the fruit.

When our mind is focussed on the fruit of action, instead of the action itself, we tend to be distracted and unable to give our full attention. Obsession with the fruit can also make us nervous, and the 'need to win drains us of power', as poetically described by Chuang Tzu[8.3]:

When an archer shoots for nothing, he has all his skill.
If he shoots for a brass buckle, he is already nervous.
If he shoots for a prize of gold, he goes blind,
Or sees two targets – he is out of his mind!
His skill has not changed, but the prize divides him.
He thinks more of winning than of shooting,
And the need to win drains him of power.

In other instances when we hanker for a certain outcome, but the outcome happens in a way contrary to our expectation, we can get into reactions of anger, hatred and revenge (*rajas*) or get into depression and grief (*tamas*). These tend to alter our attitude to work. We keep mulling over our misfortune, finding people to blame. This takes away our ability to concentrate upon and enjoy our work. An employee known to be passionate about work is likely to be a different person the day after he discovers that he has failed to get a promotion he had been eagerly expecting. The motivation to work for the organisation gets lost, and there is a tendency to slide towards inaction or to rebel and perhaps indulge in counter-productive work. When there are several disgruntled individuals like this in an organisation, competing with one another, they begin to indulge in activities that make them fail as a group. 'People who came together to help an organisation succeed actually end up delighting in each others' failures and resenting each others' successes.'[8.4]

Clearly, this is an unhealthy approach to work in any organisation. It reflects a complete absence of spirituality at work, due to the fallout of an obsession with the fruit of action.

Non-dependence on Fruit of Action and Equipoise, *samatvam*

The work that one has taken upon oneself, the 'work that needs to be done' (*karyam karma*), based on one's *svadharma*, needs to be done to perfection. This perfection is possible only by acting with one's entire being, fully concentrated on the task at hand. For this, one must not only have the relevant knowledge and skill, but also a positive striving for excellence, regardless of the outcome. This calls for care, dedication and attention to the work. The driving force is simply the urge for perfection and excellence. This can be further enhanced, as explained in the next chapter, by treating the work as an offering to the Divine.

Even if the purity of one's motivation is contaminated by a desire for the fruit of action, the recommendation is to let go of it consciously. This is the true meaning of renunciation. It is this inner renunciation that makes the *Karmayogin* equal to a *Sannyasin* (renunciate), as indicated in the following verse.

श्रीभगवानुवाच ।
अनाश्रितः कर्मफलं कार्यं कर्म करोति यः ।
स संन्यासी च योगी च न निरग्निर्न चाक्रियः ||6.1||

The Blessed Lord said:	श्रीभगवान् उवाच
Without dependence on the fruit of action,	अनाश्रितः कर्म फलं
He who does work that needs to be done,	कार्यं कर्म करोति यः
Is a true Sannyasin as well as a Yogin,	सः संन्यासी च योगी च
Not he, who's without fire or shuns work.	न निरग्निः न च अक्रियः

This kind of renunciation ends in complete detachment from whatever may result. It is further emphasised that such renunciation does not imply abandoning work in the world. So long as there is the fire of the life-force active in the individual, it must be put to creative use, through work, for a Divine purpose.

Freedom from attachment to the fruit of action is associated with an equipoise (*samatvam*) that keeps one always inwardly calm: before, during and after the action. This is described in the following verse.

योगस्थः कुरु कर्माणि सङ्गं त्यक्त्वा धनञ्जय ।
सिद्ध्यसिद्ध्योः समो भूत्वा समत्वं योग उच्यते ||2.48||

Do perform actions, steadfast in Yoga,	योगस्थः कुरु कर्माणि
Giving up attachment to fruits, Arjuna,	सङ्गं त्यक्त्वा धनञ्जय
Equipoised to success and failure,	सिद्धि असिद्ध्योः समः भूत्वा
For such equipoise is implied by Yoga.	समत्वं योग उच्यते

The result may be so-called success or failure (*siddhyasiddhyoh*) as defined by others. It does not matter. One has done one's best, and despite this, the result may have been governed by factors beyond one's control. One learns to accept these gracefully, not losing the calmness of one's inner poise. The Divine Teacher recognises that traces of attachment may cling to the fruit, as the action is performed. That should not pose a problem, if one remembers to let go of the attachment consciously (*sangam tyaktva*). Such letting go can be nurtured as a practice, whereby inner calmness is immediately experienced.

Such equipoise is implied by *samatvam yoga ucyate.* Sri Aurobindo gives a clear explanation to this primary step in *Karmayoga*, 'An entirely desireless and disinterested working of the personal will and the whole instrumental nature is the first rule of *Karmayoga*. Demand no fruit, accept whatever result is given to you; accept it with equality and a calm gladness: successful or foiled, prosperous or afflicted, continue unafraid, untroubled and unwavering on the steep path of the Divine action.'[8.5]

In the following verse, the Divine Teacher goes on to suggest that such performance of work, as a steady practice of inner renunciation, serves as means and cause, *karanam*, for ascending the hill of *Yoga*. Thus it is possible to achieve self-mastery over the lower nature.

आरुरुक्षोर्मुनेर्योगं कर्म कारणमुच्यते |
योगारूढस्य तस्यैव शमः कारणमुच्यते ||6.3||

For one seeking to rise to heights of Yoga,	आरुरुक्षोः मुनेः योगं
Work is the means of attaining self-mastery.	कर्म कारणम् उच्यते
For the sage who has thus risen in Yoga,	योग आरूढस्य तस्य एव
Equipoise (yoked to Oneness) is the way.	शमः कारणम् उच्यते

For one who has ascended the hill of *Yoga*, work is no longer the cause for continuing the journey. The calm and equipoise gained through this process then become the cause of staying *yukta*, ever-anchored in the Self, effortlessly engaging in perfect action — if, as and when required.

Lest one assumes that equipoise implies indifference to the quality of work done, the Divine Teacher emphasises in the following verse that *Karmayoga* also implies skill (expertise, efficacy) in action.

Skill in Action, *kaushalam*

बुद्धियुक्तो जहातीह उभे सुकृतदुष्कृते ।
तस्माद्योगाय युज्यस्व योगः कर्मसु कौशलम् ।।2.50।।

One drops off notions of good and evil acts,	जहाति उभे सुकृत दुष्कृते
When the intellect is yoked here to Oneness.	बुद्धि युक्तः इह
Thus, yoking yourself to this yoga practice,	तस्मात् योगाय युज्यस्व
Act with skill, for yoga is skill in action.	योगः कर्मसु कौशलम्

The term, *buddhi-yukta*, implies uniting reason and will with the One Divine Self. As explained earlier, this sense of oneness brings release from the world of dualities (*dvandva*). In a pointed reference to Arjuna's dilemma at the battlefield, the Divine Teacher points out that the enlightened being 'drops off notions of good and evil acts' (*sukritadushkrite*). It does not matter if the work involved appears so terrible as the battle at Kurukshetra. So long as one is *buddhi-yukta*, the work needing to be done is Divine and needs to be executed perfectly.

It is only when one has actualised one's talents and potential of gifts inborn (*svabhavajam*) that anyone can deliver such perfection. Till then, of course, one does the best one can. The Gita emphasises perfection and skill at work (*yogah karmasu kaushalam*) as instruments expressing spirituality at work. So there is no room for a lackadaisical or fatalistic attitude. Yes, the final outcome is not in one's hands. Yet, at the same time, one's contribution to the outcome is necessary and significant. All work, conforming to *svadharma*, needs careful planning and meticulous execution. Many projects call for team effort. So one's own inspired motivation must also serve to inspire and encourage one's colleagues. Perfection at work proceeds through love, synergy, care and attention to detail. Detachment from the fruit of action does not mean ignoring the essential goal. And thus, for genuine spirituality at work, part of that goal is to remain *yukta* (in harness) attentively. This harnessing must be achieved, while acknowledging with graceful acceptance that the final outcome is not in one's hands. Sometimes failure is needed, as it can be a tremendous source of learning. The true spiritual aspirant must surrender to the Divine will in all such matters.

One needs to be fully present in the work undertaken to achieve perfection. This means paying calm and careful attention to each detail of the work at hand. The mind needs training not to fly off either into the future or some other distraction — to which it is often prone, unless well trained. The work itself offers the perfect opportunity for such training. One will do well to devote one's fullest attention to some selected tasks for a start. Later, one may extend this habit effortlessly to all tasks. One then discovers quiet joy in simply attending to one's work: unworried about anything, including the fruit of action.

Practice Makes Perfect

Arjuna, here self-actualised as a skilled warrior, has no difficulty in understanding the need for skilled perfection in action. His difficulty pertains to the condition he finds himself in at *Kurukshetra*, where he is unnerved by an ethical dilemma. In other words, while he is comfortable with the idea of *yogah karmasu kaushalam*, he is not at ease with the idea of *samatvam yoga ucyate*. So he points to his real difficulty, which we all share — the wavering and restless (*chanchala*) nature of the mind. It is this that needs to be mastered, so as to attain equipoise as a steady state (*sthitim sthiram*). He knows, however, that this equipoise needs first to be established through meditative practice. Then only will it come in handy at work, in the battlefield.

अर्जुन उवाच ।
योऽयं योगस्त्वया प्रोक्तः साम्येन मधुसूदन ।
एतस्याहं न पश्यामि चञ्चलत्वात्स्थितिं स्थिराम् ।।6.33।।

Arjuna said:	अर्जुनः उवाच
You've described this Yoga to me,	यः अयं योगः त्वया प्रोक्तः
Krishna, with equipoise as its basis.	साम्येन मधुसूदन
But I do not see this as a steady state,	एतस्य अहं न पश्यामि
As the mind is wavering and restless!	चञ्चलत्वात् स्थितिं स्थिराम्

श्रीभगवानुवाच ।
असंशयं महाबाहो मनो दुर्निग्रहं चलम् ।
अभ्यासेन तु कौन्तेय वैराग्येण च गृह्यते ।।6.35।।

The Blessed Lord said:	श्रीभगवान् उवाच
Restraining the restless mind is very difficult.	मनः दुर्निग्रहं चलम्
Arjuna, there is no doubt indeed about this!	असंशयं महाबाहो
But it (surely) can be controlled, O Arjuna,	गृह्यते तु कौन्तेय
By regular practice and non-attachment.	अभ्यासेन वैराग्येण च

Yes, admittedly, it is very difficult to control the restless mind, confirms the Divine Teacher. Yet, it has to be done, if one wishes equipoise. Indeed, it can be done. The only way to achieve this is through regular practice (*abhyasa*) of meditation, and nurturing detachment (*vairagya*) from the tendency for attraction and aversion to sense-objects (*ragadveshau*). As the old adage goes, practice makes perfect! This is a most important point for us all to assimilate, given the tendency to look for short cuts in everything. There are no short cuts here. Our daily living itself offers the perfect opportunity to practice. We need not look out for occasions to test our equipoise. They will come to us unsolicited. The results of our tests are instantly declared by our inner reactions to various situations. How useful is it to remain inwardly calm, regardless of turmoils in the outer environment! This is the promise of the Gita's *yoga*.

In this chapter, we have explored the basic practice of *Karmayoga* — performing all actions without attachment to the fruit, free from desire (*nishkama karma*), free from dualities of attraction and aversion (*araga-dveshata*), with equipoise (*samatvam*), and with skilled perfection (*kaushalam*).

In the next chapter, we will explore how the practice can be made easier by understanding the meaning of sacrifice, *yajna*, and thereby consecrating all our actions to the Divine.

9

Consecrating Work as Sacrifice (*Yajna*)

यज्ञार्थात्कर्मणोऽन्यत्र लोकोऽयं कर्मबन्धनः |
तदर्थं कर्म कौन्तेय मुक्तसङ्गः समाचर ||3.9||

Unless work is done as sacrifice,	यज्ञ अर्थात् कर्मणः अन्यत्र
This world is imprisoned by karma.	लोकः अयं कर्म बन्धनः
Hence, Arjuna, (for liberation) do work	कर्म कौन्तेय समाचर
As an offering, free from attachment!	तत् अर्थं मुक्त सङ्गः

The concept of doing work as 'sacrifice' is a unique contribution of the Gita. Recognising that the practice of desireless action (*nishkama karma*) as difficult for most people entrapped by lower nature, the Gita shows a simple and profound way out. Whatever be the action (even motivated by desire and attachment), freedom can be gained from bondage to the lower nature, by simply offering it to the Divine. This is the meaning of sacrifice (*yajna*) in the Gita.

The Divine Teacher tells Arjuna that such an attitude to work (treated as worship) brings freedom from attachment (*muktasanga*) and from the binding consequences of acts (*karmabandhana*) that would otherwise manifest in accordance with the *law of karma*.

The term *yajna* is derived from the Sanskrit root, *yaj*, which means to offer worshipfully or to sacrifice. In the Vedic tradition, *yajna* refers to a sacred ritual, involving oblations (clarified butter, grains, wood, etc.) offered into a sacred fire (*agni*), along with recitation of various *mantras*, to invoke Divine blessings (of the gods, *devas*) for various purposes. The remains of the offering at the end of the ritual (*yajna-shishta*), typically having the forms of ash or sweet food, are distributed to all, as *prasadam*.

The concept of sacrifice, in the form of food offerings (*oblation*) as propitiation or worship has continued from time immemorial throughout the world. In many traditions (some now obsolete), the sacrifice involved ritual killing of animals to propitiate gods or the One God. Sometimes, the term 'bloodless sacrifice' is used, as in the Christian eucharist, when the food offering does not involve animal killing. The term 'sacrifice' is also used metaphorically to describe an act of giving up something voluntarily ('suffering' a short-term loss) so as to gain something far more significant and valuable. We do this commonly in a game of chess (from which the term 'sacrificial pawn' has emerged).

Both these meanings are included in the Gita's concept of *yajna* to define the right means and attitude to perform any work, *karma*. It is considered as a sacred offering (of self and its attachments) to the One Divine *Ishvara*, the *Lord of all Yoga* and worship, invisibly present everywhere and at all times, and the One recipient of all offerings. Its basic purpose is to serve the evolution of consciousness through mutually beneficial interchange between beings and powers, in the movement from darkness to light. For the human being, *yajna* broadly means sacrificing the lower nature in order to access the higher Divine nature. This letting go is not easy (and not without suffering), for there are parts in our being that are more aligned to darkness than to light.

Consecration of Work

The Gita's originality lies in applying the basic concept of *yajna* to any action. We all know from experience that any action, done with attention and care, immediately lifts up its quality. Even the simple act of eating food gets elevated when we pause to taste the food more fully, acknowledging gratefully the contributions of all those who created the food preparation. We miss this experience when we simply gobble the food, our minds engaged with something else.

When work is done as *yajna*, we not only keep our minds attentively focussed on the work at hand, we also purify it by invoking and offering its fruit to the Divine, to whom it belongs anyway. Thereby, it becomes easier to let go. We feel ennobled and blessed when we do this as a conscious offering. We do this as often as possible, by remembering to consecrate our actions, and to partake of the fruits (whatever they be) as *yajna-shishta*.

The action obviously must be the best we can do. This corresponds to the injunction of skilled perfection: *yogah karmasu kaushalam.* What kind of work can be offered as sacrifice? The following Gita verse makes it clear that all kinds of actions (including the most trivial ones we do daily) are suited for this purpose. Such actions, consecrated as *yajna*, can be life-changing.

यत्करोषि यदश्नासि यज्जुहोषि ददासि यत् ।
यत्तपस्यसि कौन्तेय तत्कुरुष्व मदर्पणम् ।।9.27।।

Whatever you do, whatever you consume	यत् करोषि यत् अश्नासि
Whatever you sacrifice, whatever you give,	यत् जुहोषि ददासि यत्
Whatever austerities you perform, Arjuna,	यत् तपस्यसि कौन्तेय
Do all that as an offering to Me (the Divine)!	तत् कुरुष्व मदर्पणम्

'Whatever you do, do as an offering to Me' (*yatkaroshi tatkurushva madarpanam*) is the simple advice of the *Purushottama* to us all — worthy of continual remembrance. Work generally involves interactions between the individual self and the outside world, and this implies either receiving (or taking) from the world or giving to the world. Both giving and taking can be translated into offerings. Even while engaging in the act of taking or consuming, we can pause and invoke the Divine residing in our own hearts. What we receive and consume is thus consecrated. Offerings to others, according to the Gita, can take three forms: sacrifice, charity and austerity (*yajna-dana-tapas*). They get consecrated when we remember to offer to the Divine residing in the hearts of others (and ever-present in the world around us).

Thus, we see that every little action in the world (whatever it may be) offers us the opportunity for consecration, thereby transforming it as a means for spirituality at work, for liberation and Self-realisation. This is made clear in the following verse.

शुभाशुभफलैरेवं मोक्ष्यसे कर्मबन्धनैः |
संन्यासयोगयुक्तात्मा विमुक्तो मामुपैष्यसि ||9.28||

Thus you'll be freed from bondage to actions, एवं मोक्ष्यसे कर्मबन्धनैः
Whose outcomes may be favourable or not. शुभ अशुभ फलैः
Renounce and be yoked to Oneness. संन्यास योग युक्तात्मा
Thus liberated, you shall come to Me! विमुक्तः माम् उपैष्यसि

When our focus shifts from attachment to the fruit of action to consecration of the action to the Divine, the nature of the actual outcome — whether favourable or not (*shubhashubhaphala*) — loses significance. It does not matter. We leave the outcome to the Divine. This then becomes an act of renunciation (of attachment to action's fruit), *sannyasa*.

It also leads to *yoking* or union (with the One Divine), *yoga*. This paves the way to liberation and the final objective of human existence: union with the Divine. Such consecration also ensures freedom from bondage to actions, *karmabandhana*.

Offering with Devotion, *Bhakti*

In order to make consecration of work a habit, it is useful to invoke a strong feeling of devotion, by making exclusive offerings to the Divine. In the following verse, we see a description of how even the most insignificant offering takes on a Divine significance. There is a Divine recipient, ever-awake and attentive, to receive our offering. It becomes a means for the descent of Divine Grace into the being of the devotee.

पत्रं पुष्पं फलं तोयं यो मे भक्त्या प्रयच्छति |
तदहं भक्त्युपहृतम् अश्नामि प्रयतात्मनः ||9.26||

Whoever offers Me with devotion, यः मे भक्त्या प्रयच्छति
Even a leaf, flower, fruit or water, पत्रं पुष्पं फलं तोयं
I accept it from that pure-hearted soul, तत् अहं अश्नामि प्रयत आत्मनः
When it is offered with sincere devotion. भक्ति उपहृतम्

The key here is the sincerity with which the offering is made. That is what ensures its acceptance by the all-knowing Divine. Will there be a return benefit from such an offering? Sri Aurobindo comments: 'The soul knows that it does not give itself to God in vain; claiming nothing, it yet receives the infinite riches of the Divine Power and Presence.'[9.1]

In another significant verse, the Divine Teacher makes it clear that different people have different conceptions of the Divine: pantheism, polytheism, monotheism, panentheism, etc. It does not matter whom they make the offering to, so long as it is done with sincere devotion. All such offerings are ultimately received by the *Purushottama*, even if it may appear that they have been rejected by the apparent deity of devotion.

ये यथा मां प्रपद्यन्ते तांस्तथैव भजाम्यहम् |
मम वर्त्मानुवर्तन्ते मनुष्याः पार्थ सर्वशः ||4.11||

In whatever way men resort to Me, ये यथा मां प्रपद्यन्ते
In that way do I devote Myself to them, तान् तथैव भजामि अहम्
In various ways do men follow, Arjuna, मनुष्याः पार्थ सर्वशः अनुवर्तन्ते
A path that eventually leads to Me. मम वर्त्म

Indeed, the Divine recognises the many different ways in which man makes offering, including apparently atheistic ways (but with the intent of altruism and charity). All are parts of the same creative evolutionary process, whose true origin and destination are the *Purushottama*. The Divine, therefore, not only receives the offerings made, in all their diverse ways, but also reciprocates in exactly the same way. It is noteworthy that the expression used here, *bhajamyaham*, describes a reciprocal devotion by the Divine to the devotee. There are different kinds of worshipful offering that can be made to the Divine, not just in the form of material objects.

Different Kinds of Offering

द्रव्ययज्ञास्तपोयज्ञाः योगयज्ञास्तथापरे |
स्वाध्यायज्ञानयज्ञाश्च यतयः संशितव्रताः ||4.28||

For some, sacrifices may take material form, अपरे द्रव्य यज्ञाः
Or the form of austerities or yoga practices, तपः यज्ञाः योग यज्ञाः तथा
Or scriptural study and knowledge sharing, स्वाध्याय ज्ञान यज्ञाः च
Made by diligent aspirants with strict vows. यतयः संशित व्रताः

In the above verse, the Divine Teacher makes it clear that the *yajna* may take the form of a material or physical offering, *dravya-yajna*, or in more subtle forms. The gross material offering typically is that which is offered by the devotee to his or her deity. This may be simple and inexpensive (*patram pushpam phalam toyam*) or expensive, or can also manifest in the form of charitable contributions (*dana-yajna*).

The subtler offerings may take the form of austerity (*tapo-yajna*) through self-discipline in various ways. As explained later in the Gita, such austerities typically pertain to the realm of the body, the use of words (as in speech) and the realm of the mind. Mention is made here in particular of practices related to disciplining the body and mind (*yoga-yajna*), which broadly includes all the eight limbs of *Rajayoga*, mentioned earlier. Indeed, all these practices have a single aim: self-mastery and freedom from the lower nature, leading to ego-transcendence and absorption with the One Divine Self.

Another form of *yajna* cited in the above verse is *svadhyaya-jnana-yajna*, which implies scriptural study motivated primarily by self-learning and reading (*svadhyaya*), as also offering of knowledge acquired and assimilated (*jnana-yajna*) by sharing it with others who are deserving and aspiring for such learning.

All such disciplined practices, carried out regularly, with renewed and avowed allegiance (*samshita-vrata*), serve to purify the being, thereby making one a fit receptacle for the descent of the Divine *Shakti*. The resulting transformation will be experienced by the individual in many ways — primarily, by a higher and enduring happiness, *Ananda*, found to be far superior to the transient ego-based enjoyment of the lower nature.

Among the different forms of sacrifice, which among them is rated to be the highest, the best? The following verse makes this clear. The subtler forms of offering, especially knowledge-offering (*jnana-yajna*), through continual learning and sharing of knowledge, are valued more highly than gross material offerings.

श्रेयान्द्रव्यमयाद्यज्ञात् ज्ञानयज्ञः परन्तप ।
सर्वं कर्माखिलं पार्थ ज्ञाने परिसमाप्यते ।।4.33।।

Superior to the material sacrifice	श्रेयान् द्रव्य मयात् यज्ञात्
Arjuna, is the knowledge sacrifice,	ज्ञान यज्ञः परन्तप
For all actions, in their entirety,	सर्वं कर्म अखिलं
Culminate in knowledge, Arjuna!	ज्ञाने परिसमाप्यते पार्थ

The material offering is rated the lowest, while the offering of wisdom is the highest. The highest knowledge referred to here goes much beyond the secular knowledge that is useful for material, scientific, social and cultural development; it points to authentic Self-knowledge.

As part of one's *sadhana* in *Karmayoga*, one must choose to engage more consciously in those activities that lead to union with the Divine. By gradually discovering the support of Divinity in all actions, this culminates in a discovery that it is none other than the Divine who keeps doing all the work. The river of *Karmayoga* finds its culmination in entering into the waters of an integral ocean of the Divine, where also merge the rivers of *Jnanayoga* and *Bhaktiyoga*. The accomplished *Karmayogin* is one who is also a *Jnani-bhakta*. There is a deeper significance to *yajna* of which the awakened sage, the *Jnani-bhakta*, is aware. It is this deeper, philosophical significance that unifies the different elements of cosmic creation, and finds its essential Oneness.

Deeper Significance of Sacrifice: Inter-being

Consecration calls for a feeling of reverence, sacredness and devotion. This is something that primitive man had in plenty, although this may have been motivated primarily by *fear* of the 'nature-spirits'. However, with the advent of science and technology and our increasing ability of controlling and harnessing nature's powers, we have lost this in our ego-centred arrogance. We therefore need to understand the deeper meaning of sacrifice, which in the Gita is described as the very basis of functioning of all creation. Such sacrifice is but another word for 'inter-change': a mutual offering of various beings in nature. By some law of mutual dependence, each being benefits and gets fostered by offerings from others, while also fostering others through self-offerings, and the ideal basis for this inter-relationship is love, not fear. Should we pause to reflect on something as simple as food (*anna*) that we consume each day for our physical survival, then we may understand how the chain operates in nature.

अन्नाद्भवन्ति भूतानि पर्जन्यादन्नसम्भवः |
यज्ञाद्भवति पर्जन्यः यज्ञः कर्मसमुद्भवः ||3.14||

Beings come forth from food;	अन्नात् भवन्ति भूतानि
Food comes forth from rain;	पर्जन्यात् अन्न सम्भवः
Rain comes forth from sacrifice;	यज्ञात् भवति पर्जन्यः
Sacrifice comes forth from work!	यज्ञः कर्म समुद्भवः

We buy food, by paying money earned through our work. We may even be grateful and say *thanks* when receiving food in exchange for the money we have offered. To whom do we offer our thanks, if at all? Do we ever pause to realise that the food that is on our plate (rice, wheat, cereal or whatever) is an outcome of a long process that connects many, many beings in this universe? Our minds may then dwell on many unknown human beings, who work in farms to grow and harvest grain. So also on those who collect, transport and sell, prepare and cook the food we consume. Also, what about the sun, the air, the water and the earth? These aspects are all represented in the above Gita verse by rain (*parjanya*), without which all this would not have been possible in the first place. Do we ever pause to thank these natural elements? We usually take all these things for granted, never pausing to even acknowledge our inter-being. All that must change, now that you are reading these verses. Acknowledge the offerings of all. Offer all your work too in this spirit of mutual beneficence!

Brahman — the Ultimate Source of all Work, all Sacrifice

कर्म ब्रह्मोद्भवं विद्धि ब्रह्माक्षरसमुद्भवम् ।
तस्मात्सर्वगतं ब्रह्म नित्यं यज्ञे प्रतिष्ठितम् ।।3.15।।

Work comes into being from Brahman;	कर्म ब्रह्म उद्भवं विद्धि
Brahman emerges from immutable Akshara.	ब्रह्म अक्षर समुद्भवम्
Thus, the all-pervading Akshara Brahman	तस्मात् सर्व गतं ब्रह्म
Is ever-present in every offering of sacrifice!	नित्यं यज्ञे प्रतिष्ठितम्

The above verse traces our work to its ultimate source — again, something that we habitually take for granted. All work, as we have seen earlier, manifests as movements in *Prakriti*, having their source in manifest *Brahman*. In Sri Aurobindo's words, 'The *Brahman* alone is, and because of It all are, for all are the *Brahman*; this Reality is the reality of everything that we see in Self and nature.'[9.2]

However, in the above Gita verse, the reference to *Brahman* is in the context of mutable existence, which itself is an emergence out of the Unmanifest and immutable *Akshara Purusha* or *Akshara Brahman*, the One Self whose all-pervading essence is *sat-chit-ananda*. This is not difficult to understand in modern scientific parlance, if we consider that the entire universe (including time and space) is believed to have emerged and expanded from the so-called *Big Bang* some 13.7 billion years ago. The only difference is that whereas Science cannot admit to the presence of anything prior to this momentous event, simply because there was nothing measurable, ancient Indian wisdom asserts the presence of *Akshara Brahman* (or *Nirguna Brahman*) even prior to all manifestation. It was not only present then, but continues to be ever-present and all-pervading — immanent in and transcending all time and space. It is that Source of everything that is ever-present in all work, in all sacrifice.

The will to create and manifest seems to have emerged, for some mysterious reason, from this immutable *Akshara Purusha*. This emergence is ascribed later in the Gita to a higher, a supreme (*Uttama*) status of *Purusha*, the *Purushottama* or *Ishvara*, described as the true Divine Source — underlying, supporting and transcending all existence.

In its immutable status, it is *Akshara*, also described as Spirit or Self, *Atman*. Yet, even in this immutable (static) status, there exists (as a tree exists potentially in its seed) a *way of becoming* or *Svabhava*, emerging as an original principle from the immutable Self, resulting in a creative process of mutable becoming, involving changes in the original *Svabhava*.

The Divine element in this becoming, hidden in all beings, is the dynamic Soul (*Kshara Purusha*) by which all the workings of nature (*Prakriti*) are rendered as *yajna*. The recipient of all *yajna* is the secret Divine *Purushottama*, dwelling in the hearts of all embodied beings.

These metaphysical concepts convey a simple truth: everything is connected with all else; all are Divine, all is *Brahman*, and all work is an offering to the Divine. This simple, yet profound, concept is captured beautifully in the following verse. The metaphor adopted here is the traditional ritual of sacrifice, in which the food offering or oblation, offered into the sacred fire by individuals in a spirit of worshipful consecration for a noble objective, are all the One Divine, *Brahman*!

ब्रह्मार्पणं ब्रह्म हविः ब्रह्माग्नौ ब्रह्मणा हुतम् ।
ब्रह्मैव तेन गन्तव्यं ब्रह्मकर्मसमाधिना ।।4.24।।

Brahman is the offering: It is the food offered ब्रह्म अर्पणं ब्रह्म हविः
By Brahman, into the sacred fire of Brahman; ब्रह्म अग्नौ ब्रह्मणा हुतम्
To serve the objective of abiding in Brahman, ब्रह्म एव तेन गन्तव्यं
Through absorption in the work of Brahman! ब्रह्म कर्म समाधिना

This knowledge of the entire unity (*brahma-vidya*) of the Self-realised soul, is that it is the same One Divine that manifests as the doer, the deed and the object of all work, as well as the knower, the knowledge and object of all knowledge. To know this, and to live and work in this consciousness of oneness is the consummation of human existence.

In this context, the role of Matter and work is explained by Sri Aurobindo as follows: 'The Spirit has made itself Matter in order to place itself there as an instrument for the well-being and joy, *yogakshema*, of created beings, for a self offering of universal physical utility and service.'[9.3]

Interchange: Giving and Taking

The well-being (*yogakshema*) of all created beings manifests from a recognition of the reality of inter-being, where all action is seen as interchange, manifesting in the form of giving and taking. This is in-built into creation, and an evolution of consciousness demands that we engage consciously with this understanding. We see this in the healthy body of a multi-cellular organism. Although each cell has its own individuality, its functioning is intended to serve the well-being of the whole body. In a similar way, the entire universe may be conceived of as an organic whole, in which every individual part, while expressing its individuality and interacting with other parts, is meant to serve the One Divine Source, from which everything has emerged. All action is thus visualised as a sacred offering of *Prakriti* to *Purusha*. While such offering is done unconsciously in most sentient beings, it is meant to be done consciously in the evolving being — as a conscious sacrifice, *yajna*. This implies an increasingly greater focus on *giving*, and a lesser focus on *taking*. Sri Aurobindo points out: 'According to the grade of consciousness and being which the soul has reached in nature, will be the Divinity it worships, the delight which it seeks and the hope for which it sacrifices.'[9.4]

At the lower end of the spectrum of human evolution, we have individuals in society, who do not seem to care to give to others, to society, to the environment, and focus entirely on taking and consuming and hoarding. This results in a 'failure to help turn the wheel of life'.

एवं प्रवर्तितं चक्रं नानुवर्तयतीह यः |
अघायुरिन्द्रियारामः मोघं पार्थ स जीवति ||3.16||

He who fails to help turn the wheel of life, न अनुवर्तयति इह यः चक्रं
Thus set in motion through mutual sacrifices, एवं प्रवर्तितं
Addicted to a life of sin and sense-pleasures, अघायुः इन्द्रिय आरामः
Arjuna, he lives in vain, wasting his life! मोघं पार्थ सः जीवति

In another verse (3.12), the Divine Teacher describes the person who enjoys the gifts of nature but does not offer anything in return as a thief. The law of interchange demands that all individual beings operate on some principle of mutual dependence, whereby all partake of the mutual benefit and prosperity. When sacrifice is not voluntarily done, nature has a way of extracting it forcefully from the ego-centred individual, thereby enforcing the principle of interchange. At the other end of the spectrum of human evolution, we have Self-realised individuals who have attained perfection through conscious self-offering.

कर्मणैव हि संसिद्धिम् आस्थिता जनकादयः ।
लोकसंग्रहमेवापि सम्पश्यन्कर्तुमर्हसि ।।3.20।।

Janaka and others have attained	आस्थिताः जनक आदयः
Perfection through work alone.	कर्मणा एव हि संसिद्धिम्
Thus, for maintaining world order,	लोक संग्रहम् एव अपि सम्पश्यन्
You are obliged to offer your work!	कर्तुम् अर्हसि

Here again, we see the Gita's emphasis on performing work, not only as a means to attain ultimate perfection (*samsiddhi*), but also after transcending the ego. Why? Simply to *keep turning the wheel of life* — for the maintenance of the world-order and evolution, *lokasangraham*. The legendary King Janaka (who was a *rajarishi*, a king who was also a sage) is cited here as the perfect example of the accomplished *Karmayogin* who is also a *Jnani-bhakta*.

Surrender, *samarpanam*

As one consciously practises the Gita's teaching of *yajna*, one gradually discovers the power in it. Whenever we see an opportunity to sacrifice our interests for the benefit of others, we will feel an inner resistance and reluctance to do so, because of the habitual entrapment of our lower nature. This requires us to overcome the resistance by letting go. We then see how viciously we cling to our ignorance, our grievances, hostilities and demands for ego-centred satisfactions.

Overcoming such inner resistance may be difficult and painful at first, but is bound to yield a higher satisfaction. It is not easy, for example, to forgive those who we believe have harmed us (or those close to us), and it is tempting to continue nursing our grievances against them. Yet, when we are truly able to forgive, it is like a burden lifting from our hearts and minds, liberating us!

Similarly, when we consciously step out to give our care, attention and assistance to others (when we are otherwise disinclined), it can do wonders to expand our hearts and minds and to invoke a feeling of joy. We then see how constricted our ordinary lives tend to be, unconnected to, and separated from, the world around us.

Sacrifice can be made much easier by the feeling of dedication to the Divine, which is essentially an expression of devotion and love. We need to invoke Divine support to help transform all the parts of our being (physical, vital and mental). This calls for not only an honest admission of our own limitations and shortcomings, but also a complete surrender (*samarpanam*) to the Divine. This is an approach of humility that wise beings adopt, knowing only too well the limitations of physical, vital and mental parts of being. In this connection, there is a traditional Indian prayer, worth recalling every now and then, invoking a sense of surrender to the Divine.

कायेन वाचा मनसेन्द्रियैर्वा बुद्ध्यात्मना वा प्रकृतेः स्वभावात् ।
करोमि यद्यत्सकलं परस्मै नारायणायेति समर्पयामि ॥

Whatever I do with body, speech, mind or senses, using intellect,
guided by my innermost being, or as conditioned by my lower
nature, I do all that as an offering, surrendering to the
One Supreme Divine!

The truth is that nothing really belongs to us, so as to give of our own. For everything belongs to the Divine, whose stock is infinite. All we need is to stay divinely yoked, which brings into our being a sense of abundance. It does not really have much to do with our actual bank balance. It has more to do with an attitude in life, where one is no longer worried by deficiency. Then one gets truly large-hearted with others: giving generously without much hesitation, wherever and whenever possible. On the contrary, even if we happen to be millionaires, remaining miserly focussed only on gaining and hoarding, we stay in fact, poor — because we continue to be obsessed by deficiency needs. True abundance is of spirit — of love reflecting oneness with others and the environment. This is facilitated by *samarpanam* — where we realise our roles as no more than caretakers and instruments of the Divine to carry out the Divine will, for the Divine mission of evolution and *lokasangraham*. Such surrender, ideally, needs to be integral, with our entire being (*sarvabhavena*).

यो मामेवमसम्मूढः जानाति पुरुषोत्तमम् ।
स सर्वविद्भजति मां सर्वभावेन भारत ।।15.19।।

He who, without any delusion,	यः एवम् असम्मूढः
Knows Me as the Purushottama,	माम् जानाति पुरुषोत्तमम्
Knowing all, thus worships Me	सः सर्व वित् भजति मां
With his entire being, Arjuna!	सर्व भावेन भारत

The Gita's *yoga* presented so far involves giving up attachment to the fruits of action, so as to focus mindfully on the work at hand, performing it with a skilled perfection that remains equipoised to success or failure. This can be supported, strengthened and advanced by consecrating the work as *yajna*. However, there is still the notion of doership, the belief that one is doing the actions that one is consecrating. In the next chapter, we will see how this false notion of doership keeps us entrapped in the lower nature, and how we are deceived by the play of the three *gunas*.

10

The Play of *Gunas* and Delusion of Doership

प्रकृतेः क्रियमाणानि गुणैः कर्माणि सर्वशः |
अहङ्कारविमूढात्मा कर्ताहमिति मन्यते ||3.27||

Actions are entirely done	कर्माणि सर्वशः क्रियमाणानि
By the modes of nature.	प्रकृतेः गुणैः
The deluded ego-self	अहङ्कार विमूढात्मा
Imagines: I am the doer!	कर्ता अहम् इति मन्यते

The notion, 'I am the doer', is something that we tend to take for granted, and which we seem to have no doubt about, unless we ask the deeper question, *Who am I?* The answer to this forms the core of true Self-realisation.

In an earlier discussion on *Who are you?* we observed that our normal identification is with our body, name, status, and so on. Yet these descriptions, made in terms of name and form (*nama-rupa*), are inadequate. We may succeed in describing some aspects (mostly superficial). However, this will not enable us to capture the essence (*sat*) of who we truly are. All identities pertain to mutable characteristics (*asat*) of a self that changes in time. Yet we know, underlying all these changes, there seems to be a constant 'I' that does not change over time. The very fact that we observe these changes (to our bodies, sensations, thoughts, emotions, desires) suggests that they are external to us (my body, my belief, my desire, my anger, etc.). They are objects, whereas who I am is the true subject who is aware of these happenings. So it is that who, in essence, is free from all that occurs.

That 'I', the pure subject, does not really do anything. It is not the doer (*karta*). It is that which is aware and conscious of all the 'doings'. It is the essence of the embodied Spirit (*dehi*) in an individual being, which acts through its instruments (*physical*, *vital* and *mental*). These instruments are part of the larger instrumentation of nature, *Prakriti* — with its diverse and multiple organic and inorganic components. It is this totality that we describe simply as 'nature'. We like to believe that man is different from nature (our frame of reference typically limited to lower nature). This, of course, is a delusion, if the workings of lower nature are examined carefully. We know that the human body, sourced in nature, goes back to nature after death. Man is just a different kind of animal — with a more evolved mental instrumentation. All instruments, without exception, are of nature.

What makes man different and superior to other sentient beings is the capacity for more intelligent and creative living, and especially, self-awareness and Self-realisation. Part of this realisation is the ability to discriminate between subject and object. This implies stepping back from our habitual object-centred awareness into the wideness of Silence, and seeing all objects truly as objects, coming and going. The True Self remains untouched by all such happenings. Eventually, we discover that everything, without exception, has its source in the One Supreme Divine, *Purushottama* or *Ishvara-Shakti.*

However, in order to ascend to this realisation, we first need to nurture the ability of separating the witnessing Spirit (*Purusha*) from the actions of Nature (*Prakriti*). This will help us clearly appreciate that the notion, 'I am the doer', is just a delusion. In this process, we become increasingly centred in our true identity with *Purusha*, thereby gaining freedom from the entrapment of lower nature.

The Play of Three *Gunas* in *Prakriti*

The Gita emphasises that all action in *Prakriti* (even apparent inaction) arises due to the interplay of the three *gunas*: *sattva*, *rajas* and *tamas*. The real doer of all action is strictly thus the *gunas*, and not the apparent individual whom we hold responsible for certain actions. For practical reasons, we need to make people responsible and accountable for their actions. This is necessary for us to gain self-control and mastery over our lower nature. Thus, we do need to ascribe *doership* to individuals. This should not blind us from seeing the deeper truth of the real impersonal actor (the *gunas* of *Prakriti*) behind the scenes, and the even deeper truth of the Divine origin of everything. By seeing constantly the interplay of the *gunas*, we can free ourselves gradually from getting attached to and entrapped by lower nature.

तत्त्ववित्तु महाबाहो गुणकर्मविभागयोः |
गुणा गुणेषु वर्तन्त इति मत्वा न सज्जते ||3.28||

But Arjuna, he who knows the truth,	तत्त्व वित् तु महाबाहो
Of how gunas are related to karma,	गुण कर्म विभागयोः
And how gunas interact with gunas,	गुणाः गुणेषु वर्तन्त
Remains unattached, knowing this.	इति मत्वा न सज्जते

The uniqueness of the ancient *Sankhya* philosophy, from which the theory of the *gunas* originates, lies in its attempt to simplify, generalise and universalise all the operations of nature in terms of just three modes (or qualities, called *gunas*). From our knowledge of physics, we know that any colour can be considered as a unique combination of the three primary colours (red, green and blue). In a similar way, any quality in nature can be considered to be a unique combination of the three *gunas* of *Prakriti*. However, while a colour can remain stable for a considerable period of time, any particular combination of the three *gunas* (defining any being or occasion) lasts but for a short duration. It is ever vulnerable to getting affected by any stimulus (internal or external), resulting in dynamic interplay among the *gunas*, thereby altering the combination. No doubt, the stability is relatively longer in material things that are predominantly *tamasic* (unlike *rajasic* impulses that last very briefly).

It may also be noted that, whereas the composition of a colour can be accurately quantified in terms of the percentages of the three primary colours, this is not possible in the case of *gunas*. The description here is essentially qualitative in nature, and not quantitative. A broad summary of the principal qualities associated with each of the three *gunas* is given in the table below:

Basic features of the three *gunas*	
Sattva	*poise, fineness, lightness, harmony, illumination, joy, balance, calmness, gentleness, care, morality, lucidity, purity, empathy, truthfulness, honesty*
Rajas	*dynamism, vitality, activity, excitation, struggle, pain, restlessness, lust, conquest, greed, instability, insatiability*
Tamas	*inertia, rigidity, mechanical nature, ignorance, delusion, coarseness, heaviness, slowness, dogmatic conservatism, sloth, laziness, dullness, grief, depression, decadence*

One may talk of something or somebody being predominantly *sattvic* or *rajasic* or *tamasic*. We may also find instances where a second *guna* is also dominant, and we may refer to such behaviour as being *tamasic-rajasic* or *rajasic-sattvic* or *tamasic-sattvic*. Detailed descriptions in the Gita of how each of these three *gunas* manifests in our day-to-day lives are given in the chapters that follow.

Seeing how all actions are conditioned by the play of the *gunas* (*guna guneshu vartanta*) provides us with a deeper insight, and brings a universality in our understanding. We then begin to see how similar we all are — regardless of our nationality, gender, religion, etc. There is an impersonality in the *gunas*, indicating that they will show up spontaneously and govern all behaviour in all beings, in a natural way — unless consciously self-controlled. The deeper message of the Gita is that who we truly are (our True Self) remains unaffected by the play of the *gunas*. It is thus imperative, if we are interested in discovering inner peace, to learn to disengage periodically from the play of *Prakriti's gunas*, thereby shifting from doing to being. We focus our attention on our innermost being or on the open wideness and Silence all around us. It is then that we can stay *yukta* (yoked to our One Divine Source).

The practical benefit of knowing about the *gunas* is that we can learn to work consciously with ourselves, so that to the extent possible, we learn to live as healthily as we can (the way we truly aspire to) rather than live helplessly vulnerable to our lower nature. Moreover, knowing about the *gunas* also helps us in dealing compassionately with others, not blaming them for being vulnerable to 'their' action (which involves the larger play of impersonal *Prakriti*). For example, when we find terrorists engaging in mindless violence, it helps to realise that they act in the manner they do, because they have allowed themselves to be possessed by extreme *tamasic* ignorance. When we find that the terrorist action has resulted in maiming or killing people whom we hold dear, and we fall into grief and sometimes get into depression for a long time, it is evident that the same *tamo-guna* has now possessed us. Any sense of vengeful anger that may get provoked in us on this account shows a strong uprising of *rajo-guna*. This is how the *gunas* play with us.

If we are on the spiritual path, and wish to live in the healthiest way possible, it is important that we recognise this, and so desist from dysfunctional behaviour ourselves. Such recognition and resulting equilibrium commonly arise on account of the *guna* of *sattva*. We know intuitively the absolute importance of developing the purifying quality of *sattva* in our lives. This can occur only by regulating significantly the influence of the other two *gunas* of *rajas* and *tamas*. That is how we can learn to live more responsibly: for our individual and collective well-being. It is also easy to see how these three *gunas* are reflected in our work culture, as summarised in the table below:

Work culture and the three *gunas*	
Sattva	*Conscience-driven motivation: doing one's 'duty', working for the 'greater good', as perfectly as possible, not worrying about the 'fruit of action', experiencing joy from within.*
Rajas	*Desire-driven motivation: struggle to achieve results, efforts driven by self-centred ambition and desire to succeed, vulnerable to 'carrot-and-stick' approach; joy depends on external reward, fearful of punishment, prone to envy, rivalry.*
Tamas	*No motivation: no drive to work for any meaningful purpose, other than survival; lazy, negligent, dull, mechanical, routine, despondent.*

All of us experience these *sattvic, rajasic* and *tamasic* states every now and then; but we tend to be predominantly centred in one of these *gunas*. The ultimate goal of the Gita's *yoga*, of course, is to go beyond the lower nature, bound by the three *gunas*, into the true freedom of higher nature (*Para Prakriti*), where the Divine itself flows out into action through its multiple instruments. This results in a sublime 'flow state' experience in the individual, where the work is performed beautifully and perfectly, without any trace of the false notion of doership ('inaction in action').

The Ego-self, *Ahankara* — a Creation of *Prakriti*

When I assert that 'I am the doer', who is this 'I' referred to? Clearly, it is not the True Self. This 'I' also cannot be entirely an impersonal *Prakriti*, acting through the three *gunas*. There is a personality involved, an individuality that I associate with myself, and which makes me identifiably different from others.

The Gita describes this personality, operating in the field of the lower nature, as *ahankara*. The term *ahankara*, is typically translated as false ego-self, which is self-deluded by the notion of doership. Yet, this deluded self also happens to be a creation of *Prakriti*, according to ancient *Sankhya* philosophy. It is conceived to be one of the four parts of the mental instrumentation, called *antahkarana* (inner organ). The other three parts are *buddhi* (intellect), *manas* (sense-mind) and *chitta* (stored memory). *Ahankara* imparts a unique mental identity, linked further to the notions of doership (*kartrtva-bhava*), ownership (*mama-bhava*) and enjoyership (*bhoktrtva-bhava*). It sustains the mental illusion of a separate and independent self. However, it is always in need of reinforcing this illusion, by comparison and contrast with others.

Fear, want and pride are the predominant motivations of the ego-self. What it wants always in me is to establish that *I am, I have* and *I know, more than others*. This gives a sense of self-esteem and pride. The value of such self-esteem should not be underestimated, for it is a basic deficiency need that must be adequately satisfied for healthy living. Besides, it imparts a sense of confidence, which is essential for pursuing higher needs. Often the value of such esteem is overlooked, especially in Indian spirituality, where *ahankara* tends to be perceived negatively. In contrast, the ego is much valued in Western psychology, where the absence of an ego points to an unstable and undeveloped individual.

It is but natural for the ego-self to expand and grow in time, along with the development of the physical, vital and mental parts of being. Indeed, there must be some purpose to nature's scheme in creating the ego-self. It is the ego-self that is driven by *thrishna* (thirst). As man exerts to quench the unending thirst of desire (*kama-thrishna* and *bhava-thrishna*), his physical, vital and mental faculties develop. This is needed for man's growth and evolution. The fruit of action (*karmaphala*) indeed provides the initial incentive for such development. It may be perceived as a kind of bribe given by Nature to seduce man into developing himself, in much the same way as sexual pleasure is nature's way of ensuring reproduction through procreation. However, this way of living (along the path of *preyas*) turns out ultimately unsatisfactory, especially when need turns into greed. A correction is called for, and this is given by the Gita's *yoga*, so that one does not grow horizontally and instead grows vertically along the path of *shreyas*.

The *Guna* of *Tamas*

Tamas seems to have been the first *guna* to manifest fully in evolution, prior to the emergence of life (signalling the *guna* of *rajas*), and the later emergence of mind (signalling the *guna* of *sattva*). It is the essential stuff of all matter, filled with an inertia of passivity. Because of this inertia, and consequent resistance to activity, *tamas* is said to be the opposite of *rajas*.

Thus, laziness and sleepiness (*alasya-nidra*) are reflective of *tamas*.

तमस्त्वज्ञानजं विद्धि मोहनं सर्वदेहिनाम् |
प्रमादालस्यनिद्राभिः तन्निबध्नाति भारत ||14.8||

Know that tamas, born out of ignorance,	तमः तु अज्ञानजं विद्धि
Deludes, confounding all embodied beings.	मोहनं सर्व देहिनाम्
By negligence, laziness and sleepiness,	प्रमाद आलस्य निद्राभिः
It binds and enslaves all beings, Arjuna!	तत् निबध्नाति भारत

Tamasic people are lethargic by nature and prone to procrastination and shirking work. They like to be inebriated and to sleep as often as possible. Our physical bodies, when we feel tired and drained of vitality, reflect this. A dead body (a *deha* devoid of the indwelling *dehi*) of course reflects this inertia in an absolute sense. Left to itself, without any external intervention, matter tends to *disintegrate*, decompose and get dispersed, following the second law of thermodynamics.

Yet, matter can be put in motion by some force (external or internal). Its *tamasic* nature has a definite preference in not getting involved consciously in the activity. If put into motion, it prefers to stay in routine and mechanical movement, unless there is an external impressed force acting upon it (Newton's law of motion). For this reason, all our mechanical ways of acting, all our habits, are reflective of the *tamo-guna*. The good news is that this applies equally to 'bad' and 'good' habits. If we wish to cultivate a new habit, such as getting up early in the morning, all we need to do is to practise daily (although this can be a struggle initially). Then after a while, the body cannot help getting up early every day! This is how we have learnt to brush our teeth in the morning! What we now need to do, to overcome *tamas* is to do the same activity mindfully — fully awake and attentive to all the movements. The Gita's *yoga* also recommends consecrating the action to the Divine.

Tamas also has a meaning of darkness and absence of light, reflecting ignorance, dullness and stupidity. In the above verse, it is said that the very birth of *tamas* is out of *ajnana*, which strictly means the opposite of knowledge, *jnana*. This suggests a deeper nescience than mere ignorance. It can do much harm by mistaking the wrong for the right, *adharma* for *dharma*, and darkness for light. For this reason, the *tamasic* individual is said to be prone to delusion (*mohanam*). This intellectual darkness of *tamas* makes it the opposite of *sattva*. Thus, *tamas* is said to be a double negative — the opposite of *rajasic vitality* as well as *sattvic lucidity*. By its dual negative action, it binds down the embodied soul. However, the evolutionary journey is unstoppable, and *tamasic* restraints are overcome, sooner or later. In the spiritually awakened human, it is overcome by the power of self-awareness and conscious self-culture.

In terms of the collective, the passive mentality of *tamas* manifests in the form of a quiet acceptance of the control by the community, as evidenced in primitive tribes in early human evolution. The *tamasic* individuality is too weak to react against established creeds with the intention of creating a new order for progressive change. For this reason, the belief in religious dogma as something inviolable and the tendency towards fanaticism and fundamentalism are seen as strong *tamasic* traits. In Sri Aurobindo's words, 'The primitive community is therefore stationary; the individual exists in it not as an individual, but as an undetachable fragment of the whole. The social organisation, even at its best, is in type and level on a par with that of the beehive and the ant-hill.'[10.1]

Tamasic ahankara is therefore reflected not in the identification and development of a unique individuality, but rather that of the group, tribe, religion, cult, community or nation. This is nature's way of ensuring conservatism and stability of the collective, even though this may be at the cost of growth — for which nature has designed the other two *gunas* of *rajas* and *sattva*.

The *Guna* of *Rajas*

Rajas seems to have been the second *guna* to manifest fully in evolution, after *tamas*. Its early manifestation is seen in the emergence of life and its vitality in biological evolution — manifesting in plant life, and more concretely in animal life, in the form of a semi-conscious seeking and activity. This later evolved into a more conscious, passionate and active seeking, motivated by desire in man. In Sri Aurobindo's words, 'The *rajasic* man is the creator, the worker, the man of industry, enterprise, invention, originality, the lover of novelty, progress and reform.'[10.1]

रजो रागात्मकं विद्धि तृष्णासङ्गसमुद्भवम् ।
तन्निबध्नाति कौन्तेय कर्मसङ्गेन देहिनम् ।।14.7।।

Know that rajas has the nature of passion,	रजः राग आत्मकं विद्धि
Arising from craving, thirst and attachment.	तृष्णा सङ्ग समुद्भवम्
It binds and enslaves the embodied soul,	तत् निबध्नाति देहिनम्
By inducing attachment to action, Arjuna.	कर्म सङ्गेन कौन्तेय

Any kind of creative human endeavour would not be possible without the *guna* of *rajas*. Herein lies its value. However, *rajas* by itself, can be like a speeding car without brakes, or (to use the metaphor given in the Gita), like an all-consuming raging fire — unless regulated by the *guna* of *sattva* or exhausted by the *guna* of *tamas*. Restlessness is a feature that we see in *rajasic* man, making him either a workaholic or addicted to some form of entertainment or other, and making him toss and turn in his attempts to rest and sleep.

The Gita specifically warns us against this danger of uncontrolled *rajas* in fanning never-ending desires, especially in the domain of sense-pleasures. *Rajasic ahankara* is also prone to arrogance, and constant comparison with others can result in either a superiority or inferiority complex. When others tend to become, have or know more than me, the ego-self in me feels threatened by an apparent loss of selfhood, and so I am inclined to react with anger, envy, worry, depression, etc. There is a constant struggle to keep up with the Joneses, resulting in tidal fluctuations of pleasure and pain, hope and despair.

It is the restless vitality of *rajas* that drives us to work, sometimes unstoppably. Even workaholism turns out to be productive, if the vitality to do work is uplifted and meaningfully directed by the *guna* of *sattva*, and especially by the light within, of the evolving soul. Alternatively, in the absence of creative engagement, the work can be routine and mechanical, where stability is introduced by the *guna* of *tamas*. We can then work like machines, even though our hearts and minds are not in the work. By itself, *rajas* does not have the quality of steady endurance, although it has kinetic energy. The *rajasic* man finds it difficult to give completion and a settled structure to any creation.

In terms of the collective, the active impulsion of *rajas* manifests in bringing about change — for better or for worse. Many activists are driven by the *rajo-guna*; they tend to be tireless crusaders looking for a cause. This, of course, can create much trouble for others and upset the existing system. While *tamas* prefers to conserve the status quo, *rajas* seeks to destroy it. There is a rebellious, anarchic spirit about it. While on the one hand, this can serve the useful purpose of breaking down obsolete and dysfunctional systems, so as to create a new order, on the other hand, it can either be destructive for the sake of destruction or not be able to converge and complete the task of establishing a new order. The *rajasic* urge manifests primarily in the individual, and the *rajasic ahankara* is not much concerned about the collective, as evidenced in history.

In Sri Aurobindo's words, 'The *rajasic* individuality was not likely to accept the traditional sanction, the communal aim as a satisfying aim and a binding sanction. The more and more he developed, the more and more strongly he would crave for the satisfaction of its expanding individual desires, ideas, activities with less and less regard to the paramount importance of social stability.'[10.1] So it is said: power tends to corrupt, and absolute power corrupts absolutely! The Gita refers frequently to the bondage caused by *rajas*, by its attachment to activity (*karmasangena*), driven by relentless thirst (*thrishna*).

Clearly, something more is needed than the passivity, dullness, dogmatic conservatism and obsolescence of *tamas*, and the creative activity and desire for increased enjoyment, growth and change of *rajas*. In order to ensure the evolutionary objective of healthy and prosperous development of both the individual and the collective, nature seems to have conceived of the creation of the *guna* of *sattva*.

The *Guna* of *Sattva*

Sattva appears to have been the third *guna* to manifest fully in evolution, after *tamas* and *rajas*. Its early manifestation is seen in the emergence of mind. A rudimentary form of mentality can be seen in plant and animal life, becoming semi-conscious in the more intelligent animals and more fully conscious in man. A growth in the *sattvic guna* can only occur by a corresponding reduction in the proportions of the other two *gunas*, and this in fact is a reflection of the evolution of consciousness. Even amongst humans, we see a wide spectrum of composition of the *gunas*: a low proportion of *sattva* indicating more animal-like behaviour, and a high proportion indicating an intellectually and morally evolved being, driven by an aspiration to know and live by impersonal and universal truths.

तत्र सत्त्वं निर्मलत्वात् प्रकाशकमनामयम् |
सुखसङ्गेन बध्नाति ज्ञानसङ्गेन चानघ ||14.6||

Among the gunas, it is sattva that is pure,	तत्र सत्त्वं निर्मलत्वात्
For it is luminous and free from any taint.	प्रकाशकम् अनामयम्
But it also binds, by attachment to joy,	सुख सङ्गेन बध्नाति
And attachment to knowledge, Arjuna!	ज्ञान सङ्गेन च अनघ

A developed mentality reflects an increased ability to think and reason, to analyse and synthesise knowledge, and to discern unity in diversity. However, the quality of *sattva* implies something more than this. There is reference to purity, luminosity and 'freedom from taint', resulting in a joy from learning and living a noble life that is quite distinct and different from the short-term vital pleasures promised by *rajas*. There is a joy in learning, as there is a joy in seeing unity and in living in accordance with this enlightened understanding. The highest ethical ideas constructed by man (such as the simple dictum of 'do unto others as you would have others do unto you') arise from a dispassionate *sattvic* understanding.

Such *sattvic* understanding is however not fruitful, unless actually put into practice. Thus the pure mind of *sattva*, is one that acts conscientiously, reflecting an alignment and integration of knowledge and will. The will power here, driven by the *buddhi*, is different from that of *rajas*, which is driven by desire. Also, the *sattvic* mentality is reflected emotionally through love and compassion, kindness and forgiveness, generosity and calm, honesty and truthfulness.

These attributes are implied in the term purity, which is the essence of *sat*, from which the term *sattva* is derived.

It is possible that there could be a high intellectual development (as in scientists and philosophers) but they could be found wanting in the purity aspect, lacking in large-heartedness and compassion for others, and vulnerable to the *rajasic* shortcomings of jealousy and hatred against rivals, and prey to dishonesty. So also there could be others well-developed in the purity aspect (large-hearted, kind, loving, compassionate, truthful and pious), but without much knowledge of the world, and of science or philosophy. A full development of *sattva*, however, implies an all-round development — morally, intellectually and spiritually.

In Sri Aurobindo's words, 'Morally it shows itself as selfless sympathy, intellectually as disinterested enlightenment and dispassionate wisdom, spiritually as a calm self-possessing peacefulness as far removed from the dull *tamasic* inertia as from the restless turbidity of *rajas*.'[10.1]

What could possibly be the shortcoming of *sattva*? The Gita points to the fact that it is still limited in potential and binding in nature. There is an ego-self concealed behind the goodness and purity, the *sattvic ahankara*, which identifies with its own goodness, and this identification often manifests through feelings of righteousness or superiority over others (who know less or appear to be less moral). The joy and knowledge inherent in *sattva* are certainly more refined and superior in quality, when compared to the crude pleasures and passions of *rajas* and the dull delusions of *tamas*, but they are nevertheless binding in nature, as they belong to the realm of lower nature (*Apara Prakriti*). The golden chains of *sattva*, no matter how refined and attractive, are nevertheless chains that fetter the embodied soul. As the Gita says, '*Sattva* binds by attachment to joy (*sukhasangena*) and attachment to knowledge (*jnanasangena*)'.

Unlike many other religious and philosophical texts, the Gita does not stop with realising the highest goodness in humanity. It urges us to go beyond, find true freedom and thus realise and manifest divinity in humanity. Man needs to realise, above all, that he is not just a human being who can contact the Divine; but that he is truly a Divine being in a human form. This realisation can make a world of difference, and this is the ultimate objective of the Gita.

In terms of the collective, the truth-abiding positive and compassionate outlook of *sattva* manifests in establishing harmony and sustaining order in civilisation, remaining open to the progressive changes brought about by *rajas*, yet regulating these in the interest of well-being for all. However, *sattva* by itself cannot bring about evolutionary growth. For that, the creative genius and individual leadership of *rajas* is needed, and the stable habit-forming adherence of the collective to the newly established order calls for the *guna* of *tamas*.

Thus, we see that the process of evolutionary growth and the rise and fall of civilisations are all attributable to the dynamic play of the three *gunas*. It is difficult to see though, except through spiritual insight, that Divinity is quietly and invisibly at work behind the scenes in this dynamic play of creation, maintenance and destruction conjoined with evolution and involution.

Clearly, we need to develop consciously the *guna* of *sattva* in us, for it gives us the light and direction needed for the evolution of consciousness. It also provides a much-needed balance between the unbridled volatile passion of *rajas* and the dull inertia and mechanical rigidity of *tamas*. This is necessary for the sake of our individual and collective well-being.

Ego-entrapment in Relationships

How easily we tend to deceive ourselves whenever we get into difficulties in our relationships — with our spouses, children, parents, colleagues, subordinates, superiors and others. It is as if we get trapped into dysfunctional behaviour, which gets reflected in a set of characteristic symptoms. These have been discussed insightfully with excellent examples in the book, '*Leadership and Self-deception*' by the Arbinger Institute.

We feel offended, we blame the other person, we self-justify our position, we fail to respect the other person's humanity, and our views of the situation get distorted, we inflate our virtues, and the faults of others. We shift responsibility, find ourselves filled with righteous indignation and a sense of victimhood.[10.2]

This is how the ego-trap operates, and once we fall in, it is difficult to come out. Seeing the other person, the whole history (our version) comes to mind, and we tend to store and nurture grievances over time. This happens unconsciously, and we do not suspect that it could all be our delusion, with our perspective biased and clouded. It takes a *sattvic* mentality to see the big picture truly and impersonally. Then this issue can be resolved — by invoking peace, love and harmony. We are usually blinded by *rajasic ahankara*. And on that basis, we tend to act from impulsive anger. Or else, we feel hurt and helpless, thus succumbing to our *tamasic ahankara*, unable to take action in our grief and depression. But even so, we retain and nurse our grievances and blame.

We will do well to acknowledge that blame of any kind is never received well by anyone. An instinctive resistance is felt. It may appear to our ego-self that in this blaming we are well intentioned and are doing what is needed to correct the other person. Sadly, our intentions may not be as noble as they appear on the surface. When frustrated, our first impulse is a need to release pent-up frustration. If the other person happens to be vulnerable (as in the case of a child or subordinate), we have no qualms directing the released emotions against them. We thus sometimes even yell: 'How many times have I told you not to do this. But you go on repeating the same mistake!'

It may well be good for us to empathise with this situation. Surely, if we were at the receiving end, we would not welcome this attempt to discipline us. The shrill tone in the voice would be upsetting enough. We would be in no mood to listen. If we could, we would retaliate directly! Typically, in such conflicts, each person will try to 'fix' the other, both getting stuck in their respective ego-traps. How would life be, if these persons need to live together for long: perhaps as husband and wife, or parent and child, boss and employee, even as two siblings, or colleagues or neighbours? Such conflicts get caught up in 'win-lose' battles, often ending up as 'lose-lose'. Similar battles are fought between two groups or communities or nations, each side blaming the other for all perceived ills arising from the interaction. The need here is to evolve out of the ego-entrapment, for the harmony and well-being of all. What is needed is a 'win-win' option — difficult, but not impossible.

With the rising of *sattva* in us, invoking wisdom about doership and the play of the *gunas*, we may succeed in holding our tongues and getting a bit of peace. But this imminent emergence from our ego-trap can easily be threatened by the provokingly accusing tone of the other person. Thus, we find ourselves sliding helplessly back into a retaliating ego-trap. Until and unless we are truly centred in the calmness of our innermost being (*yukta*), our emergence from the ego-trap cannot be sustained in a stable way. When we are so centred, our posture will no longer be seen as threatening to the other person. In fact, we will truly radiate vibrations of peace and love, which are bound to have a healing effect, as they serve to bring out the other person from such foolishly confined imprisonment.

We need to do this, regardless of provocations likely to be received from the other end. This is implied by the practices of *titiksha* (forbearance) and self-mastery recommended in the Gita. This is the surest way ahead for our mutual well-being. Instead of waiting for the other person to reform and take the initiative to come out of the ego-trap, we must be the ones to transform, unhesitatingly. For this indeed is a sign of true spirituality at work. We then realise the wisdom in Mahatma Gandhi's dictum: 'Be the change you wish to see in the world!'

In ego-conflict situations, we tend to lose focus on our noble aspirations and the meaningful purpose of our living, getting lost in narrow pettiness and blaming or finding fault with others or with the environment. When we join organisations (or enter into a marriage), we are likely to be inspired by high ideals at first. We then want to contribute our best, in sharing and working synergistically with mutual love and respect, thus prospering in all ways possible. However, it does not take too long for the sheen to wear off, as we tend to get disillusioned and discontented. If questioned about the cause of our discontent, it is most likely that we will blame others and the environment.

It is convenient for us to look upon ourselves as victims, because this provides a justification for our frustration and apparent helplessness. When organisations are filled with such frustrated employees, there is bound to be a lack of commitment, motivation, accountability and trust, along with poor teamwork and back-biting. This is very common, as observed by Stephen Covey. In his book, *The 8th Habit*, he translates his statistical findings in organisations in terms of the following metaphor: 'If, say, a soccer team had these same scores, only four of the eleven players on the field would know which goal is theirs. Only two of the eleven would care. Only two of the eleven would know what position they play and know exactly what they are supposed to do. And all but two players would, in some way, be competing against their own team members, rather than the opponent.'[10.3]

From the perspective of the *gunas*, we can visualise that the atmosphere in such organisations is pervaded with *rajas* and *tamas*, which like germs infect the unwary and the unprepared. We all tend to fall easily into the ego-trap in situations involving human interactions, and so becoming part of warring groups.

Consider, for example, people joining hands to do something noble — like bringing water or electricity to a remote village. All kinds of people are likely to be involved, including government officials, bureaucrats, engineers, NGOs, volunteers, workers and so on: all inspired initially to contribute their best to this noble cause. Yet, sooner or later, the project gets into difficulties and complications, primarily due to all kinds of inter-personal issues arising. Warring factions may emerge, blaming one another and spending energies on 'fixing' others, rather than devoting themselves to the noble mission of the project to which they had committed initially. We tend to lose sight almost completely of the noble objective, and so get distracted or even obsessed about issues relating to our ego-related pettiness. This happens when we see undeserving people getting credit, while we find ourselves overlooked or slighted. We then do not really care about the villagers getting water or electricity; we only care about the gain or loss incurred by our *ahankara*.

The typical symptoms of ego-entrapment should now be obvious to us: feeling offended, blaming others, self-justifying, having our perspective distorted, and so on. The shocking truth is that we actually wish to remain stuck in our ego-related problems, and for this, we need others to be 'blame-worthy'! Unless we recognise this harsh reality and get out of the ego-trap, we are likely to stay stuck forever and continue to keep blaming, wanting to 'fix' those whom we find deserving of blame.

We fail to realise that this is something dysfunctional, so that our immediate task should be to get out of the ego-trap, and learn to stay out. This calls for a deeply sustained self-awareness and realisation of the play of *Prakriti's gunas*. Once caught in the trap of blaming others, our focus is always on the need for them to change. They may well need such change, but this is unlikely to happen, unless we first take the initiative to change ourselves. We need to find inner peace, regaining focus on our noble life mission. Then only can we gain the competence to deal effectively with such challenging situations, which have been exacerbated by our own reactions — primarily, of our *rajasic ahankara*. If we can step back and look dispassionately at the various dramas in our lives, we can see the predictable pattern of reactions: the play of the *gunas* (*guna guneshu vartanta*). We notice that the patterns of ego-entrapment are similar in almost everybody's case, establishing the impersonal nature of *Prakriti's gunas*.

We need to withdraw from our lower nature, *Prakriti*, to our soul, *Purusha*, giving up the delusion of doership. This, along with the implications of our evolutionary journey, is discussed in the next chapter.

11

Soul and Nature: *Purusha* and *Prakriti*

कार्यकारणकर्तृत्वे हेतुः प्रकृतिरुच्यते |
पुरुषः सुखदुःखानां भोक्तृत्वे हेतुरुच्यते ||13.21||

Prakriti creates the notion of doership	कर्तृत्वे हेतुः प्रकृतिः उच्यते
And the karmic chain of cause and effect.	कार्य कारण
Purusha is the subjective experiencer	भोक्तृत्वे हेतुः पुरुषः उच्यते
Of all kinds of pleasures and pains.	सुख दुःखानां

All work and experience of life, according to the Gita, is a transaction between *Soul* (*Purusha*) and *nature* (*Prakriti*). As mentioned earlier, the nature that binds the Soul is the *lower nature* (*Apara Prakriti*), creating the delusion of doership through the *ahankara* and the play of the three *gunas*. The energy source for all the happenings in *Prakriti* is however borrowed from the *Purusha*, which although independent and inactive, tends to get identified with *Prakriti* and entrapped by it. This seemingly dynamic aspect of *Purusha* moves along with *Prakriti*, apparently sanctioning all her movements. It is called *Kshara Purusha*. Both *Purusha* and *Prakriti* function not only at the individual level (multiple souls and the respective natures), but also at the universal level (the collective) and the transcendental level (beyond manifestation).

It is the Soul, *Purusha*, that enjoys the creation and action of *Prakriti*. However, this is a limited and mixed 'enjoyment', when the action is done by the lower nature. We want this enjoyment to be in the form of pleasures (*sukha*) of various kinds (*tamasic*, *rajasic* or *sattvic*), depending on the circumstances and our preferences. These pleasures are transient, and it is the very nature of *Prakriti* to bring in a tidal action, with these pleasures giving way to their opposite. These are pains, as a consequence of the *karmic* chain of cause and effect, causing suffering, *duhkha*.

Kshara Purusha and *Akshara Purusha*

The term *bhoga* refers to experience of any kind: pleasure or pain or indifference. The experiencer here is *Kshara Purusha*, typically reflected in lower nature by *tamasic*, *rajasic* and *sattvic* forms of *ahankara*.

In our habitual object-centred awareness, the *Kshara Purusha* in us gets lost in the experience — not conscious of its sublime and Divine reality. We are fully caught in the enacted dramas, tossed and turned by the vicissitudes of life. It is only by stepping back into pure awareness that we discover our True Self, free and unaffected by all these dramas, in much the same way as a mirror is least affected by the passing images reflected in it, be they 'good' or 'bad', pretty or ugly. There is an inherent peace and quiet joy that can be experienced when we are centred in True Self. In rare moments of objectless awareness, we discover the motionless, undying and unbounded Self in us — the *Akshara Purusha*.

Some of us may find it difficult to appreciate what objectless awareness means. We may find it helpful to recall the timeless moments of deep sleep, free of dreams, that we all experience every night. When we awaken, we recall this as a blissful and untroubled state. We feel rested and refreshed, with our 'batteries' getting recharged. This is nature's way of relieving us from the tyranny and fatigue of relentless mental activity in 'waking' and 'dream' states. So in deep sleep, we get reconnected truly to our Divine

Source. We become *yukta*! Sadly, when this happens, our thoughts and emotions remain 'blank', and so we seem 'unconscious'. Nevertheless, this experience helps us to recognise that consciousness found free from all objects (physical, vital or mental) is one of deep peace and quiet joy. The world then seems to have dissolved. Along with it, the sense of personal identity too!

It is possible to enter into this state of unconditional peace, fully awake and conscious, in deep meditation (called *samadhi* in *Rajayoga*). However, it is not usually possible to abide in this state for long, even if we so wished. So we soon return to the ordinary world of external experience. The discovery of *Akshara Purusha*, and our ability to access it, will definitely change our perspective and attitude towards living. It is even possible (as happened to many sages leading solitary lives in their caves in India) that one might not welcome returning to the world of ordinary experience, which is so often perceived as *duhkha*. For such disillusioned individuals, the interacting world of personal relations may well appear to be a fancied illusion (*asat*) — to be withdrawn and disengaged from. So it is precisely this that causes many people in India (living in a world of relationships with social ties and obligations) to get worried and concerned by inclinations of family members towards spiritual enquiry.

Indeed, it is a good question to ask: *Why should we engage in work of any kind, if it is all an illusion?* If this were true, would not then our time be better spent in doing just the minimum for survival, and devoting all our energies to sitting in meditation, in order to access and abide permanently in *Akshara Purusha*? Then Arjuna would have been justified in his resolve to abandon the battlefield at Kurukshetra and to become a *Sannyasin*. We know that the Gita does not advocate such outer renunciation, motivated by escapism from the challenges and responsibilities of life. It clearly emphasises that inaction prompted by such escapism, is also not possible, as long as the purpose for which the embodiment has occurred is not fulfilled. Nevertheless, the same Gita points to the importance of attaining freedom from bondage to *Apara Prakriti* and discovering *Akshara Purusha*. This discovery of *Akshara Purusha* is advocated while one is living an active life, and not just at the time of the physical body's death. Is there then a third option of enlightened living (a third status of *Purusha* other than *Kshara* and *Akshara*), pointing to a supreme way of living a life of fulfilment?

Yes, says the Divine Teacher! It is on this supreme truth that the message of the Gita with regard to *spirituality at work* is fundamentally rooted. It is then that the Gita's *yoga* becomes complete.

This third and supreme status of the *Purusha* is the *Uttama* (defined in Gita verse 15.17). It is the status of the Supreme Divine, called *Purushottama* or *Ishvara-Shakti*, as mentioned earlier. It includes and transcends both the *Kshara* and the *Akshara*. It is the all-inclusive, all-pervading Omnipotent, Omnipresent and Omniscient *Brahman*. The aspect of the Supreme Divine (which engages in action and is subject to mutation, but is also Self-aware of its status as immutable *Akshara*) is the higher nature, *Para Prakriti* or *Shakti*, who is inseparable from the Supreme Lord she serves, *Ishvara*.

The Supreme Divine, *Purushottama* or *Ishvara-Shakti*

उपद्रष्टानुमन्ता च भर्ता भोक्ता महेश्वरः |
परमात्मेति चाप्युक्तः देहेऽस्मिन्पुरुषः परः ||13.23||

Witness, Consenter, Sustainer (of Prakriti) उपद्रष्टा अनुमन्ता च भर्ता
And Experiencer is the Almighty Lord, भोक्ता महेश्वरः
Also known as the Supreme One Self, परमात्मा इति च अपि उक्तः
The Supreme Soul seated in this body. देहे अस्मिन् पुरुषः परः

Seated in the body is a portion (*amsha*) of the Supreme Divine Lord, *Ishvara*. He is also known as the Supreme One Self in all, *Paramatma*, and as the Supreme Soul, *Purushottama*. As said clearly in the above verse, it is this portion of the Supreme Divine (*Ishvara-amsha*) that performs four distinct roles.

First, It is the quiet Witness (*Upadrashta* or *Sakshi*) to all that is happening — not only outside but also within the individual (in terms of movements in the physical, vital and mental realms). It simply watches everything, without interfering, while it clearly observes and knows. Secondly, It recognises that, being an *amsha* of the *Ishvara*, it need not remain a mute spectator. For it is empowered to withdraw giving default *sanction* to the individual's participation in all that is happening. This role as *Consenter* (*Anumanta*), which is taken for granted by *Prakriti* from the default status of the soul as *Kshara Purusha*, can be exercised by the Divine Indwelling Lord (the *Antaryami*) by a simple withdrawal of sanction, thereby arresting all action. This option is exercised when it is deemed absolutely necessary. Otherwise, It generally upholds and sustains all that is done by *Prakriti*. This is the third role of the *Ishvara-amsha*, as *Sustainer* (*Bharta*). It sustains the mutable operations of *Prakriti*, by providing the source of energy needed for this purpose.

Finally, the fourth role of the Indwelling Lord is cited as *Experiencer* (*Bhokta*). It is the *Ishvara-amsha* who is the true and ultimate experiencer and enjoyer, and yet free, of all the operations of *Prakriti*. All the actions of *Prakriti*, through her multiple instruments, are in fact, a sacrifice (*yajna*) for the enjoyment of *Ishvara*.

Self-realisation calls for knowledge of this impersonal aspect of the One Self in all. Sri Aurobindo comments: 'That is the self-knowledge to which we have to accustom our mentality before we can truly know ourselves as an eternal portion of the Eternal. Once that is fixed, no matter how the soul in us may comport itself outwardly in its transactions with Nature, whatever it may seem to do or however it may seem to assume this or that figure of personality and active force and embodied ego, it is in itself free, no longer bound to birth...'[11.1] When there is this discovery and realisation of the Divine Indweller, and the false notion of doership is entirely dispelled, then we willingly submit ourselves to whatever be the Divine will of *Ishvara*. Our instrumentation is now available for the Divine *Shakti* to operate directly through our being.

The Divine Indweller, *Antaryami*

The following Gita verse is a clear and unequivocal declaration of the Divinity ever-present in all beings (*sarvabhutanam*) as an *amsha* of *Ishvara*.

ईश्वरः सर्वभूतानां हृद्देशेऽर्जुन तिष्ठति ।
भ्रामयन्सर्वभूतानि यन्त्रारूढानि मायया ||18.61||

The Supreme Divine Being dwells	ईश्वरः तिष्ठति
In the hearts of all beings, Arjuna,	सर्व भूतानां हृत् देशे अर्जुन
Mobilising all with His mysterious power,	भ्रामयन् सर्व भूतानि मायया
Like an engine hidden in a machine!	यन्त्र आरूढानि

This divinity remains concealed (in the *cave of the heart*), and so we, in our ignorance, are not aware of this reality. Even if we acknowledge, accept and believe in God, the divinity we seek is mostly somewhere outside us, accessible perhaps in a temple or church or mosque, or in the heavens above. However, this open declaration suggests that we need not look and search outside, for the Divine is within us — so near and yet so far! This is why in traditional Indian wisdom, Self-realisation is considered as God-realisation. The Divine resides not only in my self, but in yours, too: indeed, in all sentient beings, as well as in every atom manifested in the universe, and in the formless *Akshara*, from which all manifestation has emerged. This is the essence of the *Upanishadic* saying, *ishavasyamidam sarvam* ('all This is pervaded by *Ishvara*').

In our ignorance and arrogance, we do not realise this. The ego-self (*ahankara*) in us has usurped the lordship over our beings. We point at our 'free will' as evidence of our ability to do what we want, and all our actions are thus filled with the notion of doership. We even believe that there is originality in the desires that drive us to action, little realising that it is all a play of *Prakriti's gunas*. Sri Aurobindo points to the hollowness of these fondly held and cherished beliefs, which we need to go beyond on the path to liberation: 'Our ego, boasting of freedom, is at every moment the slave, toy and puppet of countless beings, powers, forces, influences in universal nature. The self-abnegation of the ego in the Divine is its self-fulfilment; its surrender to that which transcends it is its liberation from bonds and limits and its perfect freedom.'[11.2]

This profound delusion of doership has been compared, by analogy in traditional wisdom, to grains of rice in a pot of boiling water. They jump around believing that they are creators of their wonderful kinetic energy! All sentient beings are likewise mobilised into kinetic action, fired by *Apara Prakriti*, which derives its energy source from the hidden *Kshara Purusha*. The energy source is mounted within them by the mysterious power of *Maya*, compelling them into action. It is in this way that machines operate, when switched on (*yantrarudhani*). In most beings living in ignorance, this motion is not unlike that of puppets revolving (*bhramayan*) helplessly, as in a merry-go-round, until there is a full awakening, Self-realisation and ascension to the higher nature.

Human beings, the most evolved among the sentient beings on earth, have more developed instrumentation and intelligence than animals and plants. Yet, it is they who are more prone to this delusion of doership, based on conceit, on account of *ahankara*. However, they are also the ones to have the highest potential to transcend this delusion and realise the *Antaryami* (*Ishvara-amsha*), the Divine Indweller within them. It then becomes possible to realise that it is the same Divinity all around us, sustaining all manifestation. A beautiful analogy that points to this realisation is that of an embryo within the womb of a mother. If the yet-to-be-born had the potential to Self-realise, it would know that it is entirely sustained, within and outside, by its mother. That is exactly how we too can feel the presence of *Ishvara-Shakti* — within us, and all around us!

यज्ज्ञात्वा न पुनर्मोहम् एवं यास्यसि पाण्डव |
येन भूतान्यशेषेण द्रक्ष्यस्यात्मन्यथो मयि ||4.35||

Realising this true wisdom, Arjuna,	यत् ज्ञात्वा पाण्डव
You will not fall into delusion again!	न पुनः मोहम् एवं यास्यसि
You will then see all beings	येन भूतानि अशेषेण द्रक्ष्यसि
In the One Self, then in Me!	आत्मनि अथो मयि

Realising this wisdom, while living an active life, is somewhat like waking up in a dream and knowing that it is a dream (lucid dreaming). One is then no longer deluded, and remains free of affliction of all that happens. One may still have no control over what happens (which is determined by so many *karmic* forces), but one is essentially liberated. One respects the Divinity underlying all manifestation, and plays one's assigned role in the drama of life, with freedom and skill, keeping the well-being and evolution of all (*lokasangraham*) in mind. Indeed, as Sri Aurobindo says, 'Man's highest and freest possible experience' is that of 'a quietistic inner largeness and silence reconciled with an outer dynamic active living…'[11.3]

The profound message given here by the *Purushottama*, through the Divine Teacher, is to 'see all beings in the Self, and then in Me' (*atmanyatho mayi*)! The call is for a merging of the separate self into the infinite wideness of our Divine Source. It is a call for unification, for impersonality, for seeing and respecting the *Antaryami* in all beings. The merging here implies not only an ego-transcendence into the *Akshara Purusha*, which is inactive in its Self-delight, but also a merging into *Purushottama*, implying a passage from the lower nature (*Apara Prakriti*) into the higher (*Para Prakriti*). Thus, the Divine is free to act directly through the developed individual instrumentation, as deemed fit.

The Evolutionary Journey of the Individual Soul

The soul, which is a Divine spark in sentient beings, evolves in the human being through many lives, as the *Antaratman* (or *Chaitya Purusha*), which remains veiled in man's innermost being (in the heart region). Unlike the True Self (*Atman*), which is pure Spirit unborn and not bound or affected by manifested nature, the soul serves as its projection in individual manifestation. In its early stages of evolution, the *Antaratman* even seems to assume the imperfections of the lower nature (in the manner of *Kshara Purusha*), which it supports from behind the veils. It is believed that the soul's evolution can take place only in a human form on earth, and this is the reason why a human birth is considered to be a precious gift and opportunity for the evolution of consciousness. Therefore, it is not something to be whiled away or wasted. Gradually, this soul evolves over many lifetimes and recovers its original and pristine Divine nature in its fullness, and becomes identified with the *Antaryami*. Until then, it remains in the background as a 'secret witness', according to Sri Aurobindo, who goes on to comment on its status as 'a constitutional ruler who allows his ministers to rule for him, delegates to them his empire, silently assents to their decisions and only now and then puts in a word which they can at any moment override and act otherwise.'[11.4]

Once the soul has evolved and come forward, it takes up its rightful place as the 'true monarch', the *dehi* in charge of the *deha*. In this process of emergence of the soul, it serves as the inner guru, consecrating and unifying all the divergent parts of the being (physical, vital and mental), thus facilitating the transition from the lower nature into the higher nature (*Para Prakriti*). In Sri Aurobindo's words, 'It is in its nature something that is put forth from the Divine to support the evolution and it must do so till the Divine's purpose in its evolution is accomplished. Karma is only a machinery, it is not the fundamental cause of terrestrial existence — it cannot be, for when the soul first entered this existence, it had no Karma.'[11.5]

The true *Svabhava* of the being lies in its authentic soul nature, which is a seed that lies embedded in the soul. As the soul evolves, the *Svabhava* also develops, initially through imperfection due to the play of the lower nature's *gunas*, as it gets purified and consecrated. Eventually, it begins to operate as an authentic *soul force* — a Divine *Shakti* for the Divine purpose, without any trace of doership. The self-identity shifts, through various phases, from the false ego-self to the evolved soul. At the final stage, when individuation and unification are complete, the result is an extraordinary sense of fulfilment, completion and joy (*Ananda*). In many instances, the full individuation may remain incomplete, but there is Self-realisation and absorption in the *Akshara* or a complete devotional surrender, whereby by Divine Grace, the soul is allowed to merge into the Divine Source, without seeking to serve further as an instrument. It is this that is commonly conceived to be *moksha* by those who perceive all existence to be full of sorrow (*duhkha*). The freedom thus sought is an ultimate release that finally exits from a world (*samsara*) of relentlessly cycling birth and death.

After its Divine mission and purpose in manifestation are fully served, the soul unites and merges into its source, the *Atman*. Its basic nature is one of joy (*Ananda*), which gets reflected in our actions — based on a manifestation of truth, goodness, beauty and sacredness. The evolving soul therefore provides us a direct and sure access to the Divine Indweller that it represents. Indeed, the very urge towards spirituality is an inspiration we receive from our *Antaratman*, which we need to invoke daily, in making spiritual progress and excelling in our work and in our relationships.

We need to acknowledge our present status as being entrapped in the lower nature, and then find our way into liberation. With the increasing guidance of the evolving soul within us, and a strong aspiration, this knowledge will enable us in the process of purification in our character and work — so necessary for finding fulfilment.

The Need for Balance

नात्यश्नतस्तु योगोऽस्ति न चैकान्तमनश्नतः |
न चातिस्वप्नशीलस्य जाग्रतो नैव चार्जुन ||6.16||

This yoga is not for one who over-eats,	न अत्यश्नतः तु योगः अस्ति
Nor for one who always starves;	न च एकान्तम् अनश्नतः
And not for one who sleeps too much,	न च अतिस्वप्न शीलस्य
Nor for one who gets no sleep, Arjuna.	जाग्रतः न एव च अर्जुन

One of the key features of equipoise is 'balance'. We lose our way, we lose our poise, we lose our balance, when we try taking to extremes. This is the key to the ancient *Tao* philosophy, which is said to apply to everything (including food, relationships, work, money and so on). Here the art of staying in balance, of walking the *Tao*, is one of staying in the middle, between what the Chinese refer to as doing and non-doing, *yang* and *yin*. The logic underlying this *middle path* is extremely simple. There is no stability if we try to stay with an extreme position, for we are likely to swing to the other extreme, like a pendulum. If we take to extreme starving for days, then when we find food in front of us, we would not show any etiquette or mindfulness in our eating. We would simply devour the food and gorge it down voraciously.

While fasting and other kinds of austerity (*tapas*) are considered to be very valuable in spirituality and in attaining self-mastery, they are never recommended to be followed in the extreme, as a permanent way of life. This was discovered by none other than the Buddha, who himself underwent all kinds of torturous austerities for long, including near starvation to death. Contrary to the prevailing culture among ascetics, he declared that such practices were in fact harmful and arising out of delusion. These are clearly described as being *tamasic* in the Gita. Balance, on the other hand, is the essence of the *sattvic* way of austerity. While it is always beneficial, for the purpose of learning, to experiment and touch the extremes, and to stretch the limits of our capacity, we must do this in a way that will make such learning and practice stable, healthy and helpful. Both over-eating and starving, done excessively, are reflections of *tamo-guna*. The energetic drive to these extremes, on the other hand, is reflective of *rajo-guna*. In the case of the pendulum, this is reflected by the velocity of the bob, which is high as it swings in either direction in the middle region, and drops to zero at the extremes.

The play of *rajo-guna* and *tamo-guna* are also evident in our modern consumerist culture and our high-stress lifestyles. The lack of balance is reflected in our inability to switch off our minds at will, when we need to take rest, or when we need to pay concentrated attention without getting distracted. Our restless minds tend to behave like over-used computers, with all kinds of useless programs running in a busy background that we cannot switch off. When we really need to concentrate and focus attention on some difficult task, our system tends to get paralysed and 'hangs' like an overloaded computer! We all clearly need to sometimes slow down our metabolism and pace of living, so as to make them more harmonious, steady and enjoyable. These are qualities reflective of *sattva*, which provides a balance between the restless energy of *rajas* and the dull inertia and resistance of *tamas*. For life's journey to be a harmonious and smooth drive, we need to invoke continually the intelligence of *sattva*, knowing when to press the accelerator (symbolic of *rajas*) and when to push the brakes (symbolic of *tamas*).

The lack of proper work-life balance is increasingly evident in modern times. The discipline and discrimination required for such balance are ideally to be initiated and inculcated in early education and mastered in later life. However, such self-discipline is generally found wanting even in the best of educational institutions in India (like the IITs), where students are given the best facilities and also adequate freedom. Students who should be sleeping well at night are found often hyperactive. This is not, as one might expect, related to an obsession with their studies. More commonly, they are busy indulging in all kinds of activities in their hostel rooms, such as watching films, playing digital games, getting lost in social media and other addictions (including, in a few cases, substance abuse). As a result, they wake up late, do not bathe in the morning, miss out breakfast, and come late to class, bleary-eyed and find themselves dropping off to sleep during lectures that they need to attend! This lack of sincerity and discipline, as well as poor time management, are also reflected in delayed submission of assignments (often copied from others at the last minute). There is clearly a need to develop a healthy balance between work and recreation, and to avoid falling prey to *adharma*.

It gets difficult for many students, unless inspired otherwise, to break out of a predominantly *tamasic-rajasic* culture. This often implies going against the grain of peer pressure and possible ridicule by those who are already well-entrenched, and may lead one to feel a little lost. Such pressures and doubts could be countered by developing a strong aspiration, disciplined practice (*sadhana*), and by looking for inspiration. This will help individuals break through, initially into a *rajasic-sattvic* culture, and later into a predominantly *sattvic* culture of *integral education* (physical, vital, mental and spiritual). It is such a holistic vision that needs to be understood, supported and encouraged by the teachers and administrators of our educational institutions. If this can be progressively achieved, it will serve to usher in a new order of spirituality at work in educational institutions. Students will be enabled thus to develop and spread this noble culture later on in their respective workplaces and homes, inspiring others.

The tremendous resistance offered by the prevailing *tamasic-rajasic* culture can hardly be underestimated. We see evidence of it in all walks of life in modern society. However, this has been the way in earlier societies too, as observed by the Divine Teacher in the Gita (verse 7.3): 'Among thousands of men, very few strive for perfection, and even among those who succeed, hardly anyone knows Me truly.' The reference here is to the reality that the transition from the lower to higher nature is rare to see in the world around.

Attitude and Faith, *Shraddha*

The term *shraddha* is used in the Gita (verses 17.2-4) to refer to individual *attitude* and *faith*: in thought, word and deed. This may be inspired personally by ideals in one's own religion or culture, but also by prevailing influences of peer pressure and environment. So there are bound to be pushes and pulls in the physical, vital and mental parts of our being. These parts are rarely seen acting in an integrated way, as happens when they come under the guidance and control of the innermost being (the evolved soul) representing the *Antaryami*. Until that state is attained, the *shraddha* takes the hue of the individual's predominant *guna*. It gets reflected where the individual's attention is naturally inclined.

So an individual's *shraddha* is characterised by the composition of *gunas*. These are shown variously characterised in the Gita, as follows:

1. The nature of *food* preferred (*Ahara*)
2. The nature of *renunciation* performed (*Tyaga*)
3. The nature of *sacrifice* offered (*Yajna*)
4. The nature of *giving* offered (*Dana*)
5. The nature of *austerity* offered (*Tapas*)
6. The nature of *knowledge* assimilated (*Jnana*)
7. The nature of *action* performed (*Karma*)
8. The nature of the *doer* of action (*Karta*)
9. The nature of the *intellect* in understanding (*Buddhi*)
10. The nature of the associated *resolve* (*Dhriti*)
11. The nature of *happiness* enjoyed (*Sukha*)

We shall explore each of these characteristics in detail, based on the relevant verses in the Gita. The first of these aspects, related to food preferences, is discussed in this chapter; other aspects are covered later.

Gunas and Food Preferences, *Ahara*

We have seen, according to the Gita, that everything in the lower nature, without exception, arises from the intermixing and play of the three *gunas*. Though the emphasis of the *guna* related teachings of the Gita is primarily psychological in nature, there is mention of how human psychology is also linked to the physical — as in the food we consume. Everything influences everything else with which it interacts (*guna guneshu vartanta*), and therefore our psychology is naturally affected by the food we consume. The Gita describes the *gunas* associated with different types of food generically, in terms of the distinct food preferences of those with *sattvic*, *rajasic* and *tamasic* temperaments. Their *shraddha* is towards such foods, and the consequence (vital or psychological effects) of those foods on their being are also described.

आयुःसत्त्वबलारोग्य सुखप्रीतिविवर्धनाः |
रस्याः स्निग्धाः स्थिरा हृद्या आहाराः सात्त्विकप्रियाः ||17.8||

Foods preferred by the sattvic temperament आहाराः सात्त्विक प्रियाः
Are juicy, soothing, nutritive, agreeable, रस्याः स्निग्धाः स्थिराः हृद्याः
Promoting happiness and cheerfulness, सुख प्रीति विवर्धनाः
Longevity, lucidity, strength and health. आयुः सत्त्व बल आरोग्य

The characteristics of *sattva-guna* listed in the above verse are happiness, cheerfulness, longevity, lucidity, strength and good health. Foods that promote these desirable qualities of well-being are said to be juicy, soothing, nutritive and agreeable. It is left to us to infer, through our own personal experience, as to which foods generate these qualities, imperative for keeping the body and mind fit, healthy and pure. Clearly, such food is meant to be light and easy to digest, typically vegetarian. Other texts, specifically related to the traditional Indian medical science of *Ayurveda*, refer to *sattvic* foods as those that help to maintain and restore harmony and balance in body and mind. In order to gain their full merit, they are required to be consumed fresh or freshly cooked — in moderation and mindfully.

The *rajasic* temperament is typically prone to excitement, arousal, vitality, sensuality and aggression. Thus the food preferences point to items strongly stimulating in taste. The Indian tongue is typically known to have a preference for spicy food. In *Ayurveda*, mention is made of six flavours: sweet, salty, sour, pungent, bitter and astringent. Moderate use of the sweet flavour (as in fruits), and mild use of the other five flavours, with very little use of oil, is considered to be *sattvic*.

कट्वम्ललवणात्युष्ण तीक्ष्णरूक्षविदाहिनः |
आहारा राजसस्येष्टा दुःखशोकामयप्रदाः ||17.9||

Foods preferred by the rajasic	आहाराः राजसस्य इष्टाः
Are bitter, sour, salty, very hot,	कटु अम्ल लवण अति उष्ण
Pungent, harsh and burning,	तीक्ष्ण रूक्ष विदाहिनः
Causing distress, grief, illness.	दुःख शोक आमय प्रदाः

The *rajasic* taste differs from the *sattvic* in seeking a much more pronounced and excessive use of the sour (as in fermented foods), the salty, the bitter and the pungent (as in spices, chilli, pepper, onion, garlic, pickle), so also the astringent (as in coffee, tea and dry fruit), and the use of oil. Excessive use of these foods are said to contribute feelings of distress and illness. While the *sattvic* way of eating food is one done mindfully (as a *yajna*), the *rajasic* tendency is to consume hurriedly and excitedly.

यातयामं गतरसं पूति पर्युषितं च यत् |
उच्छिष्टमपि चामेध्यं भोजनं तामसप्रियम् ||17.10||

Foods preferred by the tamasic	भोजनं तामस प्रियम्
Are stale, tasteless, unsavoury,	यात यामं गत रसं
Putrid and left-over,	पूति पर्युषितं च यत्
Rejected or spoiled.	उच्छिष्टम् अपि च अमेध्यं

The *tamasic* temperament is typically prone to sleep, heaviness, dullness, delusion and inertia. Thus the food preferences here point to items that induce these qualities. These contrast with the *rajasic* and the *sattvic*. Foods that are not freshly cooked, which are canned or pre-cooked, stale and processed, or leftover and spoiled, are considered to be *tamasic*. Foods frozen or cold, fermented, sedating or intoxicating, including some kinds of 'fast food', old meat, alcohol and drugs are all considered to be *tamasic*. Over-eating is a sign of *tamas*, as is eating with indifference or disrespect.

While considering these suggestions regarding different types of foods, we need to acknowledge the difficulties and compulsions posed by modern lifestyles, and also be open to the knowledge made available by studies on nutrition and medicine. It is becoming increasingly difficult to get fresh food and vegetables, free from impurities, given the widespread pollution in the air, in water and the earth (use of pesticides, fertilisers and chemical preservatives). Refrigeration is widely adopted, and we have little idea of what goes into the food that we consume outside. Despite this, we would do well to be sensitive to our diet, making it as *sattvic* and nutritious as possible, while carefully judging from the response in our own bodies and minds. In particular, we need caution towards 'junk food' of all kinds, which are becoming increasingly popular worldwide, despite their marked tendency to be *tamasic* or *rajasic*. Such food has been called 'supernormally stimulating', because they have been packaged to stimulate our taste buds with excess sugar, salt, fat, protein and dense calories. The young are prone specially to crave for such foods, which are now well-known to result in diseases of dietary excess.

Especially worrying is the manner in which we receive and consume the food. It should ideally be received gratefully and moderately consumed. The act of eating can be made a sacred rite: an opportunity to remember and connect with the Divine Indweller seated in our bodies, to whom the food is given as an offering. The act of preparing and serving food, likewise, can be done as a *yajna* (a sacred offering) to the same Divine Indweller seated in the hearts of many individuals. It is then that we can begin to truly feel and realise that 'all is *Brahman*'!

The *gunas* related to *Ahara* are summarised in the following table.

The three *gunas* in food preferences (*Ahara*)	
Sattva	*Foods (vegetarian) that are freshly prepared and are tasty, calming and agreeable — nourishing health, mental clarity and strength; foods consumed mindfully in moderation, and with respect and gratitude.*
Rajas	*Foods that are excessively stimulating and bitter, sour, salty, hot or burning, acrid and harsh — causing ailments, aggression and unease in the body and mind; foods consumed hurriedly (gulped down), voraciously.*
Tamas	*Foods that are cold or frozen, impure, stale, spoilt, frozen, left-over, fermented, sedating — causing dullness, lethargy, intoxication or delusion; foods taken in excess (over-eating) or with disrespect.*

In the next chapter, we shall explore in detail how the *sattvic*, *rajasic* and *tamasic gunas* get reflected in the kind of renunciation (*Tyaga*) that we practice, and in our sacrifice (*Yajna*), austerity (*Tapas*) and giving (*Dana*).

12

Gunas in Renunciation (*Tyaga*) and Offerings (*Yajna-Dana-Tapas*)

श्रीभगवानुवाच ।
काम्यानां कर्मणां न्यासं संन्यासं कवयो विदुः ।
सर्वकर्मफलत्यागं प्राहुस्त्यागं विचक्षणाः ॥18.2॥

The Blessed Lord said:	श्रीभगवान् उवाच
Relinquishing actions driven by desires	काम्यानां कर्मणां न्यासं
Is what the sages consider as Sannyasa.	संन्यासं कवयो विदुः
Relinquishing the fruit of all actions	सर्व कर्म फल त्यागं
Is what the wise declare as Tyaga.	प्राहुः त्यागं विचक्षणाः

We may recall that Arjuna appeared inclined to abdicate all work and life in the world, at the beginning of the Gita. On listening to Krishna's inspiring teaching, emphasising both action and renunciation, Arjuna seeks a clarification from the Divine Teacher in the Gita's closing chapter. It is an important clarification, given in the above verse. It is intended for all of us.

In the Indian tradition, the term *Sannyasa* is often associated with giving up all acts and relations in the world. It gets taken up by a few spiritually inclined people, usually at the last stage of their lives, when they have fulfilled all their worldly obligations and ties. So now they seek freedom from all world ties, aiming for liberation (*Moksha*) before death.

However, the Divine Teacher here gives a deeper meaning to *Sannyasa*. It does indeed point to a relinquishing of actions, but not all actions. Only those that are driven by ego-related desire. This must lead to a state of *naishkarmyam*, which implies a supreme state of inaction. It is just this that could very well be a 'flow' state of inaction in action.

In order to ascend to our higher nature, we clearly need to let go of our attachment to lower nature. This is the real objective of the Gita's renunciation — which also emphasises the importance of working for the maintenance, well-being and evolution of the world. The vast majority of us live and act in the world, neither inclined nor meant to become ascetic monks or dwellers in remote caves or on mountain tops. How then, for most of us, can renunciation be practically possible?

The Divine Teacher here points out that we need to begin with *Tyaga*. This is described as the renunciation of all attachment to the fruit of our actions. When we practise *Tyaga* consciously, we are likely to do this with a sense of doership. We are also not free from desires, which habitually motivate our actions. Yet, if we keep practising *Tyaga*, we are bound to mature and evolve spiritually. The maturing of *Tyaga* into *Sannyasa* has sometimes been compared to the natural falling of ripe fruit from a mango tree — which is significantly different from forcibly plucking unripe fruit. In a sense, the final renunciation happens by itself, although it may be inspired by a sense of supreme surrender (*samarpanam*) to the Supreme Divine. Thereafter, actions do occur through our instrumentation, but we are freed from any taint of doership, in serving as perfect channels for the flow of Divine *Shakti*.

While living in the world and carrying out assigned duties, we may do well to reflect on the theme of *Dharmakshetra* in the Gita. The field of our action (*kshetra*) is one mostly assigned to us already — through family, community, workplace and so on. It is in this *kshetra* that we need to practice the Gita's *yoga*. This leads to a happy liberation (*Moksha*) from our lower nature. That is a natural renunciation (*Sannyasa*) and dissolution of the ego-self. So also is a yoking (*Yoga*) with the infinite, blissful Supreme Divine. This is reflected in the title of the 18th and concluding chapter of the Gita: *Moksha Sannyasa Yoga*. If we recognise this, we will not seek to renounce the divinely assigned *kshetra*. There is no need to give up our jobs and families, unless there is a strong inner calling to do so. What we need to give up (to the Divine) is our attachment to the fruit of our actions and to the actions themselves.

Gunas in Renunciation, *Tyaga*

कार्यमित्येव यत्कर्म नियतं क्रियतेऽर्जुन |
सङ्गं त्यक्त्वा फलं चैव स त्यागः सात्त्विको मतः ||18.9||

When the action that needs to be done, कार्यम् इति एव यत् कर्म
Is done in a rightly regulated way, Arjuna, नियतं क्रियते अर्जुन
Relinquishing attachment and the fruit, सङ्गं त्यक्त्वा फलं च एव
Then such renunciation is called sattvic. सः त्यागः सात्त्विकः मतः

Here, the Divine Teacher clearly declares that the 'work that needs to be done' (*karyam karma*) should not be renounced. Rather it is to be rightly regulated (*niyatam*), free from attraction and aversion. What needs renouncing is the attachment to action, together with action's fruit (*sangam tyaktva phalam ca*). Such renunciation alone qualifies to be called *sattvic*. The play of *gunas* afflicts everything that is manifested. The noble concept of renunciation can also get perverted by *rajas* and *tamas*.

Sometimes we may give up our assigned duties because we perceive them to be too difficult or strenuous and painful (mentally or physically). And also we may perceive that the rewards expected from such efforts may not be worthwhile. Such 'renunciation' is declared *rajasic*, because there is a selfishness underlying such withdrawal. Not wanting to go outside our comfort zone is a *vital* weakness, and we will no doubt rationalise this with some excuse. Such *rajasic* renunciation will not reap any fruit, according to the Gita.

दुःखमित्येव यत्कर्म कायक्लेशभयात्त्यजेत् ।
स कृत्वा राजसं त्यागं नैव त्यागफलं लभेत् ।।18.8।।

Challenged by work that appears difficult, दुःखम् इति एव यत् कर्म
He who shirks, fearing physical exertion, काय क्लेश भयात् त्यजेत्
Thus performing a rajasic 'renunciation', सः कृत्वा राजसं त्यागं
Reaps no fruit from such renunciation. न एव त्याग फलं लभेत्

All work linked to our *Svadharma* needs to be carried out in a rightly regulated manner. So-called renunciation of such work is a *tamasic* act of irresponsibility, arising from a deluded understanding of *Tyaga*. Belief that such abandonment of duties would lead to liberation is sheer delusion, reflective of the *guna* of *tamas*. No less than a self-actualised person like Arjuna fell under the spell of this delusion at the battlefield. It is this that he tried to rationalise, with specious arguments.

नियतस्य तु संन्यासः कर्मणो नोपपद्यते ।
मोहात्तस्य परित्यागः तामसः परिकीर्तितः ।।18.7।।

It is inappropriate to simply abandon संन्यासः न उपपद्यते
Work that is to be rightly regulated. नियतस्य कर्मणः तु
Renunciation out of such delusion, मोहात् तस्य परित्यागः
Is declared to be tamasic in nature. तामसः परिकीर्तितः

We all may fall prey to such false notions. And our renunciation of responsibilities may sometimes also be motivated by sheer laziness and attachment to inaction — clearly reflective of a *tamasic* kind of *Tyaga*.

The *gunas* related to *Tyaga* are summarised in the following table.

The three *gunas* in renunciation (Tyaga)	
Sattva	*Renouncing attachment to actions and their fruits, while doing all that 'needs to be done' in a rightly regulated way, free from attraction and aversion.*
Rajas	*Abandoning work that is perceived to be either too difficult or strenuous and painful — mentally or physically — and not worthwhile in terms of expected rewards.*
Tamas	*Abandoning work that needs to be done in a regulated way, out of delusion that such renunciation is something noble (leading to liberation), or out of attachment to inaction.*

Acts of Offering (*Yajna-Dana-Tapas*)

यज्ञदानतपःकर्म न त्याज्यं कार्यमेव तत् ।
यज्ञो दानं तपश्चैव पावनानि मनीषिणाम् ||18.5||

Acts of sacrifice, giving and austerity,	यज्ञ दान तपः कर्म
Are to be done always, never given up!	न त्याज्यं कार्यम् एव तत्
Such acts of yajna, dana and tapas	यज्ञः दानं तपः च एव
Maintain purity in men of wisdom.	पावनानि मनीषिणाम्

Purification of our lower nature is the way forward on the spiritual path. This is an on-going process. And for this purpose, the Gita recommends that under no circumstances three of the most *sattvic* human activities should ever be given up. They are: sacrifice (*yajna*), altruistic giving (*dana*) and austerity (*tapas*).

All three activities (*yajna*, *dana* and *tapas*) involve giving away something that the ego-self associates with itself, for a noble cause. Such activities serve to relinquish expectation of and attachment to fruit. Thus rightly carried out, they serve to 'maintain purity in men of wisdom' (*pavanani manishinam*). According to Sri Aurobindo, the Gita's injunctions related to *yajna-dana-tapas* need to be understood in a much wider sense, to include all action that 'needs to be done' (*karyam karma*) by us.

Gunas in Sacrifice, *Yajna*

The Gita description of sacrifice, *yajna*, as we have seen, is deep and profound, ideally applicable to all our actions. It is a consecration of our work to the Divine, whose objective is not only to contribute to the well-being and evolution of the universe, but also to lift us up from the lower nature into our higher nature.

अफलाकाङ्क्षिभिर्यज्ञः विधिदृष्टो य इज्यते ।
यष्टव्यमेवेति मनः समाधाय स सात्त्विकः ||17.11||

Sacrifice done without craving for fruit,	अफल आकाङ्क्षिभिः यज्ञः
And in accordance with prescribed norms,	विधि दृष्टः यः इज्यते
With whole-hearted attention and care	एव इति मनः समाधाय
To the offering, is yajna that is sattvic.	यष्टव्यम् सः सात्त्विकः

The *sattvic* sacrifice is one done mindfully and whole-heartedly, without craving for the fruit (*aphalakankshibhi*). This must be with attention and care — not negligently or half-heartedly, but with an attitude of consecration.

In Sri Aurobindo's words, 'It is executed with a mind concentrated and fixed on the idea of the thing to be done as a true sacrifice imposed on us by the Divine law that governs our life...' [12.1]

The intention of the original Vedic sacrificial rite was for some specific noble purpose for the well-being of all. Although there is an expected 'fruit' from such sacrifices, it is to be impersonal in nature (not for personal benefit, including name and fame). Even this outcome should be surrendered to the Divine, and not insisted upon. The norms (*vidhi*) in the Vedic tradition involved certain rites, including invocations (in the form of *mantras*) and appropriate giving of food offerings to all, as well as fees (*dakshina*) to those performing the sacrifice. In the wider context of *yajna*, applicable to any work and in a modern context, this injunction may simply be interpreted as following the recommended specifications for the work and conforming to good practice.

Proper adherence to the prescribed norms (*vidhi*) by itself does not render the sacrifice *sattvic:* it could be *rajasic*. The difference is entirely with respect to the inner being (temperament, attitude and motivation) of the one who is credited with the performance of the *yajna*.

अभिसन्धाय तु फलं दम्भार्थमपि चैव यत् ।
इज्यते भरतश्रेष्ठ तं यज्ञं विद्धि राजसम् ||17.12||

But, if one hankers for the fruit of action,	अभिसन्धाय तु फलं
And if simply for the sake of showing off,	दम्भ अर्थम् अपि च एव यत्
The act is performed outwardly, Arjuna,	इज्यते भरत श्रेष्ठ
Know such yajna to be rajasic in nature.	तं यज्ञं विद्धि राजसम्

The primary feature of any *rajasic* activity is that it is based on a strong craving for the fruit of action and an insistent demand for reward — which is of the nature of personal gain. Sacrifice is no exception to this norm. In this case, there is the additional motive of ostentation: showing off before others and wanting to be known for one's magnanimity (*dambhartham*). In Sri Aurobindo's words, 'Wherever there is a dominating egoism in our acts, there our work becomes a *rajasic* sacrifice.'[12.1]

Finally, let us look at the Gita's description of the *tamasic yajna*, which is, both outwardly and inwardly, far removed from the *sattvic* sacrifice. Inwardly, the sacrifice is done without any sense of faith or care (*shraddhavirahitam*). And this heedlessness (a characteristic trait of *tamo-guna*) is reflected outwardly by mechanical and careless action. Even worse, the sacrifice may be done in violation of the norms (*vidhihinam*) prescribed by the prevailing *shastra*.

विधिहीनमसृष्टान्नं मन्त्रहीनमदक्षिणम् ।
श्रद्धाविरहितं यज्ञं तामसं परिचक्षते ।।17.13।।

Sacrifice done without faith or care,	श्रद्धा विरहितं यज्ञं
Violating norms, with no food offerings,	विधि हीनम् असृष्ट अन्नं
With no invocation, nor giving of fees,	मन्त्र हीनम् अदक्षिणम्
Is yajna that is regarded as tamasic.	तामसं परिचक्षते

Violating the traditional rituals of food offerings and giving of fees (*dakshina*) reflect a lack of understanding of the indispensable help and participation of all, and as Sri Aurobindo puts it, 'a wholly self-regarding thing and a violation of the true universal law of solidarity and interchange.'[12.1]

Although the symbolisms used here pertain to the traditional rituals in vogue in the external *yajna*, their inner meanings need to be understood, for us to relate to *tamasic yajna* in the context of our attitude while performing any outer work.

There is also symbolism associated with the 'deity' to whom the sacrifice is being offered as indicated in the following verse.

यजन्ते सात्त्विका देवान् यक्षरक्षांसि राजसाः ।
प्रेतान्भूतगणांश्चान्ये यजन्ते तामसा जनाः ||17.4||

Sattvic men offer sacrifices to the gods,	यजन्ते सात्त्विकाः देवान्
Rajasic men offer to spirits and demons,	यक्ष रक्षांसि राजसाः
Tamasic men offer sacrifices to ghosts,	यजन्ते तामसाः जनाः प्रेतान्
And to elemental spirits of darkness.	भूत गणान् च अन्ये

When it is stated that '*sattvic* men offer sacrifices to the gods (*devas*)', it is implied that the aspirations, thoughts and deeds (collectively, the *shraddha*) of such persons is directed towards and driven by *sattva-guna*. This points to the domain of Divine *(daivic) powers*, which is the meaning of 'gods' here.

Similarly, when it is stated that *rajasic* men offer sacrifices to the *Yakshas* (spirits supposedly governing wealth) and *Rakshasas* (powerful and evil demons), it is implied that the *shraddha* appeals to and invokes, consciously or unconsciously, unDivine *(asuric)* forces, which the Buddha described as *Mara*. These powers are forever tempting our vital being, seeking to possess us and keep us entrapped in the lower nature, by a predominance of *rajo-guna*.

Finally, the offerings of *tamasic* men are said to appeal to the elemental forces of darkness (sometimes called *Pishachas*), which are described here as *Pretas* (hungry ghosts) and *Bhutaganas* (hosts of spooky spirits). Though lacking the power of the *asuric* forces of *rajas*, they keep us bound to the nether world of ignorance, by a predominance of *tamo-guna*.

The *gunas* related to *Yajna* are summarised in the following table.

The three *gunas* in sacrifice (*Yajna*)	
Sattva	*Sacrifice done mindfully and whole-heartedly, without craving for any personal reward, as per the prescribed norms, and an attitude of consecration, dedicated to Divine (daivic) powers.*
Rajas	*Sacrifice done outwardly in keeping with norms, but with insistent craving for personal reward, and with the intention of showing off, appealing to demonic (asuric) powers.*
Tamas	*Sacrifice done without any faith or care, mechanically or rudely, in violation of all the prescribed norms, without consecration and giving, appealing to the powers of darkness.*

Gunas in Giving, *Dana*

Dana refers to giving alms or any gift in charity as a donation. As a regular spiritual practice, it is intended to nurture a happy spirit of generosity, benevolence and abundance. It serves to purify and transform the mind and reduce the acquisitive vital impulses of the ego. In the *Vedic* tradition, *dana* takes the form of formal rites, given as a rule on special occasions. The gift is usually in material form: wealth, food (*anna-dana*), medicines, clothes, land (*bhu-dana*), etc. As said earlier, the sense of abundance is an attitude (something to do with the inner being), rather than a measure of one's resources in the outer world.

The *sattvic* way of giving (as in all other acts) is without expecting a fruit of action. The giving is done graciously, simply for goodwill, and not as an expression of a favour in return (*anupakarine*): either returning a favour or gift received from someone (settling accounts, so to say), or in anticipation of some favour required from the other person. The intention must be pure and noble for it to have a *sattvic* character. Moreover, it has its true value only when given under the right conditions of time and place, to a recipient who is truly worthy, who is deserving and can be helped by this giving. It is done freely, whole-heartedly and generously, without hesitation or calculation.

दातव्यमिति यद्दानं दीयतेऽनुपकारिणे ।
देशे काले च पात्रे च तद्दानं सात्त्विकं स्मृतम् ।।17.20।।

The gift given with pure and noble intention,	दातव्यम् इति यत् दानं
Simply given, regardless of any return favour,	दीयते अनुपकारिणे
To the right person, at right place and time,	देशे काले च पात्रे च
Is dana that is considered to be sattvic.	तत् दानं सात्त्विकं स्मृतम्

The *rajasic* and *tamasic* ways of giving stand in sharp contrast to the *sattvic* way. The fruit of action invariably comes to mind when *rajo-guna* predominates. The objective of the giving here is to settle accounts: either repaying a gift received (and seen as a debt), or with an expectation and calculation of a favour in return, or given grudgingly. Such giving certainly has its value, contributing to the spirit of exchange and inter-being. However, the motive behind it lacks the purity of *sattva*.

यत्तु प्रत्युपकारार्थं फलमुद्दिश्य वा पुनः ।
दीयते च परिक्लिष्टं तद्दानं राजसं स्मृतम् ।।17.21।।

But, if the aim of the giving is to repay,	यत् तु प्रति उपकार अर्थं
Or hoping for a return favour in future,	फलम् उद्दिश्य वा पुनः
Or if the gift is given rather grudgingly,	दीयते च परिक्लिष्टं
Such dana is regarded as being rajasic.	तत् दानं राजसं स्मृतम्

अदेशकाले यद्दानम् अपात्रेभ्यश्च दीयते ।
असत्कृतमवज्ञातं तत्तामसमुदाहृतम् ।।17.22।।

The gift given at a wrong place or time,	अदेश काले यत् दानम्
Or given to a recipient who is unworthy,	अपात्रेभ्यः च दीयते
Given ungraciously or contemptuously,	असत् कृतम् अवज्ञातं
Is dana that is considered to be tamasic.	तत् तामसम् उदाहृतम्

When *tamo-guna* predominates, ignorance and delusion typically manifest, as they get reflected in outward action. Thus ignorance is reflected here in the matter of giving, by lack of consideration for the right occasion and place that is judged suited to the object given. The gift is not given with either a spirit of generosity or with a desire for exchange, but in a foolish and inconsiderate way, and to someone unworthy. Given ungraciously or contemptuously, it is likely to be ill-received or despised by the recipient. The *gunas* related to *Dana* are summarised in the following table.

The three gunas in giving (*Dana*)	
Sattva	*Giving graciously, with noble intention, simply for the goodwill of giving, and not as an expression of a favour in return or expectation in the future, to someone worthy, and at the right time and place.*
Rajas	*Giving with the objective of repaying a gift received, or with a clear expectation that the favour will be returned in equal or greater measure by the recipient, or grudgingly, unwillingly and regretfully.*
Tamas	*Giving ungraciously and contemptuously, without any consideration for the right occasion and place and object of giving, to someone unworthy.*

Gunas in Austerity (*Tapas*)

The term *tapas* is derived from the Sanskrit root, *tap*, which means heat. *Tapas*, in the spiritual context, refers to living heat energy, inwardly inspired through purifying practices of meditation, austerity and penance, called *tapasya*. In the *yogic* tradition, it is visualised as a kindling of the fire (*agni*) that burns within so as to achieve self-control, concentrated spiritual focus, simplicity, wisdom and integrity, and ultimately Self-realisation.

The Gita (verse 4.28) refers to *tapas* as a form of *yajna* (*tapoyajna*): a sacred offering to the Divine Indweller. In the Gita, three realms of *sattvic* austerity are described: of body (*shariram tapas*), speech (*vanmayam tapas*) and mind (*manasam tapas*).

देवद्विजगुरुप्राज्ञ पूजनं शौचमार्जवम् ।
ब्रह्मचर्यमहिंसा च शारीरं तप उच्यते ||17.14||

Venerating the gods, teachers and the wise,	देव द्विज गुरु प्राज्ञ पूजनं
Practising cleanliness, straight-forwardness,	शौचम् आर्जवम्
As well as sexual purity and non-violence,	ब्रह्मचर्यम् अहिंसा च
Are considered as austerities of the body.	शारीरं तपः उच्यते

Austerities of the body deal with outward actions of a physical nature. Giving reverence to the Divine, and paying respect to elders and teachers (traditionally done by bowing down and touching their feet), as well as maintaining cleanliness (in the body and one's surroundings), and staying upright and straightforward in one's dealings with the world are recommended. So too are practices of *brahmacharya*, implying discipline and self-control (especially with sexual indulgence and other sensually driven impulses, including consumption of non-*sattvic* food).

Also recommended is the practice of *ahimsa*, meaning the avoidance of killing or injuring sentient beings. Special emphasis has been given here to austerity involving the use of words (*vakyam*) — both spoken and written down.

अनुद्वेगकरं वाक्यं सत्यं प्रियहितं च यत् |
स्वाध्यायाभ्यसनं चैव वाङ्मयं तप उच्यते ||17.15||

Use of words not causing distress to others,	अनुद्वेग करं वाक्यं
Which are truthful, kind and beneficial,	सत्यं प्रिय हितं च यत्
Nurturing the practice of right learning,	स्वाध्याय अभ्यसनं च एव
Are considered as austerities of speech.	वाक् मयं तपः उच्यते

Self-control here implies being very conscious in the use of words, to ensure that they are truthful, kind, noble and helpful, not causing fear, sorrow and harm to others. Further encouraged here is the use of words for right self-learning, especially scriptural learning (*svadhyaya*). Indeed, our words truly reveal our *gunas*. Used recklessly, heedlessly, and negligently (with no regard to truthfulness or how they may distress others, or used maliciously for gossip), they reflect the *guna* of *tamas*. Used harshly, excitedly and passionately (often to attack, hurt or even abuse others), either openly or cleverly (sarcastically), words reveal how the *guna* of *rajas* is in possession of our being.

On the contrary, when we use words cautiously as a kind of *tapas*, in the manner suggested in the above verse, we invoke the *guna* of *sattva*. One practice that may be taken to immediately is to be self-aware of the words we use, so that we may avoid as far as possible (if not completely) the *tamasic* or *rajasic* use of words. Just this one practice of austerity may well bring about an inner transformation. Merely cutting down unneeded speech, we enter into a zone of silence, which in itself is spiritually uplifting, as it contributes to austerity of mind. Mental austerity includes all practices that contribute to serenity, kindness and moral perfection.

मनः प्रसादः सौम्यत्वं मौनमात्मविनिग्रहः |
भावसंशुद्धिरित्येतत् तपो मानसमुच्यते ||17.16||

Serene gladness of mind and gentleness,	मनः प्रसादः सौम्यत्वं
Practice of silence as well as self-restraint,	मौनम् आत्म विनिग्रहः
Purification of one's entire temperament,	भाव संशुद्धिः इति एतत्
Are considered as austerities of the mind.	तपः मानसम् उच्यते

Sattvic tapasya (of body, speech and mind) is that which is carried out with a deep *shraddha* — as a practice of self-discipline to gain self-control and harmony in one's nature. Like all other *sattvic* activities, the austerity here is also free from any craving for any external or personal fruit.

श्रद्धया परया तप्तं तपस्तत्त्रिविधं नरैः |
अफलाकाङ्क्षिभिर्युक्तैः सात्त्विकं परिचक्षते ||17.17||

This three-fold austerity done by men	तपः तत् त्रिविधं नरैः
With deep faith, steadfast in practice,	श्रद्धया परया तप्तं युक्तैः
Without any craving for personal reward,	अफल आकाङ्क्षिभिः
Is tapas that is considered to be sattvic.	सात्त्विकं परिचक्षते

Rajasic tapasya, on the other hand, is strongly motivated by the fruit of action, expected in the form of honour, fame and glory. This kind of austerity is put on display for others to take note of and appreciate. The lack of sincerity in such austerities makes this display of *tapas* hypocritical and ostentatious, unsteady and wavering.

सत्कारमानपूजार्थं तपो दम्भेन चैव यत् ।
क्रियते तदिह प्रोक्तं राजसं चलमध्रुवम् ।।17.18।।

Austerity performed with hypocrisy,	तपः दम्भेन यत् क्रियते
For gaining fame, honour and respect,	सत्कार मान पूजा अर्थं च एव
Wavering and transient in nature,	चलम् अध्रुवम्
Is tapas that is regarded as rajasic.	तत् इह प्रोक्तं राजसं

Tamasic tapasya is austerity based on, as Sri Aurobindo says, 'a darkness in the mind and nature, a vulgar narrowness and ugliness in the doing or a brutish instinct or desire in the aim or in the motive feeling.'[12.1]

The emphasis is on some ill-understood, but cherished dogma or ritual, involving much effort and physical self-torture. A fanatical approach, characteristic of *tamasic* religiosity, may involve causing terror and harm to others, while also harming oneself: as in suicide bomb attacks, in the firm but false belief that this is something noble and exalted. The Gita (verse 17.5-6) mentions that such 'terrible austerity' (*ghoram tapah*), and especially physical self-torture, troubles the Divine Indweller abiding in the body.

मूढग्राहेणात्मनो यत् पीडया क्रियते तपः ।
परस्योत्सादनार्थं वा तत्तामसमुदाहृतम् ।।17.19।।

Austerity performed under delusion,	मूढ ग्राहेण यत् क्रियते तपः
With much struggle and self-torture,	आत्मनः पीडया
Or with the aim of destroying others,	परस्य उत्सादन अर्थं वा
Is tapas that is regarded as tamasic.	तत् तामसम् उदाहृतम्

The *gunas* related to *Tapas* (of body, speech and mind) are summarised in the following table.

The three *gunas* in austerity (*Tapas*)	
Sattva	*Austerity practised with sincerity, deep faith and steadfastness, to gain self-control and harmony in one's nature, not expecting any personal reward.*
Rajas	*Austerity performed with hypocrisy and ostentation, for gaining fame, honour and respect, wavering and transient in nature.*
Tamas	*Austerity performed under delusion, with much struggle and self-torture, or with the aim of destroying others (as in terror attacks).*

The Gita descriptions pertaining to *rajo-guna* and *tamo-guna* reflect their untempered (pure) nature, although in reality the behaviour and character are bound to be positively influenced by the presence of *sattva*. It is important that we should not use these descriptions to be judgmental, remembering that all beings have all three *gunas*. All three are Divine in origin and each has its rightful place in manifest reality and the evolution of consciousness. *Rajas* and *tamas* certainly have their places in the Divine scheme, but they need to be refined and purified by the presence of *sattva*, and eventually transformed through a descent of the higher nature. The spiritual journey is described as a journey of consciousness from *tamas* to *jyoti,* where *tamas* may be seen as the *nadir* of lower nature, and *jyoti* (the Divine equivalent of *sattva*) as the *zenith* of higher nature. So the Gita descriptions of *tamas* and *rajas* here point to *stages* in the evolution of consciousness, and not to passing *states*.

In the next chapter, we shall explore how the *gunas* get reflected in our knowledge (*Jnana*), action (*Karma*) and sense of being the doer (*Karta*).

13

Gunas in Knowledge (*Jnana*), Action (*Karma*) and the Doer (*Karta*)

Before we plunge further into the Gita, it may help to reflect on the current status humanity finds itself in, considering our 'development'. Here, we may well reflect on the following write-up, extracted from a widely-shared essay called *The Paradox of our Age*, believed to be authored originally in 1995 by the pastor, Bob Moorehead.

> *'We have taller buildings but shorter tempers; wider freeways but narrower viewpoints; we spend more but have less; we buy more but enjoy it less; we have bigger houses and smaller families; more conveniences, yet less time; we have more degrees but less sense; more knowledge but less judgement; more experts, yet more problems; we have more gadgets but less satisfaction; more medicine, yet less wellness... We have multiplied our possessions, but reduced our values; we talk too much; love too seldom and lie too often. We've learned how to make a living, but not a life; we've added years to life, not life to years. We've been all the way to the moon and back, but have trouble crossing the street to meet the new neighbour. We've conquered outer space, but not inner space; we've done larger things, but not better things; we plan more, but accomplish less; we learned to rush, but not to wait; we have more weapons, but less peace; higher incomes, but lower morals; more parties, but less fun; more acquaintances, but fewer friends; more effort, but less success. These are the times of fast*

foods and slow digestion; tall men, but short character; steep in profits, but shallow relationships; world peace, but domestic warfare; more leisure and less fun; more kinds of food, but less nutrition; two incomes, but more divorces; fancier houses, but broken homes.' [13.1]

Neglect of Inner Development

The above 'paradox of our age' is a concern emerging from the 'developed' Western world. This is now increasingly shared by many in 'developing' countries like India. We can see how currents of modernity and post-modernity that originated in the Western world are sweeping across the globe, thus seemingly unstoppable. All countries seem helplessly driven to imitate and take on the same Western model of development, not sensibly realising how to make amends. The paradox is that, over the last century, human development has made tremendous scientific and technological progress, liberating us from religious dogma and superstition, but despite all this, we carry on so sadly unfulfilled and frustratingly confused.

The reason is conveyed in the sentence: 'We've conquered outer space, but not inner space'. Advances in science have freed us from many superstitions, but this has also sadly made us crude materialists in our world-view. We are now thus primarily concerned with the physical, material and gross 'outer' world. We see this as reality. The 'inner' world is thus taken to be secondary. Material scientists would even like to believe that all sensations, thoughts, desires, emotions and attitudes are only superficial appearances — produced materially by neuronal activity in the brain and in biochemical processes of living bodies. Many of us also believe that if only we could set things right in the external world (like having lot of money, material comforts, pleasures and so on), then we might live happily ever after. Sadly for us, the paradox of our age reveals a quite different reality.

As Jesus observed: 'Man does not live by bread alone'. He also asked, insightfully, 'For what shall it profit a man, if he shall gain the whole world and lose his own soul?' Religious people often invoke such sayings to show how our materialistic culture may lead us in the wrong direction, so that we need to reject this by returning to religious traditions. Of course, this may neither be practical nor even the truest option. There seems no right way to go back, nor even much use in romanticising the past and lamenting what now faces us. Change needs to come from within the existing system. Yes, we certainly do have the resources for this: the Gita points to the Divine Indweller residing within each of us. We have precious resources from our ancient Indian heritage, which we seem to have sadly neglected, if not regrettably disowned.

Indeed, in the interest of 'development', it would be entirely appropriate to adopt, almost in entirety, unquestioningly and blindly, as we (and others in the non-Western world) seem intent on doing, all the European (now, American) tastes, opinions, morals and intellect, if they truly point to growth, enlightenment and happiness. Unfortunately, the paradox of our age suggests that we have seriously gone wrong somewhere. Despite this awareness, we seem intent on continuing with this model of education — even in our best institutions, missing out altogether on the importance of *inner development* and the value of such timeless teachings as that of the Bhagavad Gita. The challenge before India is to realise and integrate the best of these teachings (which we have imbibed, although unconsciously, with our mothers' milk) with the best that the world has to offer. This is the renaissance that India needs to awaken to and show to the rest of the world.

Sri Aurobindo points to this as follows: 'The method of the West is to exaggerate life and to call down as much — or as little — as may be of the higher powers to stimulate and embellish life. But the method of India is on the contrary to discover the Spirit within and the higher hidden intensities of the superior powers and to dominate life in one way or another so as to make it responsive to and expressive of the Spirit and in that way increase the power of life... The work of the renaissance in India must be to make this Spirit, this higher view of life, this sense of deeper potentiality once more a creative, perhaps a dominant power in the world.'[13.2]

The teachings of the Gita point to the need to infuse our work and our lives with a spirituality, a joy, and a purpose, driven from our innermost being. We need to see the play of the *gunas* in our individual and collective lives, affecting the outer layers of our being, but incapable of touching the core Spirit in us. We need to connect to that core, our True Self, while at the same time working on purifying the workings of the *gunas* in the different parts of our being, aiming towards making them more and more *sattvic*. Clearly, the confusion reflected in the paradox of our age points to a very low proportion of the *guna* of *sattva*, and a relatively high proportion of the *gunas* of *rajas* and *tamas*.

Several aspects need to be considered while assessing the quality of our work, and determining how to improve it. The Gita emphasises, in particular, three key characteristics, in which each of the three *gunas* makes its distinctive impression: the knowledge (*jnana*) with which we do our work, the work (*karma*) itself, as well as the sense of the doer (*karta*) in us while we work. They are particularly significant in the context of spirituality at work.

Gunas in Knowledge, *Jnana*

We are concerned here with the nature of our basic *mental impulsion* to our work. According to the Gita (verse 18.18), this is determined by three factors: the knowledge (*jnana*) in our will to work, the object of our knowledge and the knower. The main factor is the nature of the knowledge itself, which can be assessed by the type of *guna* involved, and which gets reflected in the understanding of the object of knowledge and the character of the knower.

सर्वभूतेषु येनैकं भावमव्ययमीक्षते ।
अविभक्तं विभक्तेषु तज्ज्ञानं विद्धि सात्त्विकम् ||18.20||

Know that knowledge to be sattvic, तत् ज्ञानं विद्धि सात्त्विकम्
Which sees unity in apparent diversity, ईक्षते सर्व भूतेषु येन एकं
One imperishable Being in all becomings, भावम् अव्ययम्
One indivisible whole in multiple divisions. अविभक्तं विभक्तेषु

The main characteristic of *sattvic* knowledge is a constant striving to understand things in totality, seeing the part always in reference to the whole, and seeing 'unity in apparent diversity'. We see the earliest expressions of such striving in the human ability to detect what is common in apparently different entities, and in classifying and labelling them. The ability to count these entities, to introduce generic variables to describe them (mathematically, using algebra, etc.), and eventually to determine and define laws to describe natural phenomena fairly accurately is reflective of the *sattvic* tendency to unify understanding. This includes all developments in science and philosophy, resulting in a tremendous power to exercise control through the understanding of the hidden laws of nature.

Sadly, the tremendous scientific developments achieved in the past four centuries or so in the Western world have been attained at a tremendous cost — of radically separating man from nature. This separation persists strongly even today. This is far removed from *sattvic* knowledge. However, in the end, truth must naturally reveal itself. Scientists are gradually awakening to the reality of a unifying mystery that underlies everything, so that things do not rightly exist in separate isolation. This is the basic premise in the very concept of *Prakriti* (nature) in the Gita.

The seeming separation of related things is quite essential to how *Prakriti* is here conceived. The separateness is an illusion of mind, which may be used for the practical purposes of identifying and labelling. The famous constellation of seven stars called the *Big Dipper* (*saptarshi*) does not exist in separate isolation; it is an inseparable part of the heavens with its innumerable stars. As the integral philosopher Ken Wilber puts it: 'Boundaries are illusions, products not of reality but of the way we map and edit reality. And while it is fine to map out the territory, it is fatal to confuse the two.'[13.3] The map is not the actual territory! *Sattvic* knowledge is that which never loses sight of this big picture. Indeed, the very understanding of the constant interplay of the three *gunas* in all manifestation is itself reflective of *sattvic* knowing.

Sattvic knowing brings about an understanding of order in apparent chaos. It is thus of immense importance to us in understanding *dharma* at all levels (individual, social, national, world, universal). All of these, according to ancient Indian wisdom, are sustained by the cosmic order in manifest *Brahman*. Even for understanding our individual *svadharma*, it is necessary to invoke *sattvic jnana*, because we need to know our role in the larger context of the whole. This was much emphasised in the Vedic tradition, where science and spirituality were not seen to be operating, as in modern times, in separate (and sometimes conflicting) domains. Yet, they were harmoniously integrated with the clear understanding of the One imperishable Being in all becomings (*bhavamavyayam*), One indivisible whole in multiple divisions (*avibhaktam vibhakteshu*).

पृथक्त्वेन तु यज्ज्ञानं नानाभावान्पृथग्विधान् ।
वेत्ति सर्वेषु भूतेषु तज्ज्ञानं विद्धि राजसम् ।।18.21।।

Know that knowledge to be rajasic,	तत् ज्ञानं विद्धि राजसम्
Which sees all things as being divided,	पृथक्त्वेन तु यत् ज्ञानं
As multiple entities of different kinds,	नाना भावान् पृथक् विधान्
Believing that all beings are separate.	वेत्ति सर्वेषु भूतेषु

It is commonplace to see 'all things as being divided' (*prthaktvena*), and to believe that they are all separate and different entities. Indeed, this is how many of us operate in the world. The Gita refers to such knowledge as *rajasic*. It makes us see things out of their true unifying context, and makes us act egotistically. We tend to see what our ego-self wants to see, driven by its desires.

Often this inability to make our ego-centred thinking subservient to a higher ideal, based on impersonal truth introduces inconsistency and double standards in our understanding. This is also linked to the *multi-branched and endlessly distracted* (*bahushakha hyanantashca*) intellect discussed earlier (verse 2.41).

In Sri Aurobindo's words, 'This knowing is a jumble of sections of knowledge, often inconsistent knowledge, put forcefully together by the mind in order to make some kind of pathway through the confusion of our half-knowledge and half-ignorance. Or else it is a restless kinetic multiple action with no firm governing higher ideal and self-possessed law of true light and power within it.'[13.4]

It is noteworthy that while the terms science and philosophy are both associated with knowledge (ideally without boundaries), the tendency in modern times is to specialise in some narrow domain, often at the cost of missing the big picture. After spending years researching on a single topic, a so-called specialist or super-specialist often gets to a point where, as the saying goes, one cannot see the wood for the trees.

So for example, a medical super-specialist may be at a loss, when called upon to treat a neighbour for some illness, because the super-specialisation is in some narrow part of the human body. Such knowledge would come under the category of *rajasic* knowledge, especially when one tends to extrapolate, based on one's limited understanding, or worse, imagines that one has expertise in domains other than one's narrow specialisation.

The very word 'science', which is believed to be derived from the Latin word *scientia* (expert knowledge), is also said to have its root in the Greek word, *skhizein* — meaning to split, rend, cleave. Splitting of systems into sub-systems and further into sub-sub-systems is obviously necessary to improve our understanding and for the advancement of science.

What we need to put in place and always recall is the fact that we did this splitting only for our convenience in analysis, and that the reality is the system as a whole! So it is this 'big picture' understanding that brings about the real distinction between *rajasic* and *sattvic jnana*. We have less of a problem with such splitting in philosophy, which by definition, means the love of knowledge. For the very objective of *love* is to unify and heal separation.

यत्तु कृत्स्नवदेकस्मिन् कार्ये सक्तमहैतुकम् |
अतत्त्वार्थवदल्पं च तत्तामसमुदाहृतम् ||18.22||

Know that knowledge to be tamasic, तत् तामसम् उदाहृतम्
Which clings rigidly to one plan of action, यत् तु एकस्मिन् कार्ये सक्तम्
As if all-in-all, not caring for real purpose, कृत्स्न वत् अहैतुकम्
Narrow minded, not seeing the whole truth. अतत्त्व अर्थ वत् अल्पं च

The mental impulsion underlying our work takes on a *tamasic* character, when we fail to apply our discrimination. Then we act mechanically and ritualistically, not caring for the true larger purpose. In many instances this may not cause any problems (as in a factory setting, where men can be replaced by machines). However, such behaviour as a general rule can result in crises or *adharma*, when things either go wrong or call for modifying the routine way of doing things.

The larger context is always important to *integral knowing*, and the *tamasic* character (obstinate, dogmatic and fundamentalist) is simply not interested in seeing this. Nor is it capable of appreciating it. So it is said to be inflexible and rigid in clinging, by force of sheer habit, to one plan of action, as if it is 'all-in-all' (*ekasmin karye saktam*). Such knowledge is said to be 'narrow-minded, not seeing the whole truth'.

Sri Aurobindo has this comment to offer on such 'ignorant knowledge': 'The *tamasic* mind does not look for real cause and effect, but absorbs itself in one movement or one routine with an obstinate attachment to it, can see nothing but the little section of personal activity before its eyes and does not know in fact what it is doing but blindly lets natural impulsion work out through its deed results, of which it has no conception, foresight or comprehending intelligence.'[13.4]

One of the sure signs of spiritual evolution is the increasing ability to empathise with multiple perspectives, so that the sense of 'otherness' that separates us from others gradually vanishes. In this connection, it is worth recalling the wonderful ancient tale of six blind men who went to 'see' an elephant. Each person touched one part of the elephant and quickly came to a conclusion about the elephant. '*I know this elephant! It is a serpent!*' exclaimed the one who touched the trunk. This, of course, was immediately contradicted by the others, each of whom was certain about what the elephant felt like! Were they being untruthful? No, they were all 'right', given their limited perspectives — but only partially right, and in an overall sense, all far removed from the whole truth!

This story is very meaningful because it reminds us as to how wedded we tend to be to our own views and beliefs, without realising that other perspectives, including those that may be diametrically opposite to ours, may well be equally valid. It takes wisdom for us to acknowledge that we too are blind and that we do not have the openness and wherewithal to see reality in its entirety!

We all come with our different initial conditions and make strong judgements about practically everything we perceive with our limited senses, looking for compatriots who agree with our perceptions and quarrelling endlessly with (or contemptuously looking down on) those who hold completely different perspectives. The *tamasic* blindness often results in *rajasic* conflicts. If we are truly interested in discovering the truth, we must be willing to give up, at least temporarily, the positions to which we tend to cling to so tenaciously, and to explore, with genuine empathy and curiosity, other perspectives.

If we were to be the blind men in the story, we should at least ask: *Why is it that my friends are so convinced about their views regarding the elephant? Let me explore.* Then, giving up our hold on the part of the elephant we have touched, we can then walk around, and feel what others have felt, and then the wisdom will dawn: *Ah! Now I understand why they felt this way, and they are right too!* More important, we make the great and humbling discovery: *The elephant (big picture) is much more than all these views put together! It remains a supreme mystery! The whole is greater than the sum of the parts!*

The *gunas* related to *Jnana* are summarised below:

The three *gunas* in knowledge (*Jnana*)	
Sattva	*Knowledge which is synthetic, seeing unity in apparent diversity, one indivisible whole in multiple divisions.*
Rajas	*Knowledge which, ego-driven, sees all things as being separate and divided, as multiple entities of different kinds.*
Tamas	*Knowledge which narrow-mindedly clings rigidly to one plan of action, as if all-in-all, not caring for the purpose or context.*

Gunas in Action, *Karma*

According to the Gita (verse 18.18), there are three constituents that make up any work and determine its quality: the instruments used for doing the work (*karanam*), the work done (*karma*) and the doer, the agent of action (*karta*). The nature of each of these aspects can be described through the type of *guna* involved. Detailed descriptions of the *gunas* pertaining to *karma* and *karta* are given in the Gita.

नियतं सङ्गरहितम् अरागद्वेषतः कृतम् ।
अफलप्रेप्सुना कर्म यत्तत्सात्त्विकमुच्यते ॥18.23॥

That action is said to be sattvic, which is	यत् तत् सात्त्विकम् उच्यते
Well regulated and free of attachment,	नियतं सङ्ग रहितम्
Performed without attraction or aversion,	अराग द्वेषतः कृतम्
By one not craving for the fruit of action.	अफल प्रेप्सुना कर्म

Sattvic action is that which is based on an impersonal sense of duty and clear conviction of the 'work to be done', based on one's *svadharma*, regardless of the 'fruit of the action'. Free from attachment (*sangarahitam*) and free from attraction and aversion (*aragadveshata*) with regard to the work that needs to be done, one does the work in a well-regulated manner (*niyatam karma*).

यत्तु कामेप्सुना कर्म साहङ्कारेण वा पुनः ।
क्रियते बहुलायासं तद्राजसमुदाहृतम् ॥18.24॥

That action is said to be rajasic, which is	तत् राजसम् उदाहृतम्
Performed by one craving to gratify desires,	यत् तु काम ईप्सुना कर्म
Driven by selfishness (to gain possession),	स अहङ्कारेण वा पुनः
And thus motivated to apply great effort.	क्रियते बहुल आयासं

Rajasic karma is commonplace — even in the most 'successful' institutions worldwide. The incentive for the work is provided by the fruit of action, which one craves for. When the object of desire is seen to be really worthwhile, one tends to put in great effort and passionate labour (*bahulayasam*). There is a strong ego-sense of doership underlying the action, and a strong sense of possessiveness in the object attained, reflective of the *rajasic ahankara*. This forms the basis of the carrot and stick approach widely adopted in management, because it is likely to bear fruit if the employees are *rajasic* in character. Sadly, the happiness gained by such action is usually short-lived, and is easily threatened by the perception that somebody else is getting something more. Equally, there is much ego-pain in failure.

Tamo-guna, by its very nature, is prone to inertia and laziness, and so is averse to dynamic action — unless driven by habit to work mechanically. There is no application of the intellect, and the action is based largely on the instincts of the physical or lower vital being. All of us, at some time or other, tend to accept work mindlessly, without recognising whether or not we have the competence to do such work.

अनुबन्धं क्षयं हिंसाम् अनपेक्ष्य च पौरुषम् ।
मोहादारभ्यते कर्म यत्तत्तामसमुच्यते ।।18.25।।

That action is said to be tamasic, which is	यत् तत् तामसम् उच्यते
Undertaken out of delusion, without care	मोहात् आरभ्यते कर्म
And concern about one's own competence,	अनपेक्ष्य च पौरुषम्
Or consequences, loss or injury to others.	अनुबन्धं क्षयं हिंसाम्

Such *tamasic* action can have disastrous consequences, including loss or injury to others (*anubandham kshayam himsam*). If this is an occasional occurrence (for example, biting more than we can chew in terms of projects), then it could simply serve as a useful lesson, as we move on with our lives. However, for *tamasic* people, there is no such learning and such actions are routinely done out of delusion (*moha*), without care or concern for the consequences. There can be much wastage and loss arising out of such misplaced labour.

The *gunas* related to *Karma* are summarised in the following table.

The three *gunas* in action (*Karma*)	
Sattva	*Action related to the work that needs to be done, in a well-regulated way, free of attachments, free from attraction or aversion to the work, not expecting any personal reward.*
Rajas	*Action driven by desire to gain some personal reward, performed with much effort, with a strong sense of doership and possessiveness over the fruit.*
Tamas	*Action undertaken out of delusion, without care or concern about one's own competence or the damaging consequences — causing wastage, loss or injury to others.*

Gunas in the Doer, *Karta*

Having looked at the nature of the mental impulsion behind any action (based on underlying knowledge, *jnana*), so also the nature of work done (*karma*), let us explore the remaining aspect, the nature of the doer (*karta*). Although the character of the doer, described through the underlying *gunas*, is in a sense reflected in the *karanam* (instruments of action) and the *karma* (action done), the Gita accords to it a special importance — as it focusses on the motivation and behaviour of the doer, during the doing of work and after its outcome.

The *sattvic* doer displays all the noble characteristics of *sattva-guna*, while doing the assigned work. The primary characteristic is freedom from attachment (*muktasanga*), which was earlier described in connection with the action itself (*sangarahitam*).

मुक्तसङ्गोऽनहंवादी धृत्युत्साहसमन्वितः |
सिद्ध्यसिद्ध्योर्निर्विकारः कर्ता सात्त्विक उच्यते ||18.26||

A doer of work is said to be sattvic, if he is	कर्ता सात्त्विकः उच्यते
Free from attachment, and is self-effacing,	मुक्त सङ्गः अनहं वादी
Yet endowed with calm firmness and zeal,	धृति उत्साह समन्वितः
Staying unperturbed in success or failure.	सिद्धि असिद्ध्योः निर्विकारः

The work is done for a noble *dharmic* purpose, and not for any personal gain. Further, in sharp contrast with the *rajasic* nature, there is no claim of doership and possessiveness. Thus, the *sattvic* doer is described as being 'self-effacing' (*anahamvadi*), preferring to stay in the background, focussing on the work at hand, rather than seeking visibility and the limelight. The *sattvic* doer displays a steady will that remains unperturbed by the outcome of work — be it success or failure. It is this firm calmness that enables the doer to stay focussed on the task. Such impersonality and detachment shown by the *sattvic* doer does not imply indifference to work. On the contrary, the work is carried out with much enthusiasm and zeal (*utsaha*). It is driven by high purpose and concentrated energy. The attention is focussed without distraction on the task at hand, and carried out mindfully and in a well-regulated way.

The very motivation of a *rajasic* doer, is a craving for the fruit, whereby there is much attachment to the action and the perceived outcome. The *rajasic* doer is usually passionate about achieving success, seeking its rapid completion, keen on winning at any cost. This makes the individual vulnerable to corruption, insensitive to fairness and the just needs of others. It may also make the doer capable of violence and cruelty, reflective of the *Asuric* nature of pure *rajas*.

In Sri Aurobindo's words, such a *rajasic* doer is 'greedy of heart, impure of mind, often violent and cruel and brutal in the means he uses; he cares little whom he injures or how much he injures others so long as he gets what he wants, satisfies his passions and will, vindicates the claims of his ego.'[13.4]

रागी कर्मफलप्रेप्सुः लुब्धो हिंसात्मकोऽशुचिः ।
हर्षशोकान्वितः कर्ता राजसः परिकीर्तितः ||18.27||

A doer of work is said to be rajasic, if he is	कर्ता राजसः परिकीर्तितः
Full of passionate craving for the fruit,	रागी कर्म फल प्रेप्सुः
Driven by greed, aggression, corruption,	लुब्धः हिंसा आत्मकः अशुचिः
Subject to joy in success, grief in failure.	हर्ष शोक अन्वितः

Such a *rajasic* doer is bound to celebrate success in the outcome with much pride and show. Conversely, he is likely to grieve bitterly if the outcome is failure. In today's highly competitive rat race environment, where almost all the 'rats' passionately run to stay ahead, only a few are likely to celebrate success, while many are likely to grieve. Even the success celebrated is often short-lived, for its stability is precarious, in the face of stiff competition. Such is the nature of passion underlying *rajas*.

The motivation for the *tamasic* doer is based neither on the high idealism of the *sattvic* doer, nor on the passionate craving of the *rajasic* doer. The basic nature of *tamo-guna* is an inertia towards any motivated action with discipline (other than a mechanically unthinking type of action). There is also dullness and stupidity.

By nature thus, the *tamasic* doer is undisciplined (*ayukta*), obstinate (*stabdha*) and lazy (*alasa*), prone to procrastination (*dirghasutri*) and shirking work. There is also a perverse streak in the *tamasic* doer, reflected in a tendency towards being vulgar and vain (*prakrita*), deceitful (*shatha*) and insolent (*naishkritika*). The lack of inspiration often results in despondency and depression (*vishada*).

अयुक्तः प्राकृतः स्तब्धः शठो नैष्कृतिकोऽलसः |
विषादी दीर्घसूत्री च कर्ता तामस उच्यते ||18.28||

A doer of work is said to be tamasic, if he is	कर्ता तामसः उच्यते
Undisciplined, vulgar, vain and obstinate,	अयुक्तः प्राकृतः स्तब्धः
Deceitful, insolent, and lazy at work,	शठः नैष्कृतिकः अलसः
Prone to despair and procrastination.	विषादी दीर्घ सूत्री च

In Sri Aurobindo's words, 'He is obstinate in stupidity, stubborn in error and takes a foolish pride in his ignorant doing; a narrow and evasive cunning replaces true intelligence; he has a stupid and insolent contempt for those with whom he has to deal, especially for wiser men and his betters.'[13.4]

The *gunas* related to *Karta* are summarised in the following table.

The three *gunas* in the doer (*Karta*)	
Sattva	*The doer is driven by nobility and idealism, is free from attachment, and is self-effacing, yet endowed with calm firmness and zeal, staying unperturbed in success or failure.*
Rajas	*The doer is full of attachment and craving for the fruit, driven by greed, aggression and corruption, celebrating joy in success, and falling into grief in failure.*
Tamas	*The doer is undisciplined, vulgar, vain, obstinate, deceitful, insolent, and lazy at work, prone to despair and procrastination.*

In the next chapter, we shall explore in detail how the *sattvic*, *rajasic* and *tamasic gunas* get reflected in our intellect (*Buddhi*), resolve (*Dhriti*) and happiness (*Sukha*).

14

Gunas in Intellect (*Buddhi*), Resolve (*Dhriti*) and Happiness (*Sukha*)

In the previous chapter, we had *explored* in detail three key factors affecting the quality of work: the knowledge (*jnana*) with which we work, the work (*karma*) itself, and the sense of the doer (*karta*) in us. The Gita concludes its analysis of *guna* characteristics with three additional factors: the nature of human intellect (*buddhi*), the quality of resolve or determination, which is a measure of will-power and its persistence (*dhriti*), and the resulting happiness (*sukha*). We shall explore these three aspects in detail in this chapter, through the play of the three *gunas*. At the end of this chapter, we shall see how we can collate all the eleven different *guna* characteristics described in the Gita. Then we can carry out a self-assessment, including some approximate metrics, in the form of a 'psychometric *guna* chart'. This can help in increasing our self-awareness, working on specific characteristics that need improvement. Thus we can transform our lives and accelerate our spiritual evolution.

Gunas in Intellect, *Buddhi*

The primary characteristic that distinguishes humans from other sentient beings (animals and plants) is our intellectual ability. When combined with will-power, it can serve as a very potent force, creative or destructive. In Sri Aurobindo's words, 'It is the understanding power of his nature, *buddhi*, that chooses the work for him or, more often, approves and sets its sanction on one or other among the many suggestions of his complex instincts, impulsions, ideas and desires. It is that which determines for him what is right or wrong, to be done or not to be done, *dharma* or *adharma*.'[14.1]

The intellect or understanding, *buddhi*, is said to be 'right' when it is *sattvic* in nature. It then provides the right basis for action. The *Buddha* also gave much importance to right discernment, in terms of 'right view' (*samyag-drishti*) and 'right intention' (*samyag-sankalpa*). These form the first two steps in his famous eightfold path. What is the Gita's description of such right discernment? This is described in the following verse.

प्रवृत्तिं च निवृत्तिं च कार्याकार्ये भयाभये |
बन्धं मोक्षं च या वेत्ति बुद्धिः सा पार्थ सात्त्विकी ||18.30||

Arjuna, that intellect is sattvic, which knows बुद्धिः सा पार्थ सात्त्विकी
When to act and when not to act, what to do, प्रवृत्तिं च निवृत्तिं च कार्य
What not to do, what to fear and what not to, अकार्ये भय अभये
What leads to bondage and what to freedom. बन्धं मोक्षं च या वेत्ति

Knowing when to act and when not to act and what to do and what not to do (*karyakarye*) are expressions of the *sattvic* intellect. The motivation of action is usually triggered by thoughts (*sankalpa*) in the mind. However, discernment needs to be brought in by the right functioning of *buddhi* so as to decide, on the basis of an integral understanding all the relevant aspects — the right time, right place, right mode and right measure of the proposed action. The term *pravritti* here refers to a kind of law of action (*dharma*) in the world. Conforming to this, we exert ourselves outwardly. Indeed, there are occasions when the right thing to do may well be to withdraw from action, following another law of abstention from action, called *nivritti* — as suggested in the Gita's metaphor of the tortoise retracting its limbs (verse 2.58) when it perceives danger. Although this may appear to be a reflection of fear, it is also a reflection of wisdom (operating as instinct in the case of the tortoise). Knowing what to fear and what not to (*bhayabhaye*) is itself a mark of *sattvic* understanding.

Conversely, it is also a sign of the *sattvic* intellect to remain unafraid of what is not to be feared. The example widely quoted in the Indian wisdom tradition is that of mistaking a coiled rope in a dimly lit room for a dangerously poisonous snake. This seeing of a *serpent in the rope* is a classic case of false ignorance arising from the absence of truly knowing light. It is just this basic ignorance (*ajnana*) of one's own True Self that is the root cause of all our anxiety, unease and suffering. This existential ignorance appears as the stranglehold of our lower nature. Yet, it is part of the Divine will, part of the evolutionary journey of consciousness from *asat* to *sat*, from *tamas* to *jyoti*, and from *mrityu* (death) to *amritam* (immortality).

The *ajnana* here is not just the absence of knowing light preventing us from seeing reality just as it is (seeing the rope as a mere rope). It also implies the substitution of reality with a deceptive false image. This, through our existential ignorance, reflects the substitution of True Self with the false and petty ego-self. Thus nurturing a *sattvic buddhi* provides a doorway to Self-realisation, for it enables us to discern between what leads to bondage and what to freedom (*bandham moksham*). This is bound to happen naturally in the evolving journey.

Unlike the *sattvic buddhi*, the *rajasic* intellect lacks the freedom to nurture an impersonal and calm understanding of reality and truth. The vital ego-desires of *rajasic ahankara* come in the way as they must influence and colour the understanding. Truth gets distorted, so that one tends to see and understand in accordance with one's personal desires and prejudices — all too often supported by vehement arguments.

यया धर्ममधर्मं च कार्यं चाकार्यमेव च ।
अयथावत्प्रजानाति बुद्धिः सा पार्थ राजसी ।।18.31।।

Arjuna, that intellect is rajasic,	बुद्धिः सा पार्थ राजसी
Which discriminates incorrectly	यया अयथावत् प्रजानाति
Between what is right and what is wrong,	धर्मम् अधर्मं च
What should be done and what should not.	कार्यं च अकार्यम् एव च

There is an insistence in the workings of *rajas*, which sets it distinctly apart from the calm lucidity of *sattva*. In Sri Aurobindo's words, 'The *rajasic* understanding, when it does not knowingly choose error and evil for the sake of the error and evil, can make distinctions between right and wrong, between what should or should not be done, but not rightly, rather with a pulling awry of their true measures and a constant distortion of values.'[14.1]

It is this interference of the ego-self — that has its own personal agenda — which tends to muddle and distort, if not pervert, the understanding of *dharma* and *adharma*, and what should be done and what should not. For example, in recruiting or promoting employees, members of the selection committee are sometimes persuaded by their own prejudices and grudges to influence their judgement. One has to nurture a noble and disinterested understanding, with an allegiance to fairness and truth, in order to be free from such *rajasic* imperfections in understanding.

We have already seen the implications of *tamasic* understanding with regard to the widespread ignorance about who we really are, through the example of seeing the serpent in the rope. Here, there is an inversion of reality. So we fully believe in the existence of something that is not really there. While such *tamasic* ignorance is a universal phenomenon with regard to existential knowledge, the Gita refers to such misunderstanding in all other knowledge that we invoke in our day-to-day living.

अधर्मं धर्ममिति या मन्यते तमसावृता |
सर्वार्थान्विपरीतांश्च बुद्धिः सा पार्थ तामसी ||18.32||

Arjuna, that intellect is tamasic,	बुद्धिः सा पार्थ तामसी
Which enveloped in darkness,	या तमसा आवृता
Regards what is wrong to be right,	अधर्मं धर्मम् इति मन्यते
Applying this perversion to all matters.	सर्व अर्थान् विपरीतान् च

The basic nature of *tamo-guna* is to envelop true being in the darkness of ignorance. Some people are so caught in *tamasic buddhi* that it seems practically impossible to convince them that they could possibly be wrong. We encounter such *buddhi* typically in our own rigid notions and prejudices. And especially in our tendencies to reduce shades of grey into *black or white* in our judgements (*this will never work*, *she is good*, *he is a good for nothing fellow*), ignoring any evidence that points otherwise.

We are often vulnerable to lumping masses of unknown people (on the basis of religion, race, community, or even gender) into rigid categories and often demonising them, not realising that this is most unfair. In a group, this mob mentality can sometimes be fuelled into mindless rage and violence, clearly reflective of a rigid *tamasic buddhi* playing havoc. Sri Aurobindo expands on this nature as follows: 'The *tamasic* reason is a false, ignorant and darkened instrument which chains us to see all things in a dull and wrong light, a cloud of misconceptions, a stupid ignoring of the values of things and people.'[14.1]

The *tamasic* intellect is therefore dangerous when it operates, for it mistakes *adharma* for *dharma*, applying this perversion to all matters (*sarvarthan-viparitamshca*).

The *gunas* related to *Buddhi* are summarised in the following table.

The three *gunas* in the intellect (*Buddhi*)	
Sattva	*Knowing when to act and when not to act, what to do and what not to do, what to fear and what not to fear, what leads to bondage and what leads to liberation.*
Rajas	*Knowing incorrectly, with error in discrimination, as to what is right and what is wrong, and what should be done and what should not; vulnerable to ego-driven desires and prejudices.*
Tamas	*Knowing completely wrongly, believing what is wrong to be right, and applying this perversion to all matters; enveloped in darkness, unwilling to see the light.*

Gunas in Resolve, *Dhriti*

The intellect (*buddhi*) by itself cannot cause action — no matter how right the discernment is. There is a need for volition or will-power to hold on to that decision and to act (or not to act) so as to transmit it to the instruments of action (*karmendriyas*). *Dhriti* is the term used in the Gita for this resolve or determination or fortitude. It refers to a persistence of will-power as well as a consistency in it. Both are tested when obstacles emerge, as indeed they are bound to, in any enterprise. *Dhriti* is what sustains the work undertaken.

As the old proverb goes, if there is a will, there is a way. All intellectual knowledge is rendered practically ineffective, unless there is a steady, determined resolve that refuses to yield to obstacles and temptations that distract or deviate from the chosen path. We are familiar with the so-called New Year resolutions that we tend to make, with good intention and intellectual understanding, but which we often fail to sustain, for lack of support from an appropriate *dhriti*.

The Gita makes an important point regarding *dhriti* — that it can be *tamasic*, *rajasic* or *sattvic*. Unhealthy or unwise addictions are reflective of *tamasic dhriti*. Even if there is an intellectual understanding about the need to be free from such addiction, the individual is often rendered helpless by the temptation. Frequent smokers know only too well the uselessness of warnings such as 'cigarette smoking is injurious to health'. Likewise, alcoholics, drug addicts and even diabetics and obese people realise the bitter truth that the spirit may be willing, but the flesh is weak. The flesh will not remain weak, if the perceived goal is seen to be sufficiently attractive.

The vitally driven *guna* of *rajas* is capable of moving heaven and earth to get what it wants, often by hook or by crook. Thus ambition, greed and lust often provide a strong motivation to sustain a *rajasic dhriti*, which is led by a *rajasic buddhi*. The goals here are bound to be narrow and self-centred.

This *rajasic dhriti* is what predominantly drives the world today. It is primarily responsible for nearly all our technological and economic development. If the goals are noble and lofty and aligned to the evolution of consciousness, the corresponding *dhriti* will be *sattvic*.

धृत्या यया धारयते मनःप्राणेन्द्रियक्रियाः |
योगेनाव्यभिचारिण्या धृतिः सा पार्थ सात्त्विकी ||18.33||

Arjuna, that determination is sattvic, धृतिः सा पार्थ सात्त्विकी
Which, steadfast and undeviating, यया अव्यभिचारिण्या
Sustains the controlled working of the mind, धृत्या धारयते मनः
Life-force and senses by the practice of yoga. प्राण इन्द्रिय क्रियाः योगेन

Spirituality at work calls for such *sattvic dhriti*, serving as a doorway to a higher spiritual will. For the *sattvic* resolve to sustain, it must remain inspired by its noble goals as it refuses to yield to the pulls, distractions and objections raised by other demands of the lower nature. The *sattvic* resolve has to be strong and enduring enough to control and sustain its governance over the workings of the mind, life-force and senses. This calls for a steadfast and undeviating resolve by *yogic* discipline. With regard to the *sattvic dhriti*, what to do and what not to do are matters that have already been decided upon by the *sattvic* intellect.

As Sri Aurobindo puts it, 'These are the things that it follows or avoids by the persistence of its conscious will according to the degree of its light and the stage of evolution it has reached in its upward ascent to the highest Self and Spirit.'[14.1]

यया तु धर्मकामार्थान् धृत्या धारयतेऽर्जुन ।
प्रसङ्गेन फलाकाङ्क्षी धृतिः सा पार्थ राजसी ।।18.34।।

Arjuna, that determination is rajasic,	धृतिः सा पार्थ राजसी
Which is sustained and governed by	यया तु धृत्या धारयते
Selfish attachment to fruits of actions	प्रसङ्गेन फल आकाङ्क्षी
In all pursuits: dharma, kama, artha.	धर्म काम अर्थान्

Rajasic dhriti supports the intentions and understanding inculcated by the *rajasic* intellect. It is reflective of a necessary stage of evolution of consciousness, so that one gains the ability and the confidence of achieving whatever one wants.

At the heart of the *rajasic dhriti* is a self-centred attachment to the fruits of action (*prasangena phalakankshi*) in all the common human pursuits (*purushartha*): *dharma*, *artha* and *kama*. In order to satisfy the *thrishna* arising in the lower nature (for wealth and sense-pleasures, name and fame), it can go to any length and twist *dharma* according to its will.

In Sri Aurobindo's words, 'Always it is apt to put on these things the construction which will most flatter and justify its desires and to uphold as right or legitimate the means which will best help it to get the coveted fruits of its work and endeavour. That is the cause of three-fourths of the falsehood and misconduct of the human reason and will.'[14.1]

For this reason, the Gita warns us from the very beginning (verse 3.37) against the *Asuric* force of untempered *rajas*, described as being *all-devouring* and *all-corrupting* (*mahashano mahapapma*).

Tamasic dhriti is reflected essentially in an obstinacy that supports a wrong understanding. It has all the characteristics of *tamo-guna*: stupidity, irrevocable habit, inertia, sleepiness, fearfulness, grief, despair, delusion and foolish pride.

यया स्वप्नं भयं शोकं विषादं मदमेव च ।
न विमुञ्चति दुर्मेधा धृतिः सा पार्थ तामसी ||18.35||

Arjuna, that determination is tamasic,	धृतिः सा पार्थ तामसी
Which stupidly clings to, never giving up,	यया न विमुञ्चति दुर्मेधा
Excessive sleep, fearfulness and grief,	स्वप्नं भयं शोकं
Despair and intoxicated foolish pride.	विषादं मदम् एव च

In Sri Aurobindo's words, *tamasic dhriti* is 'a persistence in the satisfaction and dull pride of its ignorance' as well as 'a heavy stress of inertia and impotence, a persistence in dullness and sleep, an aversion to mental change and progress, a dwelling on the fears and pains and depressions of mind which deter us in our path or keep us to base, weak and cowardly ways.'[14.1] Such a mind is prone to taking the path of least resistance, as it is averse to any adventure or noble pursuit. Further, it is prone to justify its evasive ways and constant doubts with regard to anything new.

The *gunas* related to *Dhriti* are summarised in the following table.

The three *gunas* in resolve (*Dhriti*)	
Sattva	*Determination that is steadfast and undeviating, by which one controls and sustains the noble workings of the mind, life-force and senses, through the practice of yogic discipline.*
Rajas	*Determination driven by self-centred attachment to fruits of actions in all human pursuits; driven by ambition, lust and greed; distorting dharma to realise one's desires.*
Tamas	*Determination which stupidly and obstinately clings to inertia, sleepiness, fearfulness, grief, despair, delusion, doubt and foolish pride; averse to any adventure or noble calling.*

Gunas in Happiness, *Sukha*

It seems natural for all sentient beings to seek happiness, *sukha*, and to avoid or resist its opposite, *duhkha*. Thus the pursuit of happiness (consciously or unconsciously) is the one common characteristic of all human beings. However, there are various kinds of happiness or pleasure (*sukha*) possible. And corresponding to each kind, there is usually a flip side: an unhappiness or pain (*duhkha*).

The root cause of all lack of happiness is attributable to a sense of *separation*, which ultimately is a separation from our One Divine Source. As mentioned earlier, the meaning and purpose of the *yoga* of the Gita is to achieve union with the Divine — through the integrated practice of *Karmayoga*, *Jnanayoga* and *Bhaktiyoga*. 'Love' is another description of the feeling resulting from the healing of separation, and finds its culmination in the realisation of a union with the All.

Likewise, all forms of happiness that we usually encounter are said to be but pale reflections of the Divine *Ananda*, the ultimate happiness, which has no opposite. To discover this, we need to penetrate through the veils of ignorance fortified by our identification with the separate ego-self and the play of the *gunas* of *Prakriti*.

Of course, we need to be realistic and begin where we currently are. Fortunately, the Gita lays out a map for us, to help us recognise more-or-less where we are in this evolutionary journey. Where do we seek our happiness? Sri Aurobindo describes the direction of this conscious evolutionary process: 'The unsatisfying surface play of our feeble egoistic emotions must be ousted, and there must be revealed instead a secret deep and vast psychic heart within... all our feelings, impelled by this inner heart in which dwells the Divine, will be transmuted into calm and intense movements of a twin passion of Divine Love and manifold *Ananda.*'[14.2]

Invariably, we find ourselves seeking happiness in the world outside, in external forms, in order to quench the unending series of *kama-thrishna* and *bhava-thrishna*. While we do this, wisdom lies in reckoning with the reality that this approach will not yield us any lasting fulfilment, because our seeking is in the transient world of *asat*. Besides, they are dependent on too many external factors, and any change in the external conditions can turn happiness into sorrow, short-term or long-term. These could range from minor events such as a power failure or loss of internet connectivity to more serious ones such as an economic recession, a divorce or a life-threatening disease. Moreover, the very fact that we seem to be always pursuing some happiness in the future is a sad reflection of the reality that happiness is presently missing in our lives.

Experiencing and outgrowing the lower forms of happiness are part of an evolutionary process that we all need to go through. Indeed, the Gita recognises this, but it keeps reinforcing the fact that we also need to appreciate, aspire for and realise the true and enduring source of *Ananda*, which resides as the Divine Indweller in us. We then access the perennial source of this inner happiness and inner radiance (described respectively as *antahsukha* and *antarjyoti* in verse 5.24). The purpose of our engagement with work and life is then no longer for pursuing and gaining happiness (satisfying deficiency needs) currently missing in us. Rather, work and relationships serve as avenues for the perennial inner happiness and light to flow out into the world.

The *sattvic* individual's intellect sets noble and lofty goals, and earnestly strives to realise them with wilful determination and *yogic* discipline. There is emphasis here on an inner transformation, which is bound to be resisted by the *rajasic* and *tamasic* parts of our being, posing difficulties and challenges that need to be surmounted by a steady *sattvic buddhi* and *dhriti*. The pursuit and realisation of such long-term goals invariably demand forbearance and tolerance of short-term sufferings. This very aspect is highlighted in the Gita as the basic description of the nature of *sattvic* happiness.

यत्तदग्रे विषमिव परिणामेऽमृतोपमम् ।
तत्सुखं सात्त्विकं प्रोक्तम् आत्मबुद्धिप्रसादजम् ||18.37||

That happiness is said to be sattvic,	तत् सुखं सात्त्विकं प्रोक्तम्
Which at first seems like poison,	यत् तत् अग्रे विषम् इव
But in the end turns out to be like nectar,	परिणामे अमृत उपमम्
A calm delight emerging from one's soul.	आत्म बुद्धि प्रसाद जम्

Sattvic happiness is described here as a calm delight emerging from one's soul (*atmabuddhiprasadajam*). This is a description of *Ananda*, not directly at its source, but as reflected in the mind and heart of the individual. This corresponds to the very nature of the *sattva-guna* — a quiet happiness and contentment, with mental clarity and lucidity, moral purity, emotional goodwill, harmony and affection towards all beings. Such happiness, when it is deeply realised, is found relatively independent of external circumstances. And when it is stabilised, it can be enduring and sustainable. However, for such happiness to be won, the individual has to endure successfully the hardships of self-discipline and purification. In Sri Aurobindo's words, 'It has to be conquered by self-discipline, a labour of the soul, a high and arduous endeavour. At first this means much loss of habitual pleasure, much suffering and struggle, a poison born of the churning of our nature, a painful conflict of forces, much revolt and opposition to the change due to the ill-will of the members or the insistence of vital movements, but in the end the nectar of immortality rises in place of this bitterness.'[14.3]

The allegorical references to nectar of immortality (*amritam*) and poison (*visham*) in this Gita verse, appear to be drawn from the ancient legend of *Samudra mathanam*, in which the mythological ocean of milk was churned by the gods (*devas*) and demons (*asuras*) together, with the objective of accessing the nectar of immortality (*amritam*). Yet surprisingly, what emerged first from the elaborate process of churning was a terrible poison (*visham*), which had to be swallowed (by the Divine) before various gifts, including *amritam* (at the end) could emerge.

Anyone who has undergone the travails of inner transformation will vouch for this truth regarding *visham* turning into *amritam*. Looking back at some of these *trials by fire*, one experiences gratefulness in one's happiness. Had these difficulties and challenges not been there, one would not have evolved to one's present happy condition. The caterpillar has necessarily to endure the painful condition of the chrysalis, before it can metamorphose and transform into a beautiful winged butterfly. *Sattvic* happiness, therefore, is something that each person has to necessarily earn for oneself through self-effort and self-discipline (physical, vital, mental and spiritual). It is not something that gets received as a gift or purchased in a market. Many of the comforts and pleasures that children demand from their parents may well be better earned than provided too easily. Challenges and hardships naturally need to be borne for authentic development. It takes a *sattvic buddhi* to discern 'what is right and what is not' and a *sattvic dhriti* to help manifest what is right, firmly and lovingly, overcoming the pains that arise naturally in the process of growing up. *No pain, no gain*!

In the next verse, the Gita adopts the same metaphors of *amritam* and *visham* (but in an opposite way) to describe happiness of a *rajasic* kind.

विषयेन्द्रियसंयोगात् यत्तदग्रेऽमृतोपमम् ।
परिणामे विषमिव तत्सुखं राजसं स्मृतम् ।।18.38।।

That happiness is said to be rajasic,	तत् सुखं राजसं स्मृतम्
Which at first seems like nectar,	यत् तत् अग्रे अमृत उपमम्
But in the end turns out to be like poison,	परिणामे विषम् इव
Born from contacts of senses with objects.	विषय इन्द्रिय संयोगात्

Rajasic happiness is described here as born from contacts of senses with sense-objects. This is the most common kind of happiness that most people in the world enjoy. Unlike *sattvic* happiness, this is an enjoyment that can sometimes be purchased, although at a price. Effort is still required to get resources needed to make the purchase or to win the prize. If the prize is seen to be irresistibly attractive, the *rajasic* person will go to any extent (using means fair or foul) to acquire and enjoy the prized possession. Such pleasures essentially belong to the vital and physical realms — corresponding to Maslow's deficiency needs or the lowermost three *chakras* in the *chakra* theory. In Sri Aurobindo's words, 'The mind of the *rajasic* man drinks of a more fiery and intoxicating cup; the keen, mobile, active pleasure of the senses and the body and the sense-entangled or fierily kinetic will and intelligence are to him all the joy of life and the very significance of living.' He goes on to add insightfully, 'This joy is nectar to the lips at the first touch, but there is a secret poison in the bottom of the cup and after it the bitterness of disappointment, satiety, fatigue, revolt, disgust, sin, suffering, loss, transience.'[14.3]

In today's world we see evidence of this, for example in the consumption of junk food and drinks, which are packaged and advertised in such attractive ways, stimulating our senses and thrilling our taste buds, making us crave for more. The harmful effects of such consumption (its poisonous nature) get revealed only much later. The craving for *rajasic* happiness also tends to nurture an attitude of ends justifying the means, and we render ourselves vulnerable to all kinds of *adharmic* compromises and corrupt practices. Seeking instant gratification, we then may adopt short cuts and quick fixes, rather than put in the hard effort required for authentic development. Although we may succeed in fooling people and gaining initial success, in the long run we are bound to get exposed and suffer the results.

Despite these negative connotations, we must appreciate that the deficiency needs that drive our *rajasic* pursuits (with an insistent demand for gratification) serve the useful purpose of developing the physical, vital and mental parts of our being, even just by following the rat race. For example, to gain the satisfaction of looking good and attractive, we work out in the gym and develop our physical bodies. By way of gaining a livelihood to become rich and famous, we study and struggle through various examinations and challenges in life, thus developing our talents and our mental faculties, gaining an inner confidence and self-esteem in this process. All this eventually leads to self-actualisation in a few among us. However, the Spirit in us does not really seek the transient satisfactions that *rajo-guna* craves. Instead it is waiting to be awakened and realised (Self-realisation). As we evolve and eventually discover our higher nature, our well-developed instrumentation can be put to good use in the service of the Divine to serve the Divine will.

यदग्रे चानुबन्धे च सुखं मोहनमात्मनः ।
निद्रालस्यप्रमादोत्थं तत्तामसमुदाहृतम् ।।18.39।।

That happiness is said to be tamasic,	तत् सुखं तामसम् उदाहृतम्
Which, from the beginning to the end,	यत् अग्रे च अनुबन्धे च
Deludes one's own self, driven by	मोहनम् आत्मनः उत्थं
Sleep, indolence and negligence.	निद्रा आलस्य प्रमाद

Tamasic happiness is described here as delusional in its arising from indolent sleep and negligence. We all know the simple happiness that we derive from sleep — even though the moments of pure dreamless sleep last but for a few moments in our waking time scale (but timeless, in its own authentic experience). Indeed, such switching off is desirable for all of us, when we tend to over-exert, neglecting the rest needed by our bodies and minds, and sleep is nature's gift to all of us. Although seemingly *tamasic*, there is a Divine *Ananda* concealed in its depth, which is what makes this experience so refreshing, peaceful and delightful. Here, the turbulence of the waking world and dreaming mind are found dissolved. Sleep is meant to serve as brief period of rest, not as a way of life. Besides, remaining lazy and inactive or inebriated or sedated for long brings a stupor and dullness that is far removed from the happiness of deep sleep. Yet it is this dull *tamasic sukha* that we sometimes fall prey to. Sadly, it can be a regular way of living, in indolence and inebriation, for those steeped in *tamas*. In Sri Aurobindo's words, 'The *tamasic* mind can remain well-pleased in its indolence and inertia, its stupor and sleep, its blindness and its error. Nature has armed it with the privilege of a smug satisfaction in its stupidity and ignorance, its dim lights of the cave, its inert contentment, its petty or base joys, its vulgar pleasures.'[14.3]

There seems to be a primitive happiness in sheer survival — even amidst appalling conditions. If we do not have the energy, motivation, knowledge and will to emerge out of this condition, it is like being physically and mentally challenged. We remain stuck in the sheer survival mode, with our experience of happiness limited to *tamasic sukha*. The Gita contrasts *tamasic* happiness with the *rajasic* and *sattvic* forms of happiness, in their evolution through time in an individual's life in an interesting manner. Whereas one begins with a state of pain and ends up in a state of joy in *sattvic sukha*, and the condition is reversed in *rajasic sukha*, the condition of *tamasic sukha* remains stupidly delusional from beginning to end. The satisfaction derived from *tamasic sukha* is of a dull kind — not fiery and short-lived as in the case of *rajasic sukha*, or calm and enduring as in the case of *sattvic sukha*. The dull inertia of *tamas* can also turn sometimes into a dull grief or despondency or depression that can last long. Indulgence in self-pity reflects *tamasic sukha* laced with *rajasic sukha*.

The *gunas* related to *Sukha* are summarised below:

The three *gunas* in happiness (*Sukha*)	
Sattva	*Happiness in the form of a calm delight emerging from one's soul, which tastes like poison in the beginning, but later like the nectar of immortality; an enduring contentment.*
Rajas	*Happiness born from contacts of senses with objects, which tastes like nectar in the beginning, but later tastes like poison; driven by deficiency needs of the vital part of being.*
Tamas	*Happiness arising from sleep, indolence and negligence; delusional in nature, from beginning to end; a dull stupidity and stupor.*

If we look around worldwide, we do see people everywhere demonstrating these three *gunas* of happiness. However, there are rare souls, who have gone beyond the entrapment of all three *gunas*, and who bask in the pure joy of *Ananda*. These few, who can be a tremendous source of inspiration for the rest of humanity, define the leading edge in the evolution of consciousness, generating a subtle but powerful spiritual influence. In this regard, one *Buddha* can be said to be more worthy and influential than millions of ordinary mortals.

The Psychometric *Guna* Chart

It may help to make a self-assessment of our *guna* characteristics (not just qualitatively, but if possible, also quantitatively), since we live in a technological world where we understand the importance of measurements. Quantitative measurements of behaviours (in the field of social sciences) will obviously lack the precision that we are accustomed to in the physical sciences. But our objective here is not to do any major calculations or to give any certification based on the scores. We are simply asking ourselves to make approximate judgements of ourselves, as to how *tamasic* or *rajasic* or *sattvic* we consider ourselves to be at present. Clearly all the three *gunas* operate in every one of us, for that is how nature operates. However, what are their proportions? Which of them is most dominant, and which least?

We need to go back to the three previous chapters, and review the Gita's descriptions of how the three *gunas* operate in 11 human characteristics and give ourselves three scores — shown as percentages of *sattva*, *rajas* and *tamas* (adding up to 100), for each of the 11 characteristics. These are of course rough scores, which can be tabulated conveniently, as shown in the figure below:

Characteristics	*Guna* Percentages		
	Sattva	*Rajas*	*Tamas*
1. *Ahara*	40	40	20
2. *Tyaga*	30	50	20
3. *Yajna*	40	40	20
4. *Dana*	30	50	20
5. *Tapas*	20	60	20
6. *Jnana*	30	50	20
7. *Karma*	30	50	20
8. *Karta*	20	60	20
9. *Buddhi*	30	50	20
10. *Dhrti*	30	50	20
11. *Sukha*	30	50	20
Average Scores	30	50	20

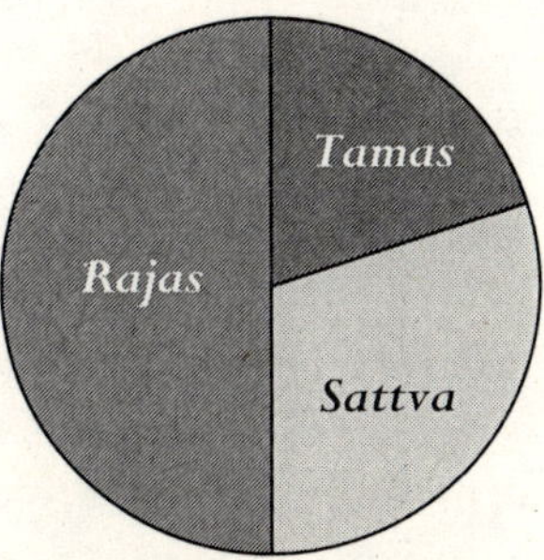

Typical Guna Composition
(self-assessed by a student)

The scores under each column head ("*Sattva*", "*Rajas*", "*Tamas*") can be averaged (adding and dividing the total by 11) and the average scores provide a rough measure of our overall *guna* nature. In the example shown (self-assessment by a student), it turns out (as indicated pictorially in the pie chart) that the individual is predominantly *rajasic* (to an extent of 50%). The *sattvic guna* comes next (30%), with the *tamo-guna* not far behind (20%). The same table can be used to plot a bar chart, depicting the functioning of the three *gunas* in the 11 characteristics. We may use the term, 'psychometric *guna* chart', to refer to this pictorial description of ourselves — our psychology.

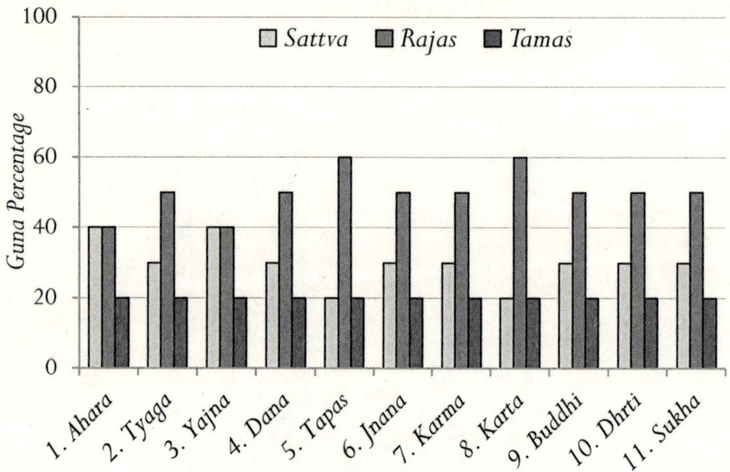

Typical Psychometric Guna Chart

The result of this example (of a student with good academic records) is not surprising as the vast majority of our population, especially young adults, are strongly driven by their vital impulses, desires and ambitions, and are naturally very competitive. They need to quench their needs of *kama-thrishna* and *bhava-thrishna* reasonably. However, while their deficiency needs have to be duly satisfied (in a *dharmic* way), they also need to make a shift from the path of *preyas* to that of *shreyas*. Their evolutionary journey of consciousness requires a conscious self-effort and course correction. Clearly this self-effort needs to be organically qualitative rather than mechanically quantitative.

We shall explore the theme of *guna* purification and transformation in detail in the next chapter.

15

Purification and Transformation of *Gunas*

We now have a fairly clear idea of how the three *gunas* function through our being, keeping us entrapped in our lower nature. The evolution of consciousness demands that we purify our being, discover our True Self and thus ascend to our higher nature. In this chapter, we shall broadly explore how this can be done through the Gita's *yoga*. First, we need to understand our present condition of entrapment in the lower nature. Then we can see where purification is needed and how it can be done.

Purification of *Gunas*

The psychometric *guna* chart (described in the previous chapter) helps in making an honest assessment of our present condition. Which of the three *gunas* is predominant in our character? What weak areas need conscious improvement to refine our character? What changes are needed in our daily practice of *sadhana*, to help us progress? The aim of purification here is to become more *sattvic.* We can revisit the psychometric guna chart to monitor our practices and progress. The proof of the pudding is in the eating. If some practices do not work with us, we must explore others. This would be a good way to live and make genuine progress. We need to reckon with the organics involved in the play of the three *gunas*, as they mutually compete to fill and possess our being. This is described in the following verse.

रजस्तमश्चाभिभूय सत्त्वं भवति भारत ।
रजः सत्त्वं तमश्चैव तमः सत्त्वं रजस्तथा ||14.10||

By prevailing over rajas and tamas	रजः तमः च अभिभूय
Does sattva predominate, Arjuna!	सत्त्वं भवति भारत
Rajas rises by overpowering sattva and tamas,	रजः सत्त्वं तमः च एव
Tamas rises by overpowering sattva and rajas.	तमः सत्त्वं रजः तथा

Our goal is not to drive out the *gunas* of *rajas* and *tamas* (which is practically impossible). It is instead to transform them as far as we can, by inclining towards *sattva* — with a *sattva-guna* score of at least 50%. Getting very high scores of *sattva* is not the real aim of *Integral Karmayoga*. For *sattva* itself needs transforming in the ascent to higher nature. Even while abiding in lower nature, what remains of *rajas* and *tamas* needs tempering and refinement, as *sattva* emerges and awakens the evolving soul. This is needed to invoke spirituality at work, aiming for perfection.

All three *gunas* originate in higher Divine nature. And so the ultimate objective of spirituality at work is to rise up into higher nature, where the *gunas* get transformed. In Sri Aurobindo's words, 'The three *gunas* become purified and refined and changed into their Divine equivalents: *sattva* becomes *jyoti*, the authentic spiritual light; *rajas* becomes *tapas*, the tranquilly intense Divine force; *tamas* becomes *shama*, the Divine quiet, rest, peace.'[15.1] The implications of this are discussed in greater detail in the next chapter.

Here, it will be helpful to see the signs of our behaviour when we are able to rise up to the summit of *sattva*, with respect to each of the 11 characteristics we had examined in detail earlier. As far as food is concerned, our aim will be to consume mostly *sattvic ahara* — mindfully, in moderation, and with respect and gratitude, perceiving the presence of divinity in the food itself, as well as beings associated with it, while offering it to the Divine Indweller.

With regard to renunciation (*tyaga*) in our work, we not only give up any obsession with the fruit of action and attachment to the work itself, but also end up renouncing all desire and ego-centred notions of doership. We do all that required work, perfectly and whole-heartedly, as a sacrifice (*yajna*) to the Divine, recognising clearly that all action is a *yajna*, an offering of *Prakriti* to *Purusha*. All our practice of *giving* (*dana*) — extending to all that is possible and appropriate (material, financial or educational) — is done graciously and nobly, simply out of goodwill, out of a heartfelt sense of self-giving of our being to the Divine manifest in the world (*atma-samarpana*). Our practices of self-discipline in the form of austerity (*tapas*) — of body, speech and mind — are done with sincerity, deep faith and steadfastness, bringing about 'a high purity of the reason and will, an equal soul, a deep peace and calm, a wide sympathy and preparation of oneness, a reflection of the inner soul's Divine gladness in the mind, life and body.'[15.2]

With regard to knowledge (*jnana*), we strive to see not only the One in all, but also the all in One, discovering that being is not different from the truth of knowing Spirit. We do all work (*karma*) that needs to be done in a well regulated way, free from attraction or aversion, not worrying about the outcome, nor expecting any personal reward. Our action gets increasingly impersonal and governed by the Spirit in us, rather than the intellect, for we aim to serve as perfect instruments of the Divine. The *karta* in us then becomes free of the delusion of ego-centred doership, and our work becomes 'the spontaneous working of the spiritual *Tapas* and at last a highest soul-force, the direct God-Power, the mighty and steadfast movement of a Divine energy in the human instrument...'[15.3] Our intellect (*buddhi*) underlying the mental impulsion to work transcends the limits of reason, accessing trans-rational intuition and direct knowledge, providing a certitude in our decisions on what to do and what not to do. This will be then supported by a persistence and consistency in will-power or resolve (*dhriti*). The mental will is replaced by a spiritual will arising out of the union with the True Self, with all parts of the being (physical, vital, mental) serving integrally its cause, without any resistance or confusion. Finally, having successfully overcome the resistances and sufferings in the short-term in our practice of the *yoga* of the Gita, we experience an enduring *sattvic* happiness as a calm delight emerging from our soul. This is said to taste like poison in the beginning, but later like the nectar of immortality. It is described by Sri Aurobindo as: 'absolute *Ananda*... the secret delight from which all things are born, by which all is sustained in existence, and to which all can rise in the spiritual culmination.'[15.3]

Spiritual Practice is Never Wasted

Over time, much conscious and dedicated effort (*sadhana*) is needed towards purification and self-discipline. This is essential for the long-term need of irreversible establishment in a timeless truth of being. What happens if we fall short or fail in our practice? This of course is a genuine question that deserves a right answer. One of the students in the *Integral Karmayoga* course posed this question: 'Yes, I want to be spiritual, but I also don't want to miss out on all the fun. 'Will I not get lost if I don't make it?'

The 'fun' referred to here is primarily *rajasic* happiness, with some elements of *tamasic* happiness. Our being may be compared to a tree, where the three *gunas* are like three different flocks of birds looking for a nesting or roosting place, where they can take shelter and also grow and multiply. However, the space is limited, and all three compete with one another to take roost. Each flock appeals to the tree for accommodation, promising its own kind of 'fun'. It is for the tree to grant permission. Yet, the tree is not very decisive — in its fickleness, it can be seduced by the appeals of each flock. Besides, the birds have already taken possession of some branches. So they will resist any attempt at getting ousted. Most of us are like that tree (not yet spiritually mature to act decisively). We need to go through an evolutionary process of maturation during which we are likely to make many mistakes, sometimes even overestimating our spiritual ardour and ignoring the just demands of our deficiency needs. In the backlash, we may forget our spiritual aspirations, moving from need to greed and so getting lost in the vital world of *rajas* and the delusion of *tamas*. What then will be our fate, when we thus 'fall'? Arjuna poses this question to the Divine Teacher, on our behalf. The question demands an assurance, which is given unhesitatingly.

अर्जुन उवाच ।
अयतिः श्रद्धयोपेतः योगाच्चलितमानसः ।
अप्राप्य योगसंसिद्धिं कां गतिं कृष्ण गच्छति ||6.37||

Arjuna said:	अर्जुनः उवाच
When one develops faith, but falls in practice,	अयतिः श्रद्धया उपेतः
With his mind straying from the path of Yoga,	योगात् चलित मानसः
Unable to attain perfection in Yoga,	अप्राप्य योग संसिद्धिं
What then is his fate, O Krishna?	कां गतिं कृष्ण गच्छति

श्रीभगवानुवाच ।
पार्थ नैवेह नामुत्र विनाशस्तस्य विद्यते ।
न हि कल्याणकृत्कश्चित् दुर्गतिं तात गच्छति ||6.40||

The Blessed Lord said:	श्रीभगवान् उवाच
Arjuna, neither in this life nor later,	पार्थ न एव इह न अमुत्र
Will he suffer any loss due to this.	विनाशः तस्य विद्यते
One who engages in noble deeds	कल्याण कृत् कश्चित्
Will never meet with misfortune.	न हि दुर्गतिं तात गच्छति

Progress is not monotonic or linear, and we all go through ups and downs, getting elated by success and depressed by failure. Should we aspire for perfection in *yoga* (*yoga-samsiddhim*), we must get fit and pace ourselves to complete a marathon journey. This is not a short sprint or something gained through crash courses or other promises of instant gratification that have got popular in present times. It is a long haul. We are divinely supported in our spiritual aspirations, no matter what challenges and temporary setbacks we may encounter.

Should we, despite our faith (*shraddha*), give up our practice and stray from the straight path, such noble efforts will not go waste. This is the assurance that the Divine Teacher gives Arjuna. What is well and truly done (*kalyana-krit*) will bear fruit — if not in this life, later in the lives to come. We need to see the evolving journey in its fullness, from start to end, through many lifetimes. For *karma* keeps on bearing fruit until ego and desire are fully transcended, and we thus arrive at *naishkarmyam* (freedom from all *karma* and its effects).

Liberation: Beyond the *Gunas* of Lower Nature

In *Jnanayoga*, what is needed is an attitude of critical enquiry concerning ultimate reality, to be nurtured as frequently as possible. This starts by nurturing how to discern what is mutable (*asat*) from what is timelessly true (*sat*). Thus, the body (*deha*) and all its constituents (physical, vital and mental), ever subject to change, is always seen as *asat*, whereas the Indwelling Spirit (*dehi*) is realised as being intimately sourced in timeless *sat*. The entire world of lower nature (*Apara Prakriti*), with its constant interplay of the three *gunas*, is also experienced as *asat*, while the unchanging principle of consciousness behind this play (*Akshara Purusha*) is perceived as the ultimate reality, *sat*. It is this immutable aspect of the True Self or Divine Indweller in us (unaffected and untouched by the unending play of the three *gunas*) that we need to realise and abide in, for liberation from the entrapment of the lower nature.

This requires us to step back from our habitual involvement with object-centred awareness to the silent Witness (*Upadrashta* or *Sakshi*). Returning undistracted here, we truly see that everything is happening of its own accord — in the mysterious and unending action of *Prakriti*. Then we witness everything as the three *gunas* at play. We also observe each ego-self (*ahankara*) tending to get involved and entrapped in this play. This is described beautifully in the following two verses.

प्रकृत्यैव च कर्माणि क्रियमाणानि सर्वशः ।
यः पश्यति तथात्मानम् अकर्तारं स पश्यति ||13.30||

By Prakriti alone are actions	प्रकृत्या एव च कर्माणि
Performed in their entirety!	क्रियमाणानि सर्वशः
The witnessing Self is not the doer.	तथा आत्मानम् अकर्तारं
One who sees this truth, truly sees!	यः पश्यति सः पश्यति

नान्यं गुणेभ्यः कर्तारं यदा द्रष्टानुपश्यति ।
गुणेभ्यश्च परं वेत्ति मद्भावं सोऽधिगच्छति ||14.19||

When the observer sees that the agency	कर्तारं यदा द्रष्टा अनुपश्यति
Causing actions is none other than gunas,	न अन्यं गुणेभ्यः
And knowing That which is beyond gunas,	गुणेभ्यः च परं वेत्ति
He turns towards Me and attains My being.	मत् भावं सः अधिगच्छति

Sustaining this witnessing ability (*sakshi bhava*) is a key practice that can lead to liberation. Only then one knows for sure that there is a sanctuary of deep peace within us that we can always access. It is of the nature of *sat*, which always safeguards us and is ever-peaceful, amidst the turmoil in the manifest world of *asat* around us.

There are several other verses in the Gita that emphasise the importance of nurturing this ability of 'true seeing', not only during the time of meditation, but also while engaging in all kinds of action. Verses 5.8 and 5.9, for example, point out that the practising *Yogin* realises: 'I' am not doing anything! While seeing, hearing, touching, smelling, eating, walking, sleeping, breathing, speaking, excreting, grasping, opening and closing eyelids and so on, the *Yogin* maintains: The senses are engaging with the sense-objects (*indriyani-indriyartheshu vartante*). Indeed, one who sees this truth truly sees (*yah pashyati sa pashyati*), and thus remains free from entanglement with the world. In order to be able to retain such witnessing awareness even while engaging in action, one needs to achieve some degree of mastery, practising it while sitting quietly in meditation. It then becomes more convenient to withdraw attention that is habitually reaching outward, and turn it inwards or upwards to That which is beyond the *gunas* (*gunebhyah param*).

While this may seem appealing, we are bound to be troubled by questions such as: *How then will work get done?* Indeed, Arjuna does pose similar questions in the Gita, for he is puzzled by the seeming contradiction between realising the truth of the immutable *Akshara Purusha* (eternally free from the *gunas* and all action) and the Divine Teacher's insistence on action (involving the play of the *gunas*). The Gita's *yoga* aims for a harmonious integration between these two. It begins with drawing our attention to what Sri Aurobindo describes as 'the desire of the fruits which is the most potent cause of the soul's bondage, and by abandoning it the soul can be free in action'. To further eliminate any attachment to the work itself, 'the resource is in that other injunction of the Gita, to give up the action itself to the Lord of works and be only a desireless and equal-minded instrument of His will...

Only so can we attain to the movement and status of the Divine, *madbhava.*'[15.4]

This status is also that of *sthitaprajna*, reflecting the impersonality and calm and immovable condition of *brahmi sthiti*, discussed earlier. It is as though one is impartially seated above (*udasinavad-asinah*), as described in the following verse.

उदासीनवदासीनः गुणैर्यो न विचाल्यते ।
गुणा वर्तन्त इत्येव योऽवतिष्ठति नेङ्गते ||14.23||

Impartial in poise, as though seated above, उदासीन वत् आसीनः
Unshaken by the ongoing play of the gunas, गुणैः यः न विचाल्यते
His inner being stands firm and never wavers, यः अवतिष्ठति न इङ्गते
For he knows that the gunas are in operation. गुणाः वर्तन्ते इति एव

The term *udasina* is often translated as being indifferent. Such indifference in the lower nature could be typically *tamasic*, *rajasic* or *sattvic.* The *tamasic* kind of indifference is often associated with laziness and lack of motivation, and may arise from failure, disappointment or weariness (*vibhava thrishna*). *Rajasic* indifference, on the other hand, typically arises from a desire and difficult struggle to look heroic like a *stoic*, unaffected by any disturbance. *Sattvic* indifference is a superior smiling indifference that arises from *sattvic jnana* and *sukha*, being able to see calmly one unifying principle in all diversity, and being content in most situations. However, it is still not the absolute impartiality that comes from being centred in the truth of the Self.

When one rises beyond the three *gunas*, and thus discovers the poise of being impartially seated above, the *udasinata* that comes spontaneously does not mean that one becomes insensitive to all that is happening around. For liberation, '*Sattva* must be transcended as well as *rajas* and *tamas*; the golden chain must be broken no less than the leaden fetters and the bond-ornaments of a mixed alloy.'[15.5]

According to the Gita's *yoga*, in addition to being the quiet Witness (*Upadrashta*), the *Purusha* also has the roles of Consenter (*Anumanta*) and Sustainer (*Bharta*). This implies giving consent to and sustaining all aspirations and actions that promote perfection and evolution of consciousness. It also implies the responsibility of withdrawing consent from, and so rejecting, all that functions in a contrary direction — including all kinds of dysfunctional habits. Such practices encourage perfection in our nature, along with liberation. *Jnanayoga* alone may not find full acceptance with temperaments that perceive it as being too impersonal, and bereft of emotions like love, compassion and adoration of the Divine. In recognition of this, the Gita also encourages a personal relationship with the Divine, which finds its purest form in the practice of unwavering and profound devotion, *Bhaktiyoga*, and leads eventually to the One Supreme Personal-Impersonal Divine, the *Purushottama*. Though the practice of sincere devotion and surrender to the Divine is suitable for persons of all temperaments (regardless of *guna* composition), it is specially so for those who are not inclined towards critical enquiry and understanding of the subtleties of *Purusha* and *Prakriti*.

मां च योऽव्यभिचारेण भक्तियोगेन सेवते |
स गुणान्समतीत्यैतान् ब्रह्मभूयाय कल्पते ||14.26||

He who serves Me, unswervingly	मां च यः सेवते अव्यभिचारेण
Practising the yoga of devotion,	भक्ति योगेन
He gets to go beyond these gunas,	सः गुणान् समतीत्य एतान्
Ready to be absorbed in Brahman.	ब्रह्म भूयाय कल्पते

Here, one goes beyond the *gunas* of lower nature (*gunan-samatitya*), but not by stepping back and being centred in the

Witness consciousness and so remaining unentangled in the passing show. Instead, this transcendence is attained here by a full involvement in all the work that needs to be done, but with one's entire being directed to the Divine, serving with devotion and adoration. This practice of the *yoga of devotion*, called *Bhaktiyoga*, is to be done unswervingly (a*vyabhicharena*). One seeks to see the Divine (with whom one has an intense personal and mystical relationship) everywhere and at all times. The transcendence that comes about, leading to absorption in *Brahman* (*brahma-bhuyaya*), is considered to be an outcome of Divine Grace. We will discuss the practice of *Bhaktiyoga* in greater detail in the penultimate chapter of this book.

In *Integral Karmayoga*, the objective is to integrate harmoniously the practices of *Karmayoga*, *Jnanayoga* and *Bhaktiyoga*, as described in the Gita. This is a triple process of action as a Divine worker, knowledge of the true Divine reality, and devoted adoration and service of the Divine. In this evolutionary journey, in addition to striving for liberation, importance is given to perfecting the individual nature and making it as *sattvic* as possible. Such purification is needed to attain perfection in work — both in the lower nature as well as in the higher nature.

Higher Nature, *Para Prakriti*

Indeed, the *gunas* cannot be purified to perfection, while we remain entrapped in the lower nature. It is only when we rise beyond the lower nature, and begin to live centred in the knowing and being of the True Self, that there is a possibility of complete transformation. On this rising beyond the three *gunas* of the lower nature (*traigunatita*), the higher Divine nature (*Para Prakriti* or *Shakti*) begins to function or flow through our being. This descent of Spirit is in fact an involution — a conscious one.

We usually talk about liberation or Self-realisation or union with the Divine as the ultimate goal of spirituality, with a focus on an evolution upwards — from darkness to light, from Matter to Spirit. Indeed in India, liberation or *Moksha* is commonly understood to mean a salvation from the tyranny of *samsara* and the cycle of rebirths. This seems meaningful and justifiable from the perspective of a fragmented and separated part of the Whole, yearning to merge permanently with its Source, the infinite Whole. The individual's spiritual journey gets consummated when one is truly able to abide in *sat*, beyond the *gunas*, never again getting entangled in the world of *asat*. However, the world of *asat* (the world of manifestation and creation) is perhaps not something to be dismissed as an illusion or delusion. One only has to contemplate on something as innocuous as a little wildflower, to realise that there is something deep and profound underlying such a marvellous manifestation. It has probably taken nature aeons of biological evolution to arrive at this degree of perfection. Are such creations meaningless, having no ultimate purpose, no reality?

Any work of art (inorganic or organic) may be *asat*, in the sense that it is perishable. Yet, it is still a wondrous and marvellous creation — an expression of truth, goodness and beauty (*satyam shivam sundaram*)! We intuitively feel it as an expression of the Divine, of Spirit in manifestation. How then, do we reconcile this fundamental difference between *sat* and *asat*, between *Purusha* and *Prakriti*, the *Unmanifest* and the *Manifest*? *Purusha* and *Prakriti* seem to be inter-mixed in everything, and in order to find our True Self, it is necessary and important (in *Jnanayoga*) to separate the subject (*Purusha*) from objective experience (*Prakriti*) and the play of the *gunas* in our ignorant lower nature. It is then that we discover our true identity as Immutable Silent and Inactive Spirit — which we call *Akshara Purusha*. It is boundless *Unmanifest Spirit*, and because it is free of all qualities, it is also known as *Nirguna Brahman*. It is from that very *Unmanifest* that all manifestation has emerged, according to traditional Indian wisdom. That is how we have the spectrum of consciousness: from gross Matter to pure formless Spirit. Spirit is hidden as the unchanging essence (*sat*) in all forms of existence. As mentioned before, *Ishvara* or the Supreme Lord, is another name for the Supreme *Purusha* (*Purushottama*), transcending and including *Akshara Purusha*, according to the Gita (verses 15.17-18). Thus, the power and will to create originally emerged from this all-knowing Divine Source.

Infinite are the possibilities of the creative potential of this Source, which is called *Para Prakriti* ('beyond lower nature') or *Shakti*. Interestingly, the term *Prakriti* literally points to the original power of action ('prior to creation'), before any manifestation. Higher nature (*Para Prakriti*) is but the creative aspect of *Purushottama*, the *Shakti* of *Ishvara*. The two (static and dynamic principles) are inseparable at the Source, and it is this essential unity that makes creation of the higher nature Divine. This is an all-knowing and all-powerful nature, not bound in ignorance, nor limited by the three *gunas*, as in the case of lower nature. This distinction between lower and higher nature is brought out clearly in the following verse, where the *Purushottama* represented by the *Avatar* of Krishna proclaims unequivocally to Arjuna and us: 'know My higher nature' (*prakritim viddhi me param*).

अपरेयमितस्त्वन्यां प्रकृतिं विद्धि मे पराम् ।
जीवभूतां महाबाहो ययेदं धार्यते जगत् ।।7.5।।

Different from this 'lower' Prakriti,	अपरा इयम् इतः तु अन्यां
Know My 'higher' Nature, Arjuna,	प्रकृतिं विद्धि मे पराम् महाबाहो
As the very life unfolding in all beings,	जीव भूतां
By which this universe is sustained.	यया इदं धार्यते जगत्

The word 'creation' does not quite capture the workings of higher nature, for it does not reflect the reality that here the creation is but a Self-extension of the Divine Creator, manifesting an infinite potential. While *sat* (true existence) is a key aspect of ultimate reality, so are *chit* (consciousness) and *ananda* (bliss). *Para Prakriti* is essentially a dynamic manifestation of *chit-shakti*, expressing its creative power joyfully in fulfilment (*ananda*). This dynamic aspect of *Brahman* is sometimes referred to as *Saguna Brahman*: with qualities, extending itself into many planes of existence. This includes the original descent into the ignorance (loss of its unitary all-knowing Self-consciousness) of the lower nature (*Apara Prakriti*), which is the world of Mind, Life and Matter, where it operates as a 'hidden essence sustaining this universe'. Gita verse 7.12, however, makes it clear that although the lower nature (with its ignorant play of the three *gunas*) has evolved (and is continuing to evolve) from this original pure essence in the all-inclusive space of *Brahman*, *Para Prakriti* is not in these secondary derivations: 'I am not in them; they are in Me!'

It is only by transcending ego and desire, and lifting ourselves beyond the three *gunas* of the lower nature, that we can glimpse the workings of higher nature and have access to integral knowing. Then, there is also the possibility of serving as a channel for the Divine to bring down the higher consciousness into Mind, Life and Matter. The physical, vital and mental parts of our being are said to find true fulfilment only when they get to serve the higher nature. But for this, the *gunas* of the lower nature in the individual need to be increasingly transformed.

According to Sri Aurobindo, the descent of higher nature is first felt in our mental being as luminous knowledge. For this reason, *sattva* is said to transform into the Divine light of *jyoti*. The next transformation is felt, as we abide in our *sadhana* and invite the descent of the higher nature, in our vital being. We need to conserve (and not dissipate) the energetic fire within us, and the descent of higher nature brings about a transformation of *rajas* into *tapas*. This leads to the emergence of 'Soul Forces' (discussed in the next chapter) as *chit-shakti*. The most difficult to transform is the *physical being*, whose basic *tamasic* nature is by habit, resistant to change at the cellular level itself. Sri Aurobindo believed that *tamas* too could be gradually transformed by the descending light of the higher nature into *shama*, the stable peace and rest of the Divine.

Indeed, this process of transformation renders the human vessel (the physical body, nervous system and mental apparatus) capable of receiving the higher Divine inspirations without cracking up. The term *adhara* is sometimes used to describe this capability and basis to serve as a vehicle of consciousness and Divine manifestation. It is this that the evolved soul uses to express itself directly in the world. A strong aspiration and spiritual *sadhana* (involving purification and transformation of the *gunas*) are needed for one to work upon oneself constantly, so that the *adhara* is increasingly prepared to receive and express the Divine *Shakti* and *Ananda* that may sporadically descend upon it.

When the *adhara* is weak (inadequately developed or vulnerable to ego-centred desires), then the sudden descent of a strong spiritual current can cause trouble — leading to loss of equilibrium (physical or psychological) and proneness to all kinds of perversion, including false notions of high spiritual attainment. Yet, if care is taken to ensure that the *adhara* grows gradually in stability and strength, always surrendered to the Divine for true guidance, then the higher nature can manifest and flow unhindered. It is always helpful to take guidance from an authentic *guru*, who also provides inspiration and support. However, the ultimate *guru* is the Divine, who is bound to support the sincere aspirant in ever-mysterious ways, from within and outside. As made clear in the Gita, the *inner guru* is ever-present as the *Antaryami*. The soul within us, the *Antaratman*, has to evolve fully for its full emergence. This implies a continual effort of purification and transformation of the *gunas*, fired by a strong and sincere spiritual aspiration.

In Sri Aurobindo's words, the sincere aspirant needs to 'open the ranges of this inner being and to live from there outward, governing his outward life by an inner light and force. In doing so he discovers in himself his true soul, which is not this outer mixture of mental, vital and physical elements, but something of the Reality behind them, a spark from the one Divine Fire. He has to learn to live in his soul and purify and orientate by its drive towards the Truth the rest of the nature. There can follow afterwards an opening upward and descent of a higher principle of the Being.'[15.6]

This message is also conveyed effectively by the Mother (Mirra Alfassa), spiritual collaborator of Sri Aurobindo: 'This is the first thing necessary — aspiration for the Divine. The next thing you have to do is to tend it, to keep it always alert and awake and living. And for that what is required is concentration — concentration upon the Divine with a view to an integral and absolute consecration to its Will and Purpose. Concentrate in the heart. Enter into it; go within and deep and far, as far as you can. Gather all the strings of your consciousness that are spread abroad, roll them up and take a plunge and sink down. A fire is burning there, in the deep quietude of the heart. It is the divinity in you — your true being. Hear its voice, follow its dictates.'[15.7]

What happens when one communes with the Divine soul in one's innermost being, the Divine Fire in the deep quietude of the heart? If one can truly listen to the inner call and follow its dictates, one begins to manifest divinity in one's being, without hindrance by the lower nature. In such 'soul-centred living', one responds directly to the Divine Will and Purpose, serving as a fit instrument for the flow of Soul Forces (*Mahashakti*).

The theme of Divine manifestations is discussed in the next chapter.

16

Divine Manifestations: Soul Forces, *Avatar* and *Vibhuti*

In the last chapter, we stressed on the importance of purification and transformation of our *gunas*, so that we can ascend from the lower nature into our higher nature. This also implies that we live more authentic inner lives, awaken our inner being and thus access the innermost *Divine soul* in the depths of our hearts. Our outer actions should emerge from and reflect the truth of our inner being. In this chapter, we explore how the higher nature can flow as *Soul Forces* (*Mahashakti*) through the transformed individual being, and how the basic nature (*svabhava*) is itself uniquely different for each one of us. We will also see the role of the Divine *Avatar* and other Divine manifestations (*Vibhuti*) in the world.

True Inner Calling

Fulfilment in life can ultimately come only when we begin to fulfil our true inner calling, for which we have taken birth. Once the calling is discovered and responded to, fulfilment follows naturally, because the Divine *Soul Forces* then begin to start flowing, with an inherent and unstoppable Divine power.

The real difficulty for most of us lies in discovering that true calling, and preparing ourselves for its working out. Clearly, we need to go beyond the deficiency needs of our lower nature, and be *self-actualised* for this purpose. Each one of us carries some unique and precious gifts in the innermost being, the soul, that we need to discover and manifest. There are plenty of hints thrown at us during our life's journey, as to what this deep calling could be, but we often do not pay attention, and we tend to get carried away by the outer world and so-called 'peer pressures'.

We had used the terms, *kama-thrishna* and *bhava-thrishna* to describe these endless thirsts arising in the physical, vital and mental parts of our outer being. These thirsts have been alternatively likened in the Vedic tradition to fires (*agni*) that seek to be quenched. Once quenched, fresh fires of hunger invariably leap up again. Besides the primordial hunger in the body for food, there are the many vital fires seeking sensual pleasures, wealth, status, power and emotional bonding. There are also the mental fires for learning and for knowledge in various domains of interest. Behind all these outer fires, there burns quietly a Divine flame in everyone's innermost being. It is this fire and its gentle message, conveyed through the silence of the deep inner peace of the soul (inner voice) that we need to attend to and nurture. However, we can gain awareness of the existence of our innermost being only when we are able to deal effectively with all our outer fires. Else, the inner voice gets easily drowned in the cacophony of the myriad physical, vital and mental noises that habitually engage our attention.

When our deficiency needs get more or less quenched (or no longer affect us), and we are discriminate enough to understand the distinction between need and greed, then it becomes easier to pay attention to the inner voice, and to kindle the little flame of the soul in the depths of our hearts. By then, the physical, vital and mental parts of our being would have been well-trained — ready for use by the *Soul Forces* appropriately.

We always get some inkling of the latent *Soul Force* potentials in us when we find ourselves naturally resonating to some quality or skill. There are some things that we naturally love to do, and sometimes we can get so joyously absorbed that we do not even notice the passage of time. There may also be occasions when we surprise ourselves and others — by demonstrating spontaneously and naturally such a quality or skill. Thus for instance, we may discover a natural talent for oration, or for creative writing or poetry, or for sketching, drawing or painting, or for music or dance, or for healing, or for playing certain games or solving puzzles, or computer coding, or for mathematical concepts, or for scientific or philosophical pursuits. There are infinite domains of creative expression of the soul — for the sheer joy of it, and for seeking and manifesting truth, goodness and beauty. Expressions of creative art (such as poetry, painting, music and dance) are naturally more directly connected to the soul (than the more cerebral activities), which is why they are sometimes described as being soulful and soul-stirring.

Yet often, the purity of such creative expressions gets contaminated by the desires of our lower nature. For the ego-self is always waiting to cash in on these talents, and often we get lost and trapped in the lower nature, whereby the authentic flow of the Soul Forces gets blocked. In a true *flow state*, there is a clear realisation that something mysteriously sublime is happening, and the individual ego has nothing to do with it. The ego-self may of course attempt to step in later, and usurp and claim ownership and doership for what happened, but a truly self-aware individual knows the truth — the fact that many forces have apparently conspired to create collectively. This is how higher nature operates, full of *happy* coincidences. The inner calling thus becomes strong and clear. The inner flame gets kindled into a sacred fire that illumines the individual being, provides constant inner guidance, and also empowers appropriate action. The individual's physical-vital-mental instrumentation is made available for the use and command of the awakened soul, without any notion of 'doership'.

The shift from the ego-centred way of living in the lower nature to a soul-centred way in the higher nature is not easy, and there are likely to be teething troubles during the transition period, which can be prolonged. In Sri Aurobindo's words, 'Not only the vital and the body, but the mind also has to learn the Divine Truth and obey the Divine rule. But because of the lower nature and its continued hold on them, they are unable at first, and for a long time, to prevent their nature from following the old ways... It is only by persistent *sadhana*, by getting into the higher spiritual consciousness and spiritual nature that this difficulty can be overcome; but even for the strongest and best *sadhaks*, it takes a long time.' [16.1]

The awakening of the soul is signalled by several signs: a deep calm and inner peace, a quiet joy for no reason, a deep love towards all beings and things, a deep trust in the essential divinity and goodness in everyone and everything, a radiance from within, a deep appreciation of beauty, a feeling of vastness and connectedness, a clear motivation and inspiring purpose in work and life, frequent insights and intuitions, guidance and warnings from deep within, a strong communion with the Divine and an unshakeable faith.

With a deepening faith and focus on the innermost being, there comes a gradual shift in the centre of consciousness — from the surface being with its many pushes and pulls to the soul within. It then becomes easier to transform and integrate all the different and divergent parts of one's being, under the command of the evolved soul. Such evolution of the soul, according to the Indian wisdom tradition, is a very long process covering many lifetimes. This gets accelerated when the slow and seemingly unconscious process of evolution is replaced by conscious attempts at living within and abiding in an inner wakefulness. Then it becomes easier to listen to the inner voice, to respond to the inner calling and to invoke the Divine Soul Forces.

The focus of our spiritual concerns so far has been on the ascending evolutionary journey (individual and collective) from *asat* to *sat*, from *tamas* to *jyoti*, and from *mrityu* to *amritam*. In the individual's spiritual journey, it could be helpful to explore what it really means to function in the higher nature.

This requires us to flip our spiritual enquiry, and turn it on its head! Instead of asking: *What do I need to do to get there and be unconditionally happy?* how about asking: *I am already there: what now?* From a conventional religious prayer perspective, this could be translated as follows. Instead of praying perpetually: *Lord, give me this, give me that, so that I can be happy!* how about asking: *I am happy. Lord, what is it that I can do for You? How may I best serve as Your instrument?* Instead of pursuing ego-centred desires endlessly and wishing: *Let my will be done!* how about: *Not my will, but Thine be done!*

But what is that Divine Will? What is the purpose of this manifestation, this human incarnation? How is it linked to the larger purpose of the universe? Surely, the Divine soul in my innermost being, connected to the One Divine, knows. By means of dedicated *tapasya*, we know that we can really get to know this. We can also pay heed to Self-realised sages, who have undergone such *tapasya*.

The Four Soul Forces, *Mahashakti*

Sri Aurobindo describes the manifestation of *Para Prakriti* in man in terms of 'a fourfold effective Power, *chaturvyuha*: a Power for knowledge, a Power for strength, a Power for mutuality and active and productive relation and interchange, a Power for works and labour and service…'[16.2] The fourfold order of human society (*chaturvarnya*) is said to have come into being, manifesting these four cosmic principles. The earliest mention of these four orders appears in the ancient Vedic hymn, *Purushasukta*, which is dedicated to *Purusha*, who is symbolised as a huge archetypal Cosmic Being and Divine Creator, having a human form. The four orders are described as having emerged from the head, arms, thighs and feet of this symbolic deity.

Sri Aurobindo comments: 'To us this is merely a poetical image and its sense is that the *Brahmins* were the men of knowledge, the *Kshatriyas* the men of power, the *Vaishyas* the producers and support of society, the *Shudras* its servants... To them, this symbol of the Creator's body was more than an image, it expressed a Divine reality... Man and the cosmos are both symbols and expressions of the same hidden Reality.'[16.3]

In Gita verse 4.13, the Divine Teacher as *Purushottama*, states: 'The four orders of human society were created by Me, according to the divisions of the quality of temperament and related work function'. This is further elaborated in the following Gita verse, where the division is described in terms of qualities that arise from the individual's intrinsic nature (*svabhava*), which follows its own law of being (*svadharma*). This system degenerated over the millennia to the crude idea of a hierarchical and rigid caste system.

ब्राह्मणक्षत्रियविशां शूद्राणां च परन्तप ।
कर्माणि प्रविभक्तानि स्वभावप्रभवैर्गुणैः ||18.41||

The functions of Brahmins and Kshatriyas,	ब्राह्मण क्षत्रिय कर्माणि
As well as Vaishyas and Shudras, Arjuna,	विशां शूद्राणां च परन्तप
Are distributed according to qualities	प्रविभक्तानि गुणैः
That arise from their intrinsic nature.	स्वभावः प्रभवै

In Sri Aurobindo's words, 'We must realise that the ancient *Aryan Rishis* meant by the *chaturvarnya* not a mere social division, but a recognition of God manifesting Himself in fundamental svabhava, which our bodily distinctions, our social orders are merely an attempt to organise in the symbols of human life, often a confused attempt, often a mere parody and distortion of the Divine thing they try to express. Every man has in himself all the four *dharmas*, but one predominates, in one he is born and that strikes the note of his character and determines the type and cast of all his actions; the rest is subordinated to the dominant type and helps to give it its complement.'[16.4]

Sri Aurobindo uses the name *Mahashakti* ('Great Force') to describe the basic Divine energy-force of all manifestation. *Shakti*, we may recall, is another name for the higher Divine nature, also referred to as *Para Prakriti* — the dynamic and creative aspect of *Purushottama*. In the Indian *Tantric* tradition, this dynamic (energy-force) aspect of Divine consciousness is deified as the 'Divine Mother' of all. The four aspects (*Soul Forces*) of *Mahashakti* are summarised below, with names given by Sri Aurobindo in parenthesis:

(1) *Soul Force of Integral Knowledge and Wisdom (Maheshvari)*
(2) *Soul Force of Courageous Strength and Power (Mahakali)*
(3) *Soul Force of Harmonious Prosperity and Enjoyment (Mahalakshmi)*
(4) *Soul Force of Devoted Service and Perfection (Mahasarasvati)*

Clearly, all four (*Knowledge*, *Strength*, *Harmony* and *Service*, in short) are needed for success in any creation, cosmic or otherwise. First, the conception of the big picture of the proposed project, with an integral understanding of the different parts (sub-systems) and their relationship to the whole (overall system) arises. This is how the concept of *Brahman* (which includes everything — transcendental, universal and individual) came into being, and from which the term *Brahmin* ('one who knows *Brahman*') was originally derived.

Then, in order to implement what is conceived, there has to be a proper administration with the power to govern and the strength and valour to overcome all kinds of obstacles and resistances that inevitably arise. This is how the concept of *Kshatriya* came into being, having a dual role: military power (akin to '*Nobles of the Sword*' in the old European tradition) and administrative power ('*Nobles of the Robe*').

Further, there is a need to supervise and monitor the actual projects to be executed in society, and to distribute the benefits arising from it, so that this brings about harmony, prosperity and enjoyment to all concerned. This is how the concept of *Vaishya* came into being.

Finally, the actual work needs to be done to perfection, laboriously and painstakingly going into every detail, with an attitude of service and devotion. This is how the concept of *Shudra* came into being.

Clearly, all four *Soul Forces*, representing different aspects of the one Divine *Mahashakti*, are equally important. It is necessary to invoke and develop all four principles in our being. Yet, it seems to have been the Divine plan in creation to give predominance to at least one of these four aspects in an individual's inborn nature (*svabhavajam*, according to the Gita), with the others complementing. It is for each of us to discover which of the four soul natures naturally predominate — which we effortlessly resonate to. Thus we find that some amongst us are natural thinkers and visionaries, but may be relatively weak in other respects. Some may be naturally fearless, strong and courageous, or inclined towards governance. Yet others may be naturally inclined towards concerns about material prosperity and harmonious well-being. Still others may find joy in devotional service, skilled workmanship and meticulous perfection in work.

Viewed in this way, these attributes turn out to be deeply meaningful and necessary in life, for a fulfilling existence. There is also a universality in these descriptions, applicable to all peoples at all times. In this respect, they are like the three *gunas*. However, the *Soul Forces* (flowing through the purified *soul natures*) transcend the *gunas* and are free from bondage to the ego-self (*ahankara*). The distinct characteristics of these four soul natures are akin to the *svabhava* of different players in a game, such as cricket. Some cricketers naturally make good batsmen, while others make good bowlers. The players also need to be good fielders, although only some have a natural talent for fielding, while others may tend to bungle. Then of course, there may be some exceptional players who make good all-rounders; yet they too will be known best for one of their skills: batting, bowling or fielding.

Indeed, in any real project, it is necessary to recognise who is good at what, and for all the players to synergise through teamwork. Thus, it is possible to assign appropriate roles to the different team players, so that they can individually perform to their best capacities. Still, this is not enough. They also need to be able to complement one another and to integrate synergistically, inspired by a common vision and dedication (*shraddha*). It is such combined teamwork that can make the team unified, so that it looks like they are inseparable parts of one being — one Soul Force in splendid manifestation. Even spectators who are outside the game, get drawn spontaneously into such powerful and uplifting 'flow state' experiences. In the art of manifesting such flow in life, it is therefore necessary to have a deep appreciation for all four Soul Forces, and not just be narrowly focussed on one alone. Indeed, in some sense, we must all aim to be all-rounders ourselves, invoking all aspects of Divine Grace in our work and life.

We all need to know our relative strengths and weaknesses, and so work on them accordingly. Individual weaknesses can and should be compensated by corresponding strengths in others. Indeed, this is the essence of good leadership, and every prime minister or president or general or CEO needs to know this, when he chooses the key team members, at different levels. The only problem commonly encountered in any organisation is the clash of egos, and this arises when we are entrapped in the lower nature. It is only when we can rise to the higher nature that competition and rivalry can give way easily to cooperation, harmony, equality and synergy. It is then that these four Soul Forces start flowing, unhindered, with a common objective and an integral approach. This is spirituality at work at its best.

Let us consider the example of producing a book, which requires the efforts and participation of individuals with all four soul natures: (1) knowledge of the text to be conveyed, including inspiration, conception and clear understanding of the content, (2) strength and power to endure and overcome obstacles and resistances, (3) aesthetics and art in the book's layout and its marketing, as well as contractual agreements between author, publisher and distributor, and (4) actual production of the book, with attention to quality of paper and printing. Even the author of the book needs to invoke in his being this fourfold soul nature, although the knowledge aspect may appear to be the most predominant. The author too needs to overcome continually resistances, both from within (such as the 'writer's block') and outside (such as discouragement by reviewers and publishers). He or she also needs to invoke harmony and beauty in the thematic contents and design of the book, and also needs to work steadily and unhurriedly every day (over many months or perhaps years), paying meticulous attention to every detail and every word, aiming for perfection. There is agony and ecstasy underlying every creation, as every mother giving birth to a baby knows. The mother also knows and gratefully acknowledges that her womb was but a vessel for a Divine creation. Such indeed is the realisation of any creative artist or knowledge worker, functioning in the higher nature. All notions of intellectual property, rooted in the false notion of doership, are thus realised to be a myth, although they have a seeming validity in the lower nature.

Finally, we may note that according to ancient wisdom, the four soul natures are linked to the four basic elements in one's being: air (for Knowledge), fire (for Strength), water (for Harmony) and earth (for Service), with the fifth (and most subtle) element of ethereal space providing the supporting spiritual background for all (and specially connected to the air element). It is also believed that, in terms of *yogic* practices, *Jnanayoga* is most conducive for the *Knowledge soul nature*, *Rajayoga* for the *Strength soul nature*, *Bhaktiyoga* for the *Harmony soul nature* and *Karmayoga* for the *Service soul nature*. For an integral development, of course, all four kinds of *yoga* are indispensable.

The Soul Force of Integral Knowledge and Wisdom

We see from the descriptions of *chaturvarnya* in the Gita an emphasis on spiritual, psychological and ethical aspects, with a focus on *svadharma* based on *svabhava*. The following verse describes the *Brahmin's* 'inborn work and nature' (*brahmakarma svabhavajam*).

शमो दमस्तपः शौचं क्षान्तिरार्जवमेव च |
ज्ञानं विज्ञानमास्तिक्यं ब्रह्मकर्म स्वभावजम् ||18.42||

Serenity, self-control, austerity, purity,	शमः दमः तपः शौचं
Forbearance as well as uprightness,	क्षान्तिः आर्जवम् एव च
Knowledge, realised wisdom and piety	ज्ञानं विज्ञानम् आस्तिक्यं
Are the Brahmin's inborn nature for work.	ब्रह्म कर्म स्वभाव जम्

This Gita description may come as a surprise to many of us, because the widely prevalent notion (dating back to the *later Vedic* period) is that *Brahmins* are priests and teachers (with rigorous training in the Vedas and various religious rituals), and that only an offspring of a *Brahmin* could be a *Brahmin*. However, in the Gita description, there is no mention of work or life occupation or heredity. The Gita's description of the *Brahmin* is that of a person endowed with the purified *sattvic* qualities of serenity, self-control, austerity, purity, forbearance, uprightness, knowledge, realised wisdom and piety. These aspects, reflective of the *Soul Force of Integral Knowledge and Wisdom*, define the inborn nature and basis for work of the *Brahmin*.

As Sri Aurobindo points out: 'This is precisely what the Gita means and says, — that these things, their development, their expression in conduct, their power to cast into form the law of the sattvic nature are the real work of the *Brahmin*: learning, religious ministration and the other outer functions are only its most suitable field, a favourable means of this inner development, its appropriate self-expression, its way of fixing itself into firmness of type and externalised solidity of character.'[16.5]

The long enduring history of the *chaturvarnya* system in India, through the 'fixing' of the *svabhava* into 'firmness of type' (in each of the four soul natures) is attributable primarily to the idea of honour in society. Such honour was impressed through the ideals of piety, purity and pursuit of knowledge in the case of the *Brahmin varna*. Later, the emphasis shifted from the inner nature (with its spiritual, psychological and ethical basis) to its outer expression, which became more and more rigid in the case of all the four *varnas*.

In Sri Aurobindo's words: 'The outward expressions of the spirit or the ideal become more important than the ideal, the body or even the clothes more important than the person. Thus in the evolution of caste, the outward supports of the ethical fourfold order, — birth, economic function, religious ritual and sacrament, family custom, — each began to exaggerate enormously its proportions and its importance in the scheme... In the full economic period of caste, the priest and the *Pundit* masquerade under the name of the *Brahmin*, the aristocrat and feudal baron under the name of the *Kshatriya*... it has become a name, a shell, a sham...'[16.6]

It is but natural that society should witness major upheavals and corrections to such a system. Underlying these upheavals in the outer world, there is a *Divine Spirit* at work, and we will do well to go within deeply and thus connect with it. We need to get back to the inner essence (*sat*), rather than focus always on the outer form, which is ever subject to change (*asat*). We need to get back to the Gita's emphasis on the inner development of the *svabhava* of the soul nature, to understand its significance in a modern and universal context. It is something intrinsic, having a Divine spiritual basis primarily, and a psychological and ethical basis secondarily. Indeed, to support the inner development of any soul nature and the flow of the corresponding Soul Force, there has to be a suitable external expression of it. And that needs to be true to the associated *svadharma* (law of being). This outer work need not be linked to a means for livelihood. For indeed, the action of the Soul Force is always an expression of self-giving.

As mentioned earlier, *sattva-guna* gets transformed into the clear light of *jyoti* in the higher nature, and it is this that mainly characterises the *Soul Force of Integral Knowledge and Wisdom*. The *Godhead* of this *Soul Force* is described by Sri Aurobindo thus: 'Imperial *Maheshvari* is seated in the wideness above the thinking mind and will... who opens us to the supramental infinities and the cosmic vastness... Tranquil is she and wonderful, great and calm forever. Nothing can move her because all wisdom is in her; nothing is hidden from her that she chooses to know; she comprehends all things and all beings and their nature and what moves them and the law of the world and its times and how all was and is and must be... the Truth of things is her one concern, knowledge her centre of power and to build our soul and our nature into the Divine Truth her mission and her labour.'[16.7]

It is by the descent of the light of this Knowledge Soul Force that the mind is able to access higher potentials and ways of knowing Truth that lie beyond the ordinary range of human mentality (i.e., logical rational thinking). These include intuitions received in mental silence, mystic illuminations and insights, leading to 'knowledge by identity' and unity consciousness — various supramental grades that Sri Aurobindo describes at length, based on his own personal realisations.

Here knowledge is received by revelation, as evidenced by the flashes of insight and intuition reported by so many artists, scientists and mathematicians. The genius mathematician, Srinivasa Ramanujan, for example, credited his mathematical findings to the Goddess of Namagiri, who appeared in his visions, proposing mathematical formulae. Nikola Tesla, the genius inventor of alternating current and many electric devices, discovered that he could clearly visualise his discoveries and even work on them in his mind. He thus conducted many virtual experiments on his devices in his imagination, to know which ones would work and which would not, with a high certitude of truth.

In the lower nature, one has to work through the play of the three *gunas*, till the *guna* composition becomes predominantly *sattvic* and ready for transformation to *jyoti* in the higher nature. It is possible for one with a Knowledge soul nature to lose one's way in the lower nature, and so function in a predominantly *rajasic* or even *tamasic* way. So even though outwardly, the life occupation may be conducive for the expression of the *Knowledge Soul Force*, the authentic expression of the soul nature may be marred in many ways, blocking any possibility of descent of the *Soul Force*. Thus, intellectuals, thinkers, teachers, academics and scientists in the modern world will do well to tend to their soul nature, in order to live fulfilling lives and make significant contributions to the world.

The Soul Force of Courageous Strength and Power

The widely prevalent notion of *Kshatriyas* is that they are kings, governors and warriors — i.e., in terms of their occupation. However, the Gita's description of the *Kshatriya* is that of a person endowed with the purified *rajasic-sattvic* qualities of heroism, fiery energy, fortitude, skill, valour in battle, generosity and majesty in conduct. These aspects, reflective of the *Soul Force of Courageous Strength and Power*, define the inborn nature and work of the *Kshatriya*. The following Gita verse describes the Kshatriya's inborn work and nature (*kshatram karma svabhavajam*), reflecting an emphasis on spiritual, psychological and ethical aspects.

शौर्यं तेजो धृतिर्दाक्ष्यं युद्धे चाप्यपलायनम् ।
दानमीश्वरभावश्च क्षात्रं कर्म स्वभावजम् ।।18.43।।

Heroism, fiery energy, fortitude, skill,	शौर्यं तेजः धृतिः दाक्ष्यं
And also not running away in battle,	युद्धे च अपि अपलायनम्
Generosity and great majesty in conduct	दानम् ईश्वर भावः च
Are the Kshatriya's inborn nature for work.	क्षात्रं कर्म स्वभाव जम्

As Sri Aurobindo points out: 'War, government, politics, leadership and rule are a similar field and means for the *Kshatriya*; but his real work is the development, the expression in conduct, the power to cast into form and dynamic rhythm of movement the law of the active battling royal or warrior spirit.'[16.5]

The social honour (which contributed much to the long endurance of the *chaturvarnya* system in India) was originally rooted, in the case of the *Kshatriya*, in the ideals of courage, strength, nobility, self-restraint and mastery. Gradually, over the millennia, these ideals lost their authenticity, and eventually, as Sri Aurobindo points out, the 'aristocrat and feudal baron' came to 'masquerade under the name of the *Kshatriya*'. Today, the concept of the noble *Kshatriya* lives mostly in legend and myth, sustained by television serials.

It is the *svabhava* of the soul nature of the *Kshatriya*, described eloquently in the Gita, that we need to understand afresh, in the present context. Some of us are naturally endowed with the *Strength soul nature*, and it is this that we need to nurture, staying true to the underlying *svadharma*. There is a strong presence of *rajo-guna* in such individuals, a fire that needs to be refined, tempered and purified with the aid of *sattva-guna*. Eventually, that fire has to be transformed into *tapas* in the higher nature, where it becomes a powerful instrument of the Divine Will — to fight injustice without fear, to give protection to goodness, to uphold virtue, to stand up for truth, to assert with confidence and power whenever required, and thus nurture the evolutionary journey of humanity from Darkness to Light. The battles that are to be fought thus are provided by life-situations in a wide variety of contexts. While, for most people faced with challenging conflicts in life, there is a 'flight or fight' option, there is but one option that comes up naturally for the Strength soul nature — and that is to fight, and never to flee from battle.

Indeed, individuals with such a *soul nature* often demonstrate their potentials of strength, courage and valour early in life. The fire element in them is clearly perceptible to all. They often surprise themselves and others when their abilities are in full flow, especially when triggered by conflict and competition. This could happen spontaneously, for example, the champion John McEnroe was known to produce his best tennis in a fiery fit of anger! Fiery speeches and writings have sometimes turned the course of human history. Battles with adversaries are not necessarily fought in a battlefield or a boxing ring or wrestling pit. This is reflected in the popular saying: the pen is mightier than the sword! An individual who has developed his or her Strength soul nature is a formidable adversary to encounter — whether in a battlefield or playground or debating platform, whether in the workplace or at home!

The power is especially strong, when it is conserved through *tapas* (and not frittered away), so that when it is unleashed, it either emerges victorious or goes down in great glory, earning the respect and admiration of all. However, it is important that the cause be noble and just, for without this *sattvic* element, such power can be dangerous. The Divine Teacher of the Gita urges the warrior Arjuna to invoke this *Soul Force of Courageous Strength and Power* at the Kurukshetra battlefield. What may appear to be violent and *destructive* (locally and temporally) is often constructive (in a global and long-term Divine perspective). Such course corrections, though painful, must be necessarily endured. However, untempered *rajas* can be all-devouring and all-corrupting (*mahashano mahapapma*). The power has to be used wisely and skilfully, and only when required. Thus, a brilliant *Samurai* warrior or a Master of the *martial arts* often walks around innocuously in the world, never displaying his or her powers, except in situations where this is truly warranted. But to arrive at this level of self-mastery, a great deal of practice (*sadhana*) and spiritual development is needed. One must be guided from within one's soul to know when to act (with seeming violence) swiftly, unhesitatingly and powerfully, and when not to.

The *svabhava* of the untempered fiery temperament is to lash out in anger (sometimes, with the tongue) at the slightest provocation, but when developed through the practice of *tapas*, it is also capable of containing and mastering the fire within (rather than releasing it impulsively or wrathfully), transforming its heat into light. Indeed, fire is a great purifier. For this reason, practices of *Rajayoga* are recommended for this soul nature, while *Jnanayoga* would obviously resonate more easily with the *Knowledge* soul nature. Some individuals, like Swami Vivekananda, are known to resonate well with both soul natures, although it would appear that the Strength Soul Force is more predominant in his case, for he truly served as a mighty spiritual warrior.

Strength (*bala* or *shakti*) can manifest in different parts of one's being: typically, as *physical* strength (*deha-bala*), *vital* strength (*indriya-bala* or *prana-bala*) or *mental* strength (*mano-bala*). Without proper control, each of these can be dangerous (as in the use of brute force or cunning). The ultimate strength is *spiritual* strength (*atma-bala*), emerging from one's innermost being. It is this soul strength that needs to be awakened, to guide and integrate the other three components of strength. It is then that the Soul Force of Courageous Strength and Power can flow effectively in the higher nature through the different instrumental parts of being. Liberated from ego-desire, the use of this strength becomes an expression of self-giving for a noble cause. Such inner strength and power can express itself outwardly in a wide variety of ways — not necessarily violent, as demonstrated by Mahatma Gandhi. There is a bold calmness and freedom from fear underlying such passive inner strength, which is capable of confronting any crisis or apparent misfortune, and it is this that needs to be nurtured through a daily *sadhana*. Gandhi advocated the principle of *Svaraj*, which is commonly understood to mean self-governance (associated with India's independence movement), but he meant it in an integral sense: 'If we become free, India is free. And in this thought you have a definition of Svaraj. It is Svaraj when we learn to rule ourselves.'[16.8]

Sri Aurobindo describes the main qualities of *Mahakali*, the Godhead of this Soul Force: 'There is in her an overwhelming intensity, a mighty passion of force to achieve, a Divine violence rushing to shatter every limit and obstacle. All her divinity leaps out in a splendour of tempestuous action; she is there for swiftness, for the immediately effective process, the rapid and direct stroke, the frontal assault that carries everything before it… She is the Warrior of the Worlds who never shrinks from the battle… her love is as intense as her wrath and she has a deep and passionate kindness… But for her what is done in a day might have taken centuries…'[16.9]

Thus, this Divine intervention through individuals with the Strength soul nature gets manifest. But clearly, this work needs to be complemented by the Knowledge soul nature for it to be rightly directed by wisdom; by the Harmony soul nature for it to be agreeable and directed towards prosperity; and also by the Service soul nature to work devotedly and steadfastly and thus achieve perfection in all that gets manifest. All four are necessary, although it is natural that there be differences in individual preferences, depending on the relative dominance of the four soul natures in any individual. The Gita instruction is to discover and be true to the primary *svabhava* and *svadharma* that one naturally resonates to in one's soul. The other soul natures are also to be developed, but remain naturally subservient to, and complement one's primary soul nature, which asserts itself effortlessly and spontaneously.

The Soul Force of Harmonious Prosperity and Enjoyment

Throughout the Gita, there is an emphasis on inner quality and spirit as the basis of expression in work, function and action in the outer world. This is also evidenced in Gita verses 18.42 and 18.43, describing in detail the intrinsic *svabhava* of the *Brahmin* and the *Kshatriya* (representing the *Knowledge* and *Strength* soul natures, respectively). Curiously, we find this missing in the following verse, which describes the *svabhava* of the other two soul natures: the *Vaishya* and *Shudra* (representing the *Harmony* and *Service* soul natures) in terms of farming, cattle-herding, commerce and service-related work respectively.

Sri Aurobindo explains: 'The work of the *Vaishya* and *Shudra* is expressed in terms of external function, and this opposite turn may have some significance. For the temperament moved to production and wealth-getting or limited in the circle of labour and service, the mercantile and the servile mind, are usually turned outward, more occupied with the external values of their work than its power for character, and this disposition is not so favourable to a sattvic or spiritual action of the nature… Nevertheless, this kind of nature too and its functions have their inner significance, their spiritual value and can be made a means and power for perfection.'[16.10]

कृषिगौरक्ष्यवाणिज्यं वैश्यकर्म स्वभावजम् ।
परिचर्यात्मकं कर्म शूद्रस्यापि स्वभावजम् ।।18.44।।

Farming, cattle-herding and commerce	कृषि गौ रक्ष्य वाणिज्यं
Are the Vaishya's inborn nature for work.	वैश्य कर्म स्वभावजम्
Work related to doing service	परिचर्या आत्मकं कर्म
Is the Shudra's inborn nature.	शूद्रस्य अपि स्वभावजम्

The social honour of the *Vaishya* was originally supported by honesty in trade, mercantile fidelity, quality of goods produced, generosity and philanthropy, while that of the *Shudra* was sustained by faithful service, obedience and subordination. The Harmony and Service soul natures seem to function largely through temperaments that seem predominantly *rajasic-tamasic* and *tamasic* respectively. While making this observation, we should refrain from being judgemental, recognising that each one of us contains all four soul natures that need to be appropriately developed. There is a Divine Soul Force underlying each, waiting to descend into and flow through the individual being in the higher nature. This calls for purification and refinement in our *guna* nature, with the aid of *sattva-guna* and Divine Grace.

The fourfold order of the *chaturvarnya* system and its subsequent deterioration, due to hardening of external structures, social hierarchy and exploitation, are not unique to India. For example, in Europe there existed broad social orders of a hierarchically conceived society, since the Middle Ages: notably the three 'estates' of clergy, nobility and commoners. The commoners got divided further into urban 'burghers' (bourgeoise), who later became rich and influential, and 'rural commoners' (peasants and serfs), the 'wage-earners', who later included industrial labour (the proletariat). Class conflicts became inevitable, and following the French Revolution in 1789 and its clarion call for 'liberty, equality and fraternity' (whose essence is truly spiritual), the world has witnessed all kinds of social, economic and political upheavals, with theocracies and monarchies getting replaced by republics and democracies.

With the advent of *globalisation*, there is now an increased focus on interchange of world views, economic trade, products and culture, and these exchanges have been tremendously accelerated by the digital revolution and the internet. All these aspects reflect a predominance of the soul nature of harmonious prosperity and enjoyment in the current world scenario. It would appear that all our modern spheres of activity, including education and science, seem to focus on this domain. Education has itself become a big business, having the primary objective of giving degree certificates that serve as a means of livelihood and a better standard of living. Almost everything is measured in terms of money, and higher paying jobs are much valued and sought after, regardless of whether the job profile resonates with one's true soul nature or not. Scientific research is also highly valued if the findings and inventions can lead to the generation of significant profits, and multinational corporations are ready to make large investments in such research, and also in the marketing and advertising of such products, often disregarding any adverse effects they may have (to human life and the environment). Market forces rule everything and determine almost all our choices in life.

The emphasis here is primarily on material and vital well-being — on wealth, physical comforts and sensual enjoyments, reflective of a focus on a *rajasic-tamasic* lifestyle, centred in the lower vital being. Sadly, such lifestyles, anchored in consumerism, materialism, high-energy consumption and high costs to the environment, are not sustainable for human society as a whole. It is therefore essential to awaken the inner being in us, instead of getting lost in the outer world. It is necessary to know the dangers of losing our way on the path of *preyas,* where we lose discrimination between need and greed (and become vulnerable to corruption), as mentioned earlier. We will then not find the fulfilment we seek. The Harmony soul nature seeks primarily to find harmony and beauty as expressions of love (whose domain is the realm of the higher vital), and not just enjoyment of pleasures (in the realm of the lower vital). This calls for developing loving relationships with others, and for generous sharing of resources for the well-being of all. Further, this soul nature calls for developing inventions and technologies with the motive of nurturing life and well-being.

Thus, there are two errors that we need to awaken to, in the present scenario we find ourselves in. Firstly, not all of us have this Soul nature of harmonious prosperity and enjoyment as our primary nature, and so we will do well to pause in the *rat race*, discover our authentic soul nature and thus be true to it. Secondly, even if this indeed happens to be our authentic soul nature, we need to realise the true objectives of this nature, and thus purify and transform our *guna* nature, and so allow for the flow of the Harmony Soul Force. We will then be able to understand our role in the big picture of unfolding Divinity in manifestation.

Sri Aurobindo outlines the main qualities of the Godhead of this Soul Force: '...all turn with joy and longing to *Mahalakshmi*... grace and charm and tenderness flow out from her like light from the sun... Harmony and beauty of the mind and soul... harmony and beauty of the life and surroundings, this is the demand of *Mahalakshmi*... But all that is ugly and mean and base, all that is poor and sordid and squalid, all that is brutal and coarse repels her advent... Life is turned in her supreme creations into a rich work of celestial art and all existence into a poem of sacred delight; the world's riches are brought together and concerted for a supreme order and even the simplest and commonest things are made wonderful by her intuition of unity and the breath of her spirit.'[16.11]

Thus, we see the qualities of harmony, beauty, love, generosity, creativity and joy in the work of this Soul Force, whose very nature is an abundant self-giving and a joyous celebration of life through creation. We do get to see different aspects of this Soul Force manifesting in great individuals. We see this in some entrepreneurs, big and small, who while setting up creative and lucrative business ventures, have also become philanthropists, pledging their money for noble causes and societal development. The planning of cities and towns must ideally reflect this larger vision of progressive harmony and aesthetic design. The Mother who conceived the international township at Auroville (to realise human unity) had this advice to offer with regard to money and its right use: 'Money is meant to increase the wealth, the prosperity and the productiveness of a group, a country or, better, of the whole earth. Money is a means, a force, a power, and not an end in itself. And like all forces and all powers, it is by movement and circulation that it grows and increases its power, not by accumulation and stagnation.'[16.12] It is this indeed that is implicit in the concept of *lokasangraham* in the Gita.

The Soul Force of Devoted Service and Perfection

We shall now look at the fourth soul nature — last but not least, often undervalued and ill-treated, but without which no work can really get done or completed. Without developing and manifesting this soul nature, it would be impossible to find fulfilment in any of the other soul natures. We will realise this when we get a deeper understanding of the essence of this soul nature. In Sri Aurobindo's words, 'The ancients held that all men are born in their lower nature as *Shudras* and only regenerated by ethical and spiritual culture... For the soul powers that belong to the full development of this force in us are of the greatest importance — the power of service to others, the will to make our life a thing of work and use to God and man, to obey and follow and accept whatever great influence and needful discipline, the love which consecrates service, a love which asks for no return... Man could not be perfect and complete if he had not this element of nature in him to raise to its Divine power.'[16.13]

It is therefore with this perspective that we will do well to view this soul nature, rather than the widespread view of the much-maligned and under-privileged *Shudra*. For indeed, it is true that if the predominant *guna* nature were to be one of untransformed *tamas*, 'the natural *Shudra* works not from a sense of the dignity of labour or from the enthusiasm of service... but for the maintenance of his existence and gratification of his primal wants, and when these are satisfied, he indulges, if left to himself, his natural indolence', whereas, 'the well-developed *Shudra* soul-type has the instinct of toil and the capacity of labour and service.'[16.13] Slowly and steadily, the practice of *Karmayoga*, when combined sincerely with *Bhaktiyoga*, can ripen into perfection, bringing the required purification and transformation. Thus, through sustained practice, it is possible for *tamas* to eventually get transformed to *shama*, the Divine and awakened peace, while work continues to be done diligently as devoted service. When the grace descends into the Service soul nature, it manifests as a Divine flow of the Soul Force of Devoted Service and Perfection.

Sri Aurobindo outlines the main qualities of *Mahasarasvati*, the Godhead of this Soul Force: 'The science and craft and technique of things are *Mahasarasvati's* province. Always she holds in her nature and can give to those whom she has chosen the intimate and precise knowledge, the subtlety and patience, the accuracy of intuitive mind and conscious hand and discerning eye of the perfect worker. This Power is the strong, the tireless, the careful and efficient builder, organiser, administrator, technician, artisan and classifier of the worlds... her action is laborious and minute and often seems to our impatience, slow and interminable, but it is persistent, integral and flawless.'[16.14]

According to our ancient wisdom, underlying all manifestation (involving creation, maintenance and destruction), there is a Divinity at work. Even what appears to be devastating destruction (sometimes brought about by the Godhead of Courageous Strength and Power) serves a Divine purpose that seems inscrutable to the limited human understanding. Invariably, it is the Godhead of Devoted Service and Perfection, who continues work under all circumstances, converting even seeming destruction eventually into a perfect and beautiful construction. It is akin to the work of a sculptor chipping away pieces from a block of stone, steadily and laboriously — the statue that gets sculpted to perfection gets revealed and marvelled at, only much later.

A striking example of the Service soul nature is Mother Teresa, who dedicated herself completely and wholeheartedly to the service of the poor, in response to a deep inner calling. She was deeply inspired spiritually and moved by compassion. Similarly, when the inspiration is drawn from a great Master (representing the One Divine), to whom all work is consecrated and carried out to perfection, in absolute obedience, the Service Soul Force is bound to flow. In the great Indian epic, *Ramayana*, this aspect is powerfully depicted by the character of Hanuman, who is an epitome of this Soul nature of dedicated service and perfection, but is also one in whom all the other soul natures are also exceptionally well developed, especially Knowledge and Strength.

Developing the Service soul nature is thus indispensable for a perfect manifestation of spirituality at work, regardless of what one's basic soul nature may be. This forms the core of the *yoga* of the Gita.

Brilliant Manifestation of the Divine, *Vibhuti*

To gain fulfilment at the individual level, it is often said (notably, by Stephen Covey and others) that there has to be a confluence of four factors. First, one has to recognise and develop one's unique talents (what you're good at). Secondly, one has to develop and sustain a passion for doing work related to the expression of these talents (what you love to do). Thirdly, the work that one has taken upon oneself must be *sattvic* in nature, having the sanction and approval of one's innermost being, one's soul (what you know truly to be your inner calling). Finally, this work must satisfy some great *need* (or address some serious shortcoming or suffering) in society or in the world at large, necessary for course correction or to promote well-being, for the sake of *lokasangraham* (what the world needs). When all these four aspects converge in the self-actualised individual, who is ready to ascend to the higher nature, the individual concerned becomes a *Vibhuti*, through whom the Divine Soul Forces choose to flow.

There is an entire chapter (chapter 10) in the Gita, titled *Vibhuti Yoga* (*Yoga of Divine Manifestation*), in which the Divine Teacher as the *Avatar*, gives various examples of the Divine power manifesting in many forms in the universe, and especially in *human* forms over the ages. The Gita's intent here is to reveal the Divine potential and destiny in man, who can realise and manifest this divinity by breaking through the veils of ignorance of ego-entrapment in the lower nature, and attaining union with the Divine. It is through examples of the human *Vibhuti* that we can glimpse our own potentials awaiting realisation.

यद्यद्विभूतिमत्सत्त्वं श्रीमदूर्जितमेव वा ।
तत्तदेवावगच्छ त्वं मम तेजोंऽशसम्भवम् ||10.41||

Whatever being manifests splendour, यत् यत् विभूति मत् सत्त्वं
Great beauty or power and glory, श्री मत् ऊर्जितम् एव वा
Know all that brilliance to emerge तत् तत् एव अवगच्छ त्वं सम्भवम्
As a fraction of My potent energy! मम तेजः अंश

In verse 10.37, the Divine Teacher names Arjuna as a *Vibhuti* ('I am Arjuna among the Pandavas') through whom the Divine Strength Soul Force is waiting to unleash itself. And indeed, it is for this purpose that Krishna has chosen to be his charioteer. Yet, time seems to be running out at the Kurukshetra battlefield, and Arjuna is not yet fully convinced of the Divine purpose. Hence, the Divine Teacher has to resort to a final and most convincing demonstration of his own divinity, by bestowing on Arjuna a vision of the *World-Purusha* (in the eleventh chapter of the Gita).

तस्मात्त्वमुत्तिष्ठ यशो लभस्व जित्वा शत्रून् भुङ्क्ष्व राज्यं समृद्धम् ।
मयैवैते निहताः पूर्वमेव निमित्तमात्रं भव सव्यसाचिन् ||11.33||

Hence, raise yourself, win glory! तस्मात् त्वम् उत्तिष्ठ यशः लभस्व
Conquering the enemies, enjoy जित्वा शत्रून् भुङ्क्ष्व
Prosperity in the kingdom! राज्यं समृद्धम्
They have already been killed निहताः पूर्वम् एव
By My will; just be the occasion, मया एव एते निमित्त मात्रं भव
Just be the instrument, Arjuna! सव्यसाचिन्

Seeing is believing, as the old saying goes. So, Arjuna has to see, in advance, to believe the enormity of his Divine role in the cosmic play, in making *Kurukshetra* truly into a *Dharmakshetra*. In that vision, Arjuna gets to foresee that all the enemies that he is required to slay have already met with their end. All that remains for Arjuna is to 'be the occasion, the Divine instrument' (*nimittamatram bhava*).

The question each one of us needs to ask here is: 'What is my role, my life purpose?' The answer to this question can get revealed to any sincere aspirant, by posing it directly to the Divine, who abides in our own innermost being, in the soul. It is by discovering and developing our respective soul natures, and consecrating our lives to the One Divine, that we get to be shown the way for the Godhead to emerge in our being, to serve the Divine Will and the big picture that the human instrument can barely get to glimpse.

It is not as if everything is pre-planned for us to execute. On the contrary, the situation is dynamic and organic, full of infinite possibilities, where awakened human souls are required to assist in a Divine co-creation. The inner light shows the way, not all at once, but a step at a time. It is like holding a candle in the dark. The way is lit but for a short distance. But that is adequate for us to move with confidence and inner certitude, if we are soul-centred. For as we progress, we find that our entire path gets illuminated and revealed to us in stages. At some stage, everything becomes spontaneous and effortless — the physical, vital and mental parts of our being serve as instruments of a Divine flow. This is the ultimate expression of spirituality at work.

The Role of the *Avatar*

The higher nature is ever willing to descend upon us, if only we are capable of receiving that Grace, by preparing ourselves for it. The Sanskrit term for such descent is *avatarana*, from which the term *Avatar* is derived. While the *Avatar* represents divinity descended upon humanity as a Divine incarnation (of *Ishvara-Shakti*) in human form (always anchored in the higher nature), the human *Vibhuti* refers to one who is able to ascend into the higher nature during his or her lifetime.

Sometimes, the work done by *Vibhutis* (and other partial and temporal manifestations of the Divine power) is inadequate to serve the purpose of evolution of consciousness — to inspire human beings to evolve consciously. The *Purushottama* then chooses to opt for a more direct Divine intervention, by descending on earth in appropriate forms, fully Self-aware of the Divine purpose.

It is thus we have such Divine incarnations in human form, *Avatars*, at various times and in various places, to serve various purposes. However, because of the embodiment in the human form, the *Avatar* is naturally constrained by the human body's limitations, and so also has to undergo the joys and sorrows that humans experience. These apparent limitations also tend to conceal their '*Avatarhood*', except when they choose to break out of them occasionally, by performing so-called miracles.

In Sri Aurobindo's words, 'The Divine takes upon himself the human nature with all its outward limitations and makes them the circumstances, means, instruments of the Divine consciousness and the Divine power, a vessel of the Divine birth and the Divine works.'[16.15]

Thus the *Avatar* is not one who is a miracle performer or supernormal magician, but one who shows how the human can ascend to the Divine. The *Avatar* also undergoes human suffering — but even such suffering can serve as a means of redemption, as demonstrated by Christ and Buddha in their different ways. In the Gita, the *Avatar* of Krishna reveals his identity with none other than the *Purushottama* to Arjuna and shows the way of the *Karmayogin* through his own personal example.

न मे पार्थास्ति कर्तव्यं त्रिषु लोकेषु किञ्चन ।
नानवाप्तमवाप्तव्यं वर्त एव च कर्मणि ।।3.22।।

There's no work to be done by Me	न मे अस्ति कर्तव्यं किञ्चन
In all the three worlds, Arjuna,	त्रिषु लोकेषु पार्थ
Nothing unattained for Me to gain,	न अनवाप्तम् अवाप्तव्यं
And yet, I engage in work!	वर्त एव च कर्मणि

Clearly, the Self-aware *Avatar* has no personal need or desire to work, for there is nothing to be gained that the Divine is not already in possession of. Yet, the *Avatar* of Krishna works relentlessly, but without any ego-identity. That is the way of the *Karmayogin*, and the *Avatar* here sets the standard for such work.

There is another specific purpose for the *Avatarhood* of Krishna, as revealed in the following two celebrated Gita verses — to re-establish *Dharma*, again and again.

A superficial reading of these verses may suggest that the descent of the *Avatar* is intended primarily to punish the wicked and protect the good. This could well be achieved by other means of Divine omnipotence. There is a higher purpose, and a higher *Dharma*, not evident to ordinary humans.

यदा यदा हि धर्मस्य ग्लानिर्भवति भारत ।
अभ्युत्थानमधर्मस्य तदात्मानं सृजाम्यहम् ।।4.7।।

Arjuna, whenever there is	यदा यदा हि भवति भारत
A decadence of dharma,	धर्मस्य ग्लानिः
Unrighteousness uprising,	अभ्युत्थानम् अधर्मस्य
Then I manifest Myself.	तदा आत्मानं सृजामि अहम्

परित्राणाय साधूनां विनाशाय च दुष्कृताम् |
धर्मसंस्थापनार्थाय सम्भवामि युगे युगे ||4.8||

For the protection of the good	परित्राणाय साधूनां
And the destruction of evil-doers,	विनाशाय च दुष्कृताम्
For re-establishing the dharma,	धर्म संस्थापन अर्थाय
I come into being, age after age!	सम्भवामि युगे युगे

The real *Dharma* that the *Avatar* seeks to establish is not mere *justice*, but something special through personal example: 'Each Incarnation holds before men his own example and declares of himself that he is the way and the gate; he declares too the oneness of his humanity with the Divine being, declares that the Son of Man and the Father above from whom he has descended are one, that Krishna in the human body... and the supreme Lord and Friend of all creatures are but two revelations of the same Divine Purushottama...'[16.16]

In the next chapter, we will explore the power of *Bhaktiyoga*: the path of devotion, which is essential in *Integral Karmayoga*.

17

The *Yoga* of Devotion, *Bhaktiyoga*

अपि चेत्सुदुराचारः भजते मामनन्यभाक् ।
साधुरेव स मन्तव्यः सम्यग्व्यवसितो हि सः ||9.30||

If even one with extremely evil conduct	अपि चेत् सुदुराचारः
Worships Me with undivided devotion,	भजते माम् अनन्य भाक्
He should be deemed as virtuous,	साधः एव सः मन्तव्यः
Because his will is rightly resolved!	सम्यक् व्यवसितः हि सः

The above Gita verse points to the power of the path of devotion, which can serve as a saving grace for anyone, even if, trapped in the depths of our lower nature, we find ourselves indulging in wicked ways. For, as the Gita explains, even so-called sinful or evil behaviour is but the action of *Asuric* forces that we have allowed to enter into our being (often helplessly). The resulting unbridled play of the *gunas* of *rajas* and *tamas* can cause much havoc. When we are thus possessed by the powers of darkness and ignorance, it is difficult for the light of self-awareness and *sattva-guna* to awaken in us and purify us. Nevertheless, we are bound to feel the ill effects of the dysfunctional nature of our behaviour, and be dimly aware that we need help to save ourselves.

There is a Divine Indweller abiding in the depths of all our hearts, waiting to be called upon, and any movement in this direction is considered to be a right resolve. When we thus realise our folly and resolve to make amends sincerely, we arrest our fall. We aspire to align ourselves to the evolutionary movement of consciousness, which is divinely supported: from *asat* to *sat*, from *tamas* to *jyoti*, and from *mrityu* to *amritam*. The only problem is that we may not quite know what to do — how to actually make amends.

Under such circumstances, devotion to the Divine is a powerful way (some would say — *the only way*) to save ourselves. If the devotion is heartfelt and sincere, it is bound to get rewarded. The Divine Indweller is said to be like a mother eager to help the misguided child, no matter how wicked, for the mother's love is boundless. The Divine Teacher of the Gita goes on to suggest that if this devotion develops and becomes strong, such individuals should be deemed to be on par with the virtuous (*sadhu*), regardless of the apparent wickedness in their outer behaviour. The transformation in the behaviour at the outer level is likely to be slow at the early stages, but it is bound to manifest as the devotion grows and becomes one-pointed and undivided (*ananyabhak*). The saint begins to unfold in the sinner.

This is the assurance given with respect to the path of devotion as the way forward for the extremely wicked. How much easier then it would be for those who are not-so-wicked (especially those endowed with a predominance of *sattva-guna*), to be thus rightly resolved. Devotion (*bhakti*) is considered to be the easiest and most direct way to awaken the soul in the depths of our hearts, for the seat of the soul is said to be located close behind the heart *chakra* (seat of deep emotions). Such devotion can be developed into a means of practice (*yoga*) for soul-centred living (as against the default ego-centred living). When developed fully, it arrives at its culmination in an irrevocable union with the Divine (which is the higher meaning of *yoga*). Thus, the term *Bhaktiyoga* refers to both the sustained practice of devotion and its ultimate realisation. In this sense, *Bhaktiyoga* is profoundly different from mere *bhakti* (devotion).

Intellectual minds, given to rational thinking, may not find the path of devotion appealing initially, and may even be inclined to look down on it with some degree of condescension. It is sometimes mocked at as blind faith, as something naive and stupid. However, as they advance spiritually through alternative paths more suited for their temperament, particularly the practice of the *yoga of knowledge* (*Jnanayoga*), they discover that they are dealing here with a supreme Divine mystery, which transcends the limits of the mind and its associated intellectual arrogance.

The discovery and realisation of oneness is something that is felt integrally in one's being, not just intellectually, but also emotionally as love. There is also a deep sense of sacredness experienced. Devotion is just another name for this sacred love. It manifests in the soul as a profound longing — a yearning of the separate self to serve and surrender, and eventually merge with the One Divine Source. In the path of *Karmayoga*, devotion is naturally implied in the consecration required of the work and its fruit to the Divine (as a sacrifice, *yajna*), although here the emphasis is on the underlying attitude and quality of work done. There is bound to be a growing awareness of the validity of different paths of *yoga*, suitable for different soul natures, with all the apparently different streams flowing into the same Divine ocean. There are clear indications in the Gita that all three paths (*Karmayoga*, *Jnanayoga* and *Bhaktiyoga*) are inter-dependent and need to be integrated. The ultimate objective is to rise above the entrapments of the lower nature and to settle into our higher Divine nature.

Purification of the *gunas* by means of a steadily growing *sattvic* impulse is essential for this. Sri Aurobindo observes that 'while the soul is enlarging into Self-knowledge, it has also to increase in devotion. For it has not only to act in a large spirit of equality, but to do also sacrifice to the Lord, to that Godhead in all beings which it does not yet know perfectly, but which it will be able so to know, integrally...

Equality and vision of unity once perfectly gained... a supreme *bhakti*, an all-embracing devotion to the Divine, becomes the whole and the sole law of the being.'[17.1]

In the absence of such supreme *bhakti*, there is the danger in the path of *Jnanayoga* of an escapism into excessive quietism, absorption in the Immutable and consequent abandoning of work that needs to be done. Similarly, in the path of *Karmayoga*, there is the danger of excessive engagement in work and getting tossed and turned by the dualities of the lower nature, owing to the inability to act in a large spirit of equality. Thus, the insistence of *Bhaktiyoga* in the *yoga* of the Gita provides a necessary correction to both *Jnanayoga* and *Karmayoga*. In its culmination, the *yoga* of the Gita calls for an integral knowledge and an integral self-giving, by means of a complete surrender to, and union with, the *Divine Purushottama*.

Four Kinds of Devotees

चतुर्विधा भजन्ते मां जनाः सुकृतिनोऽर्जुन ।
आर्तो जिज्ञासुरर्थार्थी ज्ञानी च भरतर्षभ ||7.16||

Fourfold are people who do good deeds,	चतुः विधाः जनाः सुकृतिनः
Devoted to Me in different ways, Arjuna:	भजन्ते मां अर्जुन भरतर्षभ
The distressed, the seeker of wealth,	आर्तः अर्थ अर्थी
The knowledge-seeker and the jnani.	जिज्ञासुः ज्ञानी च

There are, of course, many levels or kinds of devotion (*bhakti*) possible at various stages of spiritual development, and it is instructive to be able to discern these different types, without being too judgemental, for all are declared in the Gita to be rightly aligned. They are referred to as people who do good deeds (*sukritina*) in the above verse — in contrast to the evil-doers (*dushkritina*), who are described as being deluded (*mudha*) in the previous Gita verse (7.15).

The Divine Teacher of the Gita refers to four kinds of devotees (*bhaktas*) here. The first and most common category is that of the distressed, *arta*, who turn to the Divine, looking for refuge from sorrow. When we are full of unbearable suffering and there is no one else to turn to for solace, we seek help and relief from the Divine. Here, the motivation may be essentially a seeking of relief from suffering (such as a chronic illness), rather than a positive desire to gain something. How frequently we turn to the Divine for this purpose depends a lot on our own ability to tolerate suffering. Some people are internally strong and can put up with a lot of pain and suffering. They do not seek help and trouble others, including the Divine, for what they consider to be bearable (and perhaps, necessary, for growth), and instead focus their efforts on positive actions. Even they find themselves turning to the Divine when they encounter the unbearable. There are others, of course, who are full of sorrow all the time, and constantly turn to the Divine with endless pleas. Their ability to do good deeds (*sukriti*) in a *sattvic* spirit, gets hindered to the extent they get concerned with their own distress (or distress to their near-and-dear ones). Often, this category of people is emotionally driven, having a strong 'vital-emotional and affective nature', as Sri Aurobindo points out, which is different from the '*bhakti* of ecstatic love' that 'is at its roots psychic in nature'.

The second category of devotees (*artharthi*) comprises those who seek Divine help to get material benefits or wealth (*artha*), which they consider to contribute to the 'good things in life'. They are the 'practical' people, engaged in the world, seeking happiness in material welfare, while acknowledging this to be a Divine blessing. Hence, they pray for Divine support to satisfy their material needs, which are regarded as essential for prosperity. Such individuals tend to have a strong vital nature, with a focus on lower and central vital aspects.

In contrast, the third category of devotees are those with a relatively strong mental nature, with a focus on reason and intellect. They are the knowledge-seekers (*jijnasu*), who find joy in pursuing knowledge of all kinds, including spiritual knowledge. They seek the blessings of the Divine in terms of knowledge, rather than material things or solace from suffering.

Finally, there is the highest category of devotees — those who are Self-realised, the *jnani-bhaktas.* They can no longer be said to be seekers, for they have found the ultimate object of their seeking — union with the Divine. Indeed, such souls are very rare on earth, while the seekers of worldly boons (material or knowledge) and those seeking relief from suffering constitute the vast majority.

The Supreme Devotee, the *Jnani-Bhakta*

उदाराः सर्व एवैते ज्ञानी त्वात्मैव मे मतम् ।
आस्थितः स हि युक्तात्मा मामेवानुत्तमां गतिम् ||7.18||

Noble indeed are all these kinds of devotees. उदाराः सर्वे एव एते
But the jnani I regard to be My very Self, ज्ञानी तु आत्मा एव मे मतम्
For he abides with his soul yoked to Me, आस्थितः सः हि युक्त आत्मा
Holding Me as his supreme goal and way! माम् एव अनुत्तमां गतिम्

The Divine Teacher, as *Purushottama*, declares in unequivocal terms that the *jnani* alone qualifies to have the highest status. This is not simply a realised knowledge (*jnana*) of the Impersonal Divine, but one that is *integral* in nature (including *vijnana*), and naturally full of devotion (*bhakti*) to the Transcendent *Purushottama*. Here, the realisation includes development, purification and integration of all parts of being (physical, vital and mental), so that the entering into the Supreme Divine is done with the whole being (*sarva-bhavena*), and not just intellectually.

In Gita verse 7.17, the Divine Teacher makes it clear that this is indeed a supreme state of permanent abiding in union with the Divine (*nitya-yukta*), arising from the fusion of knowledge with devotion to the 'One Divine' (*ekabhakti*), whose Divine presence is seen and felt in all manifestation and as the formless.

All other expressions of devotion, although high and noble (*udara*), are but preparatory in nature to this ultimate realisation. In the case of all other categories, the devotee worships not the One Divine *Purushottama*, but some lower godheads, for satisfying some deficiency needs of the lower nature. In Sri Aurobindo's words, 'the devotee does not approach the Divine in His integral all-embracing truth... but constructs imperfect names and images of the Godhead, which are only reflections of his own need, temperament and nature, and he worships them to help or appease his natural longings.' [17.1]

Eventually, the devotee advances to the highest state of the *jnani-bhakta*, realising that all other forms of devotion (for the purpose of gratifications in the lower nature) are limited in nature, obscured by ignorance, yielding only transient fruits. It is then that the *bhakta* begins to seek the One Divine, transcendent and yet immanent in all forms. In this process, the knowledge, faith, trust and joy in the Divine become so strengthened that the *bhakta* begins to see divinity in all manifestations. It is then that devotion becomes one with knowledge. Does this mean that the individual is no longer vulnerable to the play of the three *gunas*?

Sri Aurobindo explains: 'There is a place also for the three lesser seekings even after the highest attainment, but transformed, not narrowly personal, — for there can still be a passion for the removal of sorrow and evil and ignorance and for the increasing evolution and integral manifestation of the supreme good, power, joy and knowledge in this phenomenal nature.' [17.1] In this way, the Supreme becomes both the goal and the way (*anuttamam gatim*), in whom the devotee takes refuge completely.

Sri Aurobindo clearly speaks from authentic personal experience, when he goes on the describe the unique nature of the *jnani's* devotion (*ekabhakti*): 'This single devotion is his whole law of living and he has gone beyond all creeds of religious belief, rules of conduct, personal aims of life. He has no griefs to be healed, for he is in possession of the All-blissful. He has no desires to hunger after, for he possesses the highest and the All and is close to the All-Power that brings all fulfilment.' [17.1]

The Supreme Divine is All That is, *Vasudevah sarvamiti*

बहूनां जन्मनामन्ते ज्ञानवान्मां प्रपद्यते ।
वासुदेवः सर्वमिति स महात्मा सुदुर्लभः ।।7.19।।

Towards the end of innumerable births,	बहूनां जन्मनाम् अन्ते
The jnani takes refuge in Me and realises:	ज्ञानवान् मां प्रपद्यते
The Supreme Divine is all that is!	वासुदेवः सर्वम् इति
Such a great soul is rare indeed!	सः महात्मा सुदुर्लभः

The *jnani-bhakta's* devotion is anchored in a deep knowing of the supremacy of the One Divine as the source of everything. Although this knowing has been glimpsed through insight during mystic moments, it has a strength and stability to endure at all times, especially when the mystic peak experience is no longer there. It is then sustained by remembrance, sheer faith and unflinching trust. One then consciously seeks to see and feel the Divine in all manifestation, knowing the hidden presence of the divinity. It is like knowing that the sun is always present somewhere above or below in the sky during the day-time, even if one cannot see the sun directly, even if there are clouds shielding the sun, or even if it is night-time. It is like knowing the reality of one's ever-present breath, even when one is caught up in various thoughts, emotions and actions.

Krishna, the Divine Teacher of the Gita, also happens to be known as *Krishna Vasudeva*. However, here, he is playing the role of the complete *Avatar*, representing the Supreme *Purushottama*, abiding everywhere and in all things. This meaning is also embedded etymologically in the word *Vasudeva*, which literally means indwelling or all-abiding God. The highest truth is *Vasudevah sarvamiti*: The Supreme Divine is all that is! This is the deep realisation of the *jnani-bhakta*. Indeed, it is extremely rare (*sudurlabha*) to find such a great soul (*mahatma*), who manifests only after evolving through innumerable births.

सर्वभूतस्थितं यो मां भजत्येकत्वमास्थितः |
सर्वथा वर्तमानोऽपि स योगी मयि वर्तते ||6.31||

Established in oneness, he who worships	यः भजति एकत्वम् आस्थितः
Me as the One abiding in all beings,	मां सर्व भूत स्थितं
That Yogin always abides in Me,	सः योगी मयि वर्तते
Whatever be his engagements.	सर्वथा वर्तमानः अपि

The experience of the *jnani-bhakta*, of devotedly seeing and experiencing One Divine in all, is truly a profoundly liberating experience. In Sri Aurobindo's words, 'He will see all things and every creature living, moving and acting in the One, contained in the Divine and eternal Existence. But he will also see that One as the Inhabitant in all, their Self, the essential Spirit within them without whose secret presence in their conscious nature they could not at all live, move or act...'[17.2]

In other words, even trying circumstances will not confuse or shake the ever-yoked (*nitya-yukta*) condition of the one who truly knows *Vasudevah sarvamiti*. Even if the situation appears confusing or 'untoward', all is surrendered to the One Divine, in the supreme faith that this is the way things are to unfold and that one's role in what needs to be divinely done will be revealed spontaneously — not only from within, but also from signs outside, for all is the Divine. Such a *Yogin* is always supported by the *Purushottama*, who proclaims in verse 7.17: 'I am the beloved of the *jnani*, and he too is My beloved!'

This profound love which is fully reciprocated by the Supreme Divine is what gives the *Integral Karmayoga* of the Gita a distinctive edge over traditional *Rajayoga* or *Jnanayoga*, whose summit is seen as a dissolution into an Impersonal and infinite Oneness. In Sri Aurobindo's words, 'The indefinable Oneness accepts all that climb to it, but offers no help of relation and gives no foothold to the climber. All has to be done by a severe austerity and a stern and lonely individual effort. How different is it for those who seek after the *Purushottama* in the way of the Gita! When they meditate on him with a *Yoga* which sees none else, because it sees all to be *Vasudeva*, he meets them at every point, in every movement, at all times, with innumerable forms and faces, holds up the lamp of knowledge within and floods with its Divine and happy lustre the whole of existence.'[17.3]

Qualities of the Devotee Beloved to the Divine

Devotion facilitates a unique personal relationship between the individual and the Divine. Its ultimate objective is to heal the separation introduced by ego-consciousness, and thereby to enter into a union with the Divine

Purushottama. As the transcendent reality of *Purushottama* is difficult to access, most individuals need to relate to some representative name and form of that Supreme Divine. The chosen deity, in the Indian tradition, is called *ishta devata*, literally meaning 'cherished deity', and should ideally represent the One Divine, rather than some inferior godhead. One is free to relate to and worship the Divine in any manner one wishes to, conforming to one's temperament or religion. For example, the same Krishna is commonly conceived of and worshipped in India in multiple ways: as a Godchild, a mischievous prankster, a model lover, a Divine hero, a Divine Teacher (of the Gita), or directly as the Supreme *Purushottama*. Whatever be the mode of relationship one may prefer, the common features are a deep longing and a mystic love and adoration, which can turn to be ecstatic. Such ecstasy, of course, lies beyond the understanding of the thinking rational mind! The purity of such devotion in the *jnani-bhakta* is underlined by the fact that it does not seek anything in return, especially related to ego-desires.

As mentioned in the Gita, whatever be the level of the devotee, as long as the devotion is authentic, sincere and deep, it is bound to be answered appropriately. As the quality of the devotion becomes more intense and pure, one begins to feel the presence of the Divine more and more frequently and proximately. God is not out there somewhere in some sacred place (temple, church or mosque), to be accessed at some auspicious times, but is in here in our innermost being and also in the hearts of all beings, and in all forms. The *jnani-bhakta* also discovers that there are infinite ways of seeking and finding the Divine, and all are meaningful in their own ways.

Just as we are entitled to our own personal preferences in our conception of the Divine, we must be able to respect equally those of others, especially other religious groups, and even the preference of the atheist. Notions of exclusivity, as well as sectarianism and fanaticism, which define *tamasic*-

rajasic forms of religiosity, are out of place here, for they reflect an immaturity and ignorance far removed from the realisation of *Vasudevah sarvamiti*.

The soul's longing for union with the Divine gets answered by Divine Grace, at an appropriate time, when the devotee is ready. Hence, the sincere devotee will do well to nurture especially those qualities that are beloved to the Divine. The list of qualities enumerated in the Gita begins with a clear and unequivocal emphasis on equality, freedom from ego-centred desires, and love and compassion for all.

अद्वेष्टा सर्वभूतानां मैत्रः करुण एव च |
निर्ममो निरहङ्कारः समदुःखसुखः क्षमी ||12.13||

Without hatred to any being,	अद्वेष्टा सर्व भूतानां
Friendly and compassionate,	मैत्रः करुणः एव च
Free from the sense of 'I' and 'mine',	निर्ममः निरहङ्कारः
Equal to joy and sorrow, forgiving.	सम दुःख सुखः क्षमी

Freedom from hatred to all beings (*adveshta sarvabhutanam*) at all times is possible only in the presence of kinship and friendship, which emerge spontaneously when one discovers the presence of the One Divine in all. Empathy, compassion and forgiveness then follow naturally, extending to all. This feeling of unity with all beings becomes stable as one gets liberated from the ego-entrapments of the lower nature and their binding notions of 'I' and 'mine' (*nirmamo nirahankarah*). The sense of tranquil equality also extends naturally to freedom from attraction and repulsion to the dualities; one thus becomes equal to joy and sorrow (*samaduhkhasukhah*).

These attributes of *calm equality* have been emphasised from the very beginning in the Gita; they are foundational in nature and are imperative for the ascent of the *Yogin* into the higher nature. Calm equality, free from turbulent desires, is naturally rooted in ever-present contentment (*santushtah satatam*) and demands mastery in self-control. This is of course difficult, but can be made easy, by a devotional surrender to the Supreme Divine of one's entire being, and especially the mind and intellect, which need to struggle against the pulls of the vital being.

सन्तुष्टः सततं योगी यतात्मा दृढनिश्चयः ।
मय्यर्पितमनोबुद्धिः यो मद्भक्तः स मे प्रियः ||12.14||

Always contented and yoked to Me,	सन्तुष्टः सततं योगी
Self-controlled, resolute in decisions,	यत आत्मा दृढ निश्चयः
With mind and intellect surrendered to Me,	मयि अर्पित मनः बुद्धिः
Such a devotee of Mine is beloved to Me!	यः मत् भक्तः सः मे प्रियः

The *Purushottama* is the source of all wisdom under all circumstances, and provides the *Yogin* refuge and support, especially in testing times. It is only with such a reliable and unshakeable support, and inner guidance and inspiration, that one can remain unconfused and resolute in decisions (*drdhanishcaya*). Here in the yoked state, knowledge unites with will-power, and one is able to act fearlessly and decisively. The key, of course, lies in being able to remain inwardly calm, centred and connected to the Divine. This calmness in the midst of living in the world is again elaborated upon in the next verse.

यस्मान्नोद्विजते लोकः लोकान्नोद्विजते च यः ।
हर्षामर्षभयोद्वेगैः मुक्तो यः स च मे प्रियः ||12.15||

One by whom the world is not afflicted,	यस्मात् न उद्विजते लोकः
And who is not afflicted by the world,	लोकात् न उद्विजते च यः
Free from waves of exultation and rage,	हर्ष आमर्ष मुक्तः यः
Fear and anxiety, he is beloved to Me!	भयः उद्वेगैः सः च मे प्रियः

The *jnani-bhakta* seeks only to fulfil the *Divine dharma* in the world, and has no personal cravings to satisfy, no axe to grind, no need to win for the sake of the ego. Being centred in calmness and feeling the presence of divinity all around, such an individual therefore neither afflicts the world nor gets afflicted by the world. It is only when one is entrapped in the lower nature that we are vulnerable to periodic 'waves of exultation and rage, fear and anxiety'. Therefore, freedom from subjugation to these tidal waves is a clear sign of a high state of liberation. For that, one needs to only submit to that One Divine, and do whatever one is required to do, without any worry. The Divine Teacher of the Gita proclaims here that such a soul at peace is beloved to the *Purushottama*. The next verse elaborates on the right attitude to work by the integral *jnani-bhakta-karmayogin*.

अनपेक्षः शुचिर्दक्ष उदासीनो गतव्यथः |
सर्वारम्भपरित्यागी यो मद्भक्तः स मे प्रियः ||12.16||

Free from expectation, pure, skilled,	अनपेक्षः शुचिः दक्षः
Who is unprejudiced and unworried,	उदासीनः गत व्यथः
Who has given up ego-motivated work,	सर्व आरम्भ परित्यागी
Such a devotee of Mine is beloved to Me!	यः मत् भक्तः सः मे प्रियः

For the devotee to serve as a perfect instrument of the Divine, he or she must be free from ego-expectations of the fruit of actions (*anapeksha*), and thus be pure-minded and pure-hearted (*shuchi*). Moreover, he or she needs to be self-actualised and therefore skilled (*daksha*) in the talent or potential the person is endowed with. This skill enables the 'flow' state in one who allows the Divine knowledge and will to flow through the individual being, unhindered by personal ego-desires.

In the next two verses, the Divine Teacher reiterates the importance of transcending the dualities, in a true spirit of equality. Free from attachment and aversion (*ragadveshau*), the devotee who is beloved to the Supreme Divine does not rejoice unduly upon meeting with the pleasant nor despise whatever comes across as unpleasant. Hence, he or she neither grieves nor hankers.

यो न हृष्यति न द्वेष्टि   न शोचति न काङ्क्षति |
शुभाशुभपरित्यागी   भक्तिमान्यः स मे प्रियः ||12.17||

Who neither over-enjoys nor hates, यः न हृष्यति न द्वेष्टि
Who neither grieves nor hankers, न शोचति न काङ्क्षति
Neutral to things favourable or unfavourable, शुभ अशुभ परित्यागी
Such a one, full of devotion, is beloved to Me! भक्ति मान् यः सः मे प्रियः

समः शत्रौ च मित्रे च   तथा मानापमानयोः |
शीतोष्णसुखदुःखेषु   समः सङ्गविवर्जितः ||12.18||

Who is alike to both foe and friend, समः शत्रौ च मित्रे च
And equal to honour and dishonour, तथा मान अपमानयोः
Alike to cold and heat, pleasure and pain, शीत उष्ण सुख दुःखेषु समः
Who is fully free from all attachments. सङ्ग विवर्जितः

Whatever be the nature of the unfolding events, whether favourable or unfavourable, the devotee receives all things equally, seeing the Divine in all. Thus, such a person is equal to friend and foe, honour and insult, heat and cold, pleasure and pain, and all such dualities, being free from all attachments. This is further elaborated in the next verse.

The calm equality extends to praise and censure, and is reflected in silence and inner contentment with things as they are (yet open to inner direction as to how to bring about evolutionary change).

तुल्यनिन्दास्तुतिर्मौनी सन्तुष्टो येन केनचित् ।
अनिकेतः स्थिरमतिः भक्तिमान्मे प्रियो नरः ||12.19||

Who is alike to censure and praise,	तुल्य निन्दा स्तुतिः
Silent and content with everything,	मौनी सन्तुष्टः येन केनचित्
With no secure residence, steadfast in thought,	अनिकेतः स्थिर मतिः
Such a one, full of devotion, is beloved to Me!	भक्ति मान् मे प्रियः नरः

Anchored in unshakeable devotion to the Supreme Divine, the devotee has no obsessive attachment to anything, be it person or thing. The only secure residence that such a devotee seeks is in being *nitya-yukta* to the Supreme Divine, and not in some external property or particular surroundings.

Thus, these are the characteristics that make a devotee beloved to the Supreme Divine. Sri Aurobindo sums them up as follows: 'Equality, desirelessness and freedom from the lower egoistic nature and its claims are always the one perfect foundation demanded by the Gita for the great liberation… And the crown of this equality is love founded on knowledge, fulfilled in instrumental action, extended to all things and beings, a vast absorbing and all-containing love for the Divine Self who is Creator and Master of the universe…'[17.3]

There is a concluding verse (12.20) in Chapter 12 of the Gita, which we shall take up in the next and final chapter of this book, for it pertains to the Gita's final teaching on the *immortal dharma*.

18

The Final Supreme Teaching: Immortal *Dharma*

ये तु धर्म्यामृतमिदं यथोक्तं पर्युपासते ।
श्रद्दधाना मत्परमा भक्तास्तेऽतीव मे प्रियाः ||12.20||

Those who follow, as described here,	ये तु यथा उक्तं पर्युपासते
Tenets of this immortalising dharma,	धर्म्य अमृतम् इदं
With perfect faith, with Me as the supreme aim,	श्रद्दधानाः मत् परमाः
Such devotees are exceedingly beloved to Me!	भक्ताः ते अतीव मे प्रियाः

The *yoga* of the Gita, which integrates knowledge and devotion with action, aims at complete fulfilment. To the extent the spiritual aspirant is able to realise, through the challenges presented in daily life, the attributes of equality, desirelessness and freedom from the lower egoistic nature and the flow of the higher Divine nature, to that extent, the individual is beloved to the Supreme Divine. These tenets of the Gita comprise the basic *dharma* that need to be followed. If truly followed, it will lead to the culmination of the evolutionary journey of consciousness in the individual — from *asat* to *sat*, from *tamas* to *jyoti*, and from *mrityu* to *amritam*. For this reason, this is referred to here in this verse as an *immortalising Dharma* (*dharmyamritam*).

All those who attempt to follow this *dharma* are no doubt dear to the *Purushottama*, but exceedingly beloved are those who actually implement the tenets successfully, and being *nitya-yukta*, are truly able to perceive the One Divine Self everywhere (*Vasudevah sarvamiti*). Liberated from the lower nature, and abiding in higher nature, they serve as perfect instruments for the flow of the Soul Forces, and this is what makes them so endearing to the Supreme Divine. Emerging completely from the ignorance of the lower nature, and discovering oneness with *Purushottama*, such *jnani-bhakta-karmayogins* become Divine co-creators.

Sri Aurobindo explains the significance of the immortal dharma referred to in the above verse, comparing it with the ordinary *dharmas*, as follows. '*Dharma* in the language of the Gita means the innate law of the being and its works and an action proceeding from and determined by the inner nature, *svabhava-niyatam karma*. In the lower ignorant consciousness of mind, life and body, there are many *dharmas*, many rules, many standards and laws, because there are many varying determinations and types of the mental, vital and physical nature. The immortal *Dharma* is one; it is that of the highest spiritual consciousness and its powers, *Para Prakriti*.'[18.1]

In the concluding 18th chapter of the Gita, the Divine Teacher sums up the implications of this immortal *Dharma*, for here alone lies the final and complete answer to Arjuna's original question pertaining to *dharma* (verse 2.7: *What is my true dharma?*). Herein lies the final clarity to all our confusions. Indeed, here also lies the clear message regarding the true meaning of *liberation*, and how such liberation can be sustained even in the full flood of action, in the battlefields of life, as at Kurukshetra.

Supreme Perfection and Freedom in Action

The grip of the lower nature is powerful. It casts a spell on us and keeps us bound, by the tyranny of the play of the three *gunas*, to ignorance and ego-desires. We are then drawn compulsively to engagement with the outer world, tossed and turned relentlessly by the tidal waves of pleasure and pain, hope and fear, etc. We get absorbed in this ego-centred world. Yet, liberation and fulfilment are impossible in this way of living. It is therefore imperative that we learn to withdraw from this obsession with outer engagement (*pravritti*) and enter into the quietude of our innermost being through inaction (*nivritti*), learning to balance our lives between these two modes. However, to enter into *nivritti*, we need to free ourselves, at least temporarily, from the 'hooks' of the world. This is possible when we begin with a clear intellectual conviction of the truth of what is required. As this understanding gets strengthened through reflection and clarity, it becomes easier to detach the mind and the vital being from their relentless engagement with various sense-objects. This is referred to in the following verse as *asaktabuddhih sarvatra*.

असक्तबुद्धिः सर्वत्र जितात्मा विगतस्पृहः ।
नैष्कर्म्यसिद्धिं परमां संन्यासेनाधिगच्छति ।।18.49।।

One whose intellect is unattached everywhere,	असक्तः बुद्धिः सर्वत्र
Who is self-conquered and free from cravings,	जित आत्मा विगत स्पृहः
Attains through the practice of renunciation	संन्यासेन अधिगच्छति
Supreme perfection of freedom from action.	नैष्कर्म्य सिद्धिं परमां

It is imperative, according to the *yoga* of the Gita to nurture such an unattached *buddhi*. Also, by living more and more in the present, without worrying about the imagined future or dwelling over the dead past, one becomes more and more tuned to the presence of the Divine One Self in all things and beings. This also calls for self-mastery and an ability to stay anchored in inner stillness, not yielding to the various pulls of ego-desires. Such self-conquest (*jitatma*) is accompanied by a natural falling off of all kinds of obsessive cravings (*vigatasprha*). This is the true meaning of renunciation (*sannyasa*), according to the Gita. It is an *inner* renunciation (also called *tyaga*), by entering into an inner stillness and passivity from all ego-motivated action. It is this that provides for supreme perfection and freedom from action (*naishkarmya-siddhim paramam*). Entry to the higher Divine nature (*Para Prakriti*) is facilitated through this passage into the inner stillness and immutability of *Akshara Purusha*, and proceeding beyond to the realm of the *Purushottama*.

This state of becoming one with impersonal *Brahman* is described in the Gita (verse 14.26) as *brahma-bhuyaya*. But the Gita makes it clear that while the inner quietude of *naishkarmyam* is essential, it is neither appropriate nor possible for all to give up action in the outer world, enamoured by the *brahma-bhuyaya* state. This is because there is a higher principle beyond impersonal *Brahman* — that of the *Purushottama*, which includes but transcends the static immutable reality of the Self, and engages in dynamic manifestation. This dual aspect (static as well as dynamic) is present in the very core of our being, and this is what makes it possible to be inwardly in the quiet state of *naishkarmyam* and yet be in the flow of Divine action. Without the inner connection to impersonal *Brahman*, when we act in the world, it is generally in the ignorance of the lower nature, and with a notion of doership. By withdrawing into the impersonal silent Self, we observe that all action is done — not by the soul, but by the play of the three *gunas* of *Prakriti* in the lower nature, and it is this vivid perception that imparts an impersonal equality in all things. By purification and transformation of the *gunas*, and by accessing the impersonal *Brahman*, one discovers the dynamism of higher nature as the work of the Divine *Soul Forces* of *Para Prakriti*, while still being anchored in *naishkarmyam*.

The Gita offers us many avenues of spiritual growth, depending on our individual preferences and temperaments. The practice of *Jnanayoga*, combined with the meditative practices of *Rajayoga*, are most conducive in developing the understanding unattached to things (*asakta-buddhi*) as well as self-mastery and liberation from cravings of the lower nature (*jitatma vigatasprha*), which are necessary for attaining the state of *naishkarmyam*. Yet, the Gita also insists on the practice of *Karmayoga* and *Bhaktiyoga*, whereby we nurture the attitude of sacrifice and self-giving to the Supreme Divine in all our actions. This enables the continuity of skilled action in the higher nature, but without the contamination of ego-desires, to serve the higher Divine purpose.

What is that Divine purpose? How can it be discerned? This is addressed in the closing verses of the Gita. The only way of discovering the immortal *Dharma*, after realising the state of *naishkarmyam*, is by a supreme *surrender* to the *Purushottama* in complete devotion, for *jnana* ultimately remains incomplete without the supreme *bhakti* inasmuch as *bhakti* remains incomplete without the supreme *jnana*. Completion, perfection and fulfilment are attained only by oneness in being with the *Purushottama*, and this according to the *Gita*, necessarily implies an ascent from the lower nature to the impersonal *Brahman* (*Akshara Purusha*), and beyond to the higher Divine nature of *Para Prakriti*.

Supreme Surrender

मच्चित्तः सर्वदुर्गाणि मत्प्रसादात्तरिष्यसि ।
अथ चेत्त्वमहङ्कारात् न श्रोष्यसि विनङ्क्ष्यसि ||18.58||

Being one with Me, by My grace,	मत् चित्तः मत् प्रसादात्
You shall overcome all difficulties!	सर्व दुर्गाणि तरिष्यसि
But if, out of self-conceit, you choose	अथ चेत् त्वम् अहङ्कारात्
Not to listen, you will get destroyed!	न श्रोष्यसि विनङ्क्ष्यसि

The summit of spiritual growth is reached only by becoming one with the Supreme *Purushottama*, and this manifests by Divine Grace, as indicated in the above verse. By the term *macchitta* is implied oneness in consciousness in all parts of one's being — an integral oneness with the *Purushottama*. It is with such an integral consciousness alone that one can deal with and overcome all difficulties that present themselves in the battlefield of life. 'The crux of the spiritual problem', is according to Sri Aurobindo, 'the character of this transition of which it is so difficult for the normal mind of man to get a true apprehension, turns altogether upon the capital distinction between the ignorant life of the ego in the lower nature and the large and luminous existence of the liberated *Jiva* in his own true spiritual nature. The renunciation of the first must be complete, the transition to the second absolute. This is the distinction on which the Gita dwells here with all possible emphasis.'[18.2]

Having disclosed this comprehensive knowledge to Arjuna, the Divine Teacher issues a warning at the end. Not to heed to the supreme calling at this critical moment at the *Kurukshetra* battlefield would clearly imply a fall into the ego-driven world of the lower nature, and this would be self-destructive. Not doing what one needs to do out of ignorance and confusion is perhaps forgivable, but after knowing the truth, if one still refuses to rise to the occasion, then that would be sinful. However, this warning is followed by strongly motivating and inspiring verses.

मन्मना भव मद्भक्तः मद्याजी मां नमस्कुरु |
मामेवैष्यसि सत्यं ते प्रतिजाने प्रियोऽसि मे ||18.65||

Become one with Me in mind and heart,	मत् मनाः भव मत् भक्तः
Offer all your work, surrendering to Me!	मत् याजी मां नमस्कुरु
Thus, truly, you shall come to Me,	माम् एव एष्यसि सत्यं
I promise, for you are dear to Me!	ते प्रतिजाने प्रियः असि मे

All human weakness gets eliminated by the simple act of whole-hearted self-surrender to the Supreme Divine. By this simple device of authentically surrendering to the *Purushottama*, and acting in accordance to the directions of the inner Divine voice (and in the case of Arjuna here, outer voice too!), the surrender of the devotee culminates in the ultimate fulfilment — being integrally one in consciousness in mind and heart (*manmana bhava madbhakta*). There is a complete assurance given here: 'truly you shall come to Me'. It is an assurance given by the Supreme Divine to the *jnani-bhakta-karmayogin* who earnestly practises the supreme wisdom revealed here.

Sri Aurobindo explains the significance of such surrender: 'That which surrenders here is the *Jiva*... delivered from the limiting and ignorant ego-sense who knows himself not as a separate personality but as an eternal portion and power and soul-becoming of the Divine... It is this central spiritual being in us who thus enters into a perfect and closely real relation of delight and union with the origin and continent and governing Self and Power of our existence. And he who receives our surrender is no limited Deity but *the Purushottama*, the one eternal Godhead, the one supreme Soul of all that is and of all nature, the original transcendent Spirit of existence.'[18.2]

Most Supreme *Dharma*

सर्वधर्मान् परित्यज्य मामेकं शरणं व्रज ।
अहं त्वा सर्वपापेभ्यः मोक्षयिष्यामि मा शुचः ।।18.66।।

Let go of all your notions of dharma, सर्व धर्मान् परित्यज्य
Take refuge in Me alone for guidance! माम् एकं शरणं व्रज
From all evils I shall liberate you. अहं त्वा सर्वपापेभ्यः मोक्षयिष्यामि
Trust Me fully and do not worry! मा शुचः

We return to the closing word of the Gita on *dharma*, the immortal *Dharma*, its supreme secret — which brings about a rather surprising turn to the teachings presented so far, where there was so much emphasis on knowledge and practice through dedicated self-discipline.

No matter how much the human being may progress in self-knowledge and self-discipline, there is always bound to be some limitation and imperfection arising from self-effort. No such limitation or imperfection exists in the *Purushottama*, who declares here in a unique message to Arjuna that the *Purushottama* can directly take up and execute this perfect action, even in the most trying circumstances (as at Kurukshetra), through the instrumentation of the concerned individual, provided the surrender to the *Purushottama* is total.

Sri Aurobindo expands here on the *Purushottama's* message: 'All this personal effort and self-discipline will not in the end be needed, all following and limitation of rule and dharma can at last be thrown away as hampering encumbrances if thou canst make a complete surrender to Me, depend alone on the Spirit and Godhead within thee and all things and trust to his sole guidance. Turn all thy mind to Me and fill it with the thought of Me and My presence. Turn all thy heart to Me, make thy every action, whatever it be, a sacrifice and offering to Me. That done, leave Me to do My will with thy life and soul and action…'[18.2]

The two key phrases here, in this final supreme teaching are: '*Let go of all your notions of dharma*' (*sarvadharman-parityajya*) and '*Take refuge in Me alone as your guide*' (*mam-ekam sharanam vraja*). Although these two phrases appear simple, giving a complete solution, they are in fact not so easy to implement, unless one has made significant progress in the *Integral Karmayoga* of the Gita, especially being able to invoke the supreme devotion implied in *Bhaktiyoga*. The very same ego-sense in us, which gets confused with regard to our *dharma*, is also likely to come in the way of a complete surrender. Indeed no matter how evolved in terms of self-knowledge or self-actualisation we may be, bewildering conflicts in *dharma* are bound to come our way, as in the case of Arjuna at the battlefield of Kurukshetra. The limitations of our physical-vital-mental apparatus tend to cloud our understanding and obstruct the execution of a perfect action under these circumstances. In such circumstances, we will do well to abandon all our notions of *dharma* and to take a complete refuge in the *Purushottama*. This of course assumes that we have previous experience in accessing the Supreme Divine through our daily meditative and devotional practices.

The Instrument, the Worker and the Master

In this book, we have covered many aspects of spirituality at work, based on the teachings of the Gita. At the end, we realise that there is only One Divine Spirit at work in diverse forms in the entire universe, at various levels of self-awareness and self-knowledge (or ignorance). At the highest level, all action is done integrally, with perfection and delight, by the dynamic aspect of *Purushottama* (*Ishvara-Shakti*), who is the *Master* of all work. In terms of spirituality at work, one could conceive of an intermediate level of the Divine *Worker*, and a lower level of the *Instrument* of work. These three stages of spirituality at work, manifesting through the evolving human individual, have been beautifully described by Sri Aurobindo in an essay titled *The Delight of Works*. Some excerpts from this essay are given below, summing up the various levels of spirituality at work.

'Learn thou first to be the instrument of God and to accept thy Master. The instrument is this outward thing thou callest thyself; it is a mould of mind, a driving-force of power, a machinery of form, a thing full of springs and cogs and clamps and devices... Accept thyself humbly, yet proudly, devotedly, submissively and joyfully as a Divine instrument. There is no greater pride and glory than to be a perfect instrument of the Master. Learn thou first absolutely to obey. The sword does not choose where it shall strike, the arrow does not ask whither it shall be driven, the springs of the machine do not insist on the product that shall be turned out from its labour. These things are settled by the intention and working of nature and the more the conscious instrument learns to feel and obey the pure and essential law of its nature, the sooner shall the work turned out become perfect and flawless. Self-choice by the nervous motive power, revolt of the physical and mental tool can only mar the working...

'Know thyself next as the Worker. Understand thy nature to be the worker and thy own nature and All-nature to be thyself. This nature-self is not proper to thee nor limited. Thy nature has made the sun and the systems, the earth and her creatures, thyself and thine and all thou art and perceivest... But in thee there is a special movement, a proper nature and an individual energy. Follow that like a widening river till it leads thee to its infinite source and origin. Know therefore thy body to be a knot in Matter and thy mind to be a whirl in universal Mind and thy life to be an eddy of Life that is forever. Know thy force to be every other being's force and thy knowledge to be a glimmer from the light that belongs to no man and thy works to be made for thee and be delivered from the error of thy personality... The Worker has the joy of her works and the joy of her Lover for whom she works. She knows herself to be His consciousness and His force, His knowledge and His reserving of knowledge, His unity and His self-division, His infinity and the finite of His being...

'Know last the Master to be thyself; but to this self put no form and seek for it no definition of quality. Be one with That in thy being, commune with That in thy consciousness, obey That in thy force, be subject to That and clasped by it in thy delight, fulfil That in thy life and body and mentality. Then before an opening eye within thee there shall emerge that true and only Person, thyself and not thyself, all others and more than all others, the Director and Enjoyer of thy works, the Master of the worker and the instrument, the Reveller and Trampler in the dance of the universe and yet hushed and alone with thee in thy soul's silent and inner chamber. The joy of the Master possessed, there is nothing else for thee to conquer. For He shall give thee Himself and all things and all creatures' gettings and havings and doings and enjoyings for thy own proper portion, and He shall give thee that also which cannot be portioned. Thou shalt contain in thy being thyself and all others and be that which is neither thyself nor all others. Of works this is the consummation and the summit.'[18.3]

The Ending of the Gita: Transformation of Arjuna

The Divine Teacher of the Gita ends his teaching with a final piece of advice to Arjuna (and to all of us). After having revealed the supremely secret wisdom (*jnanam guhyad-guhyataram*) leading to the immortal *Dharma*, the Divine Teacher tells us that we have the freedom of choice: to walk the path revealed (and so act decisively) or not to do so.

इति ते ज्ञानमाख्यातं गुह्याद्गुह्यतरं मया ।
विमृश्यैतदशेषेण यथेच्छसि तथा कुरु ।।18.63।।

Thus, the supremely secret wisdom	इति ज्ञानम् गुह्यात् गुह्य तरं
Has been revealed to you by Me.	ते आख्यातं मया
Reflecting on it fully,	विमृश्य एतत् अशेषेण
Act as you deem fit!	यथा इच्छसि तथा कुरु

This is not a dogma to be followed blindly or adopted out of fear, but a profound teaching to be reflected upon fully and internalised. It cannot be a dogma, for listening to the voice of the Supreme Divine in our innermost being (accessing the immortal *Dharma*) is a living dynamic truth of being, unique for each individual, and not simply a prescriptive set of commandments. The question of such choice — whether to abide by this immortal supreme *Dharma* or the confused notions of *dharma* of our ego-centred outer being — is a privilege that arises only for those who are on the path to being *jnani-bhakta-karmayogins*. It is after reflecting thus, we are advised to act as we deem fit.

So what does Arjuna decide? We recall that at the beginning he was extremely dejected, confused and demoralised and was not inclined to engage in the battle at Kurukshetra. However, he was wise enough to realise his confusion and sought the advice of Krishna, his charioteer and friend, whom he trusted to give sage advice. This is how Krishna takes on the role of the Divine Teacher, and reveals to Arjuna (and to us) the message of the Bhagavad Gita as well as his *Avatarhood*.

Arjuna makes clear his decision in the following verse.

अर्जुन उवाच ।
नष्टो मोहः स्मृतिर्लब्धा त्वत्प्रसादान्मयाच्युत ।
स्थितोऽस्मि गतसन्देहः करिष्ये वचनं तव ||18.73||

Arjuna said:	अर्जुनः उवाच
I have shed delusion and gained wisdom	नष्टः मोहः मया स्मृतिः लब्धा
Through Your Divine grace, O Krishna!	त्वत् प्रसादात् अच्युत
I stand firm, with my doubts dispelled.	स्थितः अस्मि गत सन्देहः
I shall now act, abiding by Your words!	करिष्ये वचनं तव

Arjuna has no doubts left, for he is now totally convinced about what needs to be done. Transformed from his state of dejection, he is now highly inspired, for he knows his role as a key instrument of the Divine in this divinely decreed battle between the forces of good and evil. He is now internally yoked to the *Purushottama*, who is also physically present close to him in the form of his charioteer!

As students of the Gita, we too need to choose our path and abide by it whole-heartedly. The teachings of the Gita make it amply clear as to what we need to do in terms of daily practice, so that we too can become yoked to the Supreme Divine. We too have a Divine charioteer to guide our journey, for the *Purushottama* resides in our innermost being.

The last four verses of the Gita take us back from the battlefield of Kurukshetra to the palace at Hastinapura, to Sanjaya, who has been narrating the dialogue between Arjuna and Krishna to his king, Dhritarashtra. Sanjaya cannot help but feel privileged and grateful at having been given this miraculous opportunity of a 'live telecast'. He expresses his sense of absolute wonder at having being able to witness the proceedings and so receive, although vicariously, the profound message of the Gita. We too need to be grateful to the character of Sanjaya in the Mahabharata, for having been the agent of transmission of the Gita to us. Although his role is that of a mere assistant to the king, he is no ordinary person. He has an intuitive wisdom of his own, which he reveals in this last verse of the Gita.

यत्र योगेश्वरः कृष्णः यत्र पार्थो धनुर्धरः |
तत्र श्रीर्विजयो भूतिः ध्रुवा नीतिर्मतिर्मम ||18.78||

Wherever there is Krishna, Lord of Yoga,	यत्र योगेश्वरः कृष्णः
Wherever there is Arjuna, the Archer,	यत्र पार्थः धनुर्धरः
There shall be glory, victory, prosperity	तत्र श्रीः विजयः भूतिः ध्रुवा
And righteousness: this is my conviction!	नीतिः मतिः मम

Sanjaya declares his intuitive conviction fearlessly to his own king that Arjuna, with Krishna by his side (their enemies at the battle at Kurukshetra), are bound to emerge victorious. Clearly, inspired by the teachings of the Gita, Sanjaya seems to have no doubt in his mind about right and wrong in this instance. For the law of righteousness (*niti*) rests ultimately and without doubt with the Supreme Divine, who is evidently manifest as *Purushottama* in the *Avataric* form of Krishna. Sanjaya observes here that Krishna himself is a great exemplar and Lord (*yogeshvara*) of the *yoga* he teaches. Moreover, inspired by the teachings of the Gita, Arjuna has risen above his confused lower nature, and is clearly now inspired to take up willingly his divinely ordained role as a *Vibhuti*. The combination of *Avatar* and *Vibhuti* is clearly invincible, and the outcome is bound to manifest as glory, victory and prosperity.

Thus ends the Gita.

Its message is clear and profound. We live ordinarily in a confused state of ignorance and lack of fulfilment, primarily because we are not in touch with the Supreme Divine, who abides secretly everywhere, including the core of our innermost being. The *Integral Karmayoga* of the Gita, which combines knowledge and devotion with consecrated action (*Jnanayoga, Bhaktiyoga* and *Karmayoga*), gives us a way to awaken to the living presence of the Supreme Divine and stay yoked to it, while developing and purifying various parts of our being (physical, vital and mental). This liberates us from the bondage of action and ego-entrapment, keeps us connected to a profound and mystic stillness, and enables us to abide in a higher Divine nature, from which creative action flows. Staying so yoked, we discover fulfilment and bliss, in action and inaction. Our human life becomes *divinised*.

We then see and experience the Supreme Divine manifesting secretly everywhere, in all beings and at all times.

ॐ वासुदेवः सर्वमिति

Om Vasudevah sarvamiti

References

1.1 Sri Aurobindo, *The Life Divine - I*, The Complete Works of Sri Aurobindo (Vol. 21), Sri Aurobindo Ashram Trust, Pondicherry, 2005, p. 398.

1.2 A P J Abdul Kalam with Arun Tiwari, *Wings of Fire: An Autobiography*, Universities Press (India) Private Limited, Hyderabad, 1999, p. iv.

1.3 Carl Sagan, *The Demon-Haunted World*, Ballantine Books (The Random House Publishing Group), 1996, p.29.

1.4 Ken Wilber, *A Theory of Everything*, Shambhala Publications, 2000, p. 104.

1.5 Albert Einstein, *Letter of 1950*, quoted in The New York Times (29 March 1972) and The New York Post (28 November 1972) [Source: https://en.wikiquote.org/wiki/Albert_Einstein].

1.6 Sri Aurobindo, *Essays on the Gita*, The Complete Works of Sri Aurobindo (Vol. 19), Sri Aurobindo Ashram Trust, Pondicherry, 1997, p. 204.

2.1 *Ibid.*, p. 54.

3.1 Arthur Osborne, *Ramana Maharshi and the Path of Self-Knowledge*, Jaico Publishing House, 1970, pp. 7-8.

3.2 Sri Aurobindo, *Essays on the Gita*, The Complete Works of Sri Aurobindo (Vol. 19), Sri Aurobindo Ashram Trust, Pondicherry, 1997, p. 62.

4.1 *Ibid.*, p. 240.

4.2 Sri Aurobindo, *Letters on Yoga - II*, The Complete Works of Sri Aurobindo (Vol. 29), Sri Aurobindo Ashram Trust, Pondicherry, 2013, p. 140.

4.3 Eckhart Tolle, *Stillness Speaks*, Yogi Impressions, 2003, p. 3.

5.1 Sri Aurobindo, *Essays on the Gita*, The Complete Works of Sri Aurobindo (Vol. 19), Sri Aurobindo Ashram Trust, Pondicherry, 1997, p. 199.

6.1 Sri Aurobindo, *The Life Divine - II*, The Complete Works of Sri Aurobindo (Vol. 22), Sri Aurobindo Ashram Trust, Pondicherry, 2005, p. 762.

6.2 Advaita Ashrama, *The Vairagya Satakam (The Hundred Verses on Renunciation)*, Mayavati, Almora, 1916, p. 19.

7.1 Sri Aurobindo, *Essays on the Gita*, The Complete Works of Sri Aurobindo (Vol. 19), Sri Aurobindo Ashram Trust, Pondicherry, 1997, p. 99.

7.2 Puran Bair, *Living from the Heart*, Three Rivers Press, New York, 1998.

7.3 The Mother, *Questions and Answers: 1957-1958*, Collected Works of the Mother (Vol. 9), second edition, Sri Aurobindo Ashram Trust, Pondicherry, 2004, p. 360.

7.4 Devdas Menon, *Stop Sleepwalking through Life!*, Yogi Impressions, 2004, p. 75.

7.5 Sri Aurobindo, *Essays on the Gita*, The Complete Works of Sri Aurobindo (Vol. 19), Sri Aurobindo Ashram Trust, Pondicherry, 1997, p. 79.

8.1 Abraham H. Maslow, *Motivation and Personality*, Harper and Row, 1954.

8.2 Sri Aurobindo, *Essays on the Gita*, The Complete Works of Sri Aurobindo (Vol. 19), Sri Aurobindo Ashram Trust, Pondicherry, 1997, p. 498.

8.3 Devdas Menon, *Stop Sleepwalking through Life!*, Yogi Impressions, 2004, p. 60.

8.4 The Arbinger Institute, *Leadership and Self-Deception*, Magna Publishing Co. Ltd., Mumbai, 2002, pp. 106-107.

8.5 Sri Aurobindo, *Essays on the Gita*, The Complete Works of Sri Aurobindo (Vol. 19), Sri Aurobindo Ashram Trust, Pondicherry, 1997, p. 586.

9.1 Sri Aurobindo, *The Synthesis of Yoga - I*, The Complete Works of Sri Aurobindo (Vol. 23), Sri Aurobindo Ashram Trust, Pondicherry, 1999, p. 109.

9.2 Sri Aurobindo, *The Life Divine - I*, The Complete Works of Sri Aurobindo (Vol. 21), Sri Aurobindo Ashram Trust, Pondicherry, 2005, p. 339.

9.3 Sri Aurobindo, *The Life Divine - II*, The Complete Works of Sri Aurobindo (Vol. 22), Sri Aurobindo Ashram Trust, Pondicherry, 2005, p. 1022.

9.4 Sri Aurobindo, *Essays on the Gita*, The Complete Works of Sri Aurobindo (Vol. 19), Sri Aurobindo Ashram Trust, Pondicherry, 1997, p. 125.

10.1 Sri Aurobindo, *Isha Upanishad*, The Complete Works of Sri Aurobindo (Vol. 17), Sri Aurobindo Ashram Trust, Pondicherry, 2003, pp. 288-298.

10.2 The Arbinger Institute, *Leadership and Self-Deception*, Magna Publishing Co. Ltd., Mumbai, 2002, pp. 64-79.

10.3 Stephen R. Covey, *The 8th Habit: From Effectiveness to Greatness*, Free Press, Simon and Schuster Inc., New York, 2004, p. 3.

11.1 Sri Aurobindo, *Essays on the Gita*, The Complete Works of Sri Aurobindo (Vol. 19), Sri Aurobindo Ashram Trust, Pondicherry, 1997, p. 418.

11.2 Sri Aurobindo, *The Synthesis of Yoga - I*, The Complete Works of Sri Aurobindo (Vol. 23), Sri Aurobindo Ashram Trust, Pondicherry, 1999, p. 60.

11.3 Sri Aurobindo, *Essays on the Gita*, The Complete Works of Sri Aurobindo (Vol. 19), Sri Aurobindo Ashram Trust, Pondicherry, 1997, p. 548.

11.4 Sri Aurobindo, *The Life Divine - II*, The Complete Works of Sri Aurobindo (Vol. 22), Sri Aurobindo Ashram Trust, Pondicherry, 2005, p. 934.

11.5 Sri Aurobindo, *Letters on Yoga - I*, The Complete Works of Sri Aurobindo (Vol. 28), Sri Aurobindo Ashram Trust, Pondicherry, 2012, p. 537.

12.1 Sri Aurobindo, *Essays on the Gita*, The Complete Works of Sri Aurobindo (Vol. 19), Sri Aurobindo Ashram Trust, Pondicherry, 1997, pp. 486-488.

13.1 Bob Moorehead, *The Paradox of our Age* in *Words Aptly Spoken*, Overlake Press, 1995.

13.2 Sri Aurobindo, *The Renaissance in India and Other Essays on Indian Culture*, The Complete Works of Sri Aurobindo (Vol. 20), Sri Aurobindo Ashram Trust, Pondicherry, 1997, pp. 15-16.

13.3 Ken Wilber, *No Boundary*, Shambhala Publications, 1979, p. 31.

13.4 Sri Aurobindo, *Essays on the Gita*, The Complete Works of Sri Aurobindo (Vol. 19), Sri Aurobindo Ashram Trust, Pondicherry, 1997, pp. 499-502.

14.1 *Ibid.*, pp. 502-504.

14.2 Sri Aurobindo, *The Synthesis of Yoga - I*, The Complete Works of Sri Aurobindo (Vol. 23), Sri Aurobindo Ashram Trust, Pondicherry, 1999, pp. 90-91.

14.3 Sri Aurobindo, *Essays on the Gita*, The Complete Works of Sri Aurobindo (Vol. 19), Sri Aurobindo Ashram Trust, Pondicherry, 1997, pp. 505-506.

15.1 Sri Aurobindo, *Letters on Yoga - I*, The Complete Works of Sri Aurobindo (Vol. 28), Sri Aurobindo Ashram Trust, Pondicherry, 2012, p. 49.

15.2 Sri Aurobindo, *Essays on the Gita*, The Complete Works of Sri Aurobindo (Vol. 19), Sri Aurobindo Ashram Trust, Pondicherry, 1997, p. 489.

15.3 *Ibid.*, pp. 502-506.

15.4 *Ibid.*, p. 432.

15.5 Sri Aurobindo, *The Synthesis of Yoga - I*, The Complete Works of Sri Aurobindo (Vol. 23), Sri Aurobindo Ashram Trust, Pondicherry, 1999, p. 238.

15.6 Sri Aurobindo, *Autobiographical Notes and Other Writings of Historical Interest*, The Complete Works of Sri Aurobindo (Vol. 36), Sri Aurobindo Ashram Trust, Pondicherry, 2006, p. 548.

15.7 The Mother, *Questions and Answers: 1929-1931*, Collected Works of the Mother (Vol. 3), second edition, Sri Aurobindo Ashram Trust, Pondicherry, 2003, p. 1.

16.1 Sri Aurobindo, *Letters on Yoga - IV*, The Complete Works of Sri Aurobindo (Vol. 31), Sri Aurobindo Ashram Trust, Pondicherry, 2014, pp. 251-252.

16.2 Sri Aurobindo, *The Synthesis of Yoga - III*, The Complete Works of Sri Aurobindo (Vol. 24), Sri Aurobindo Ashram Trust, Pondicherry, 1999, p. 742.

16.3 Sri Aurobindo, *The Human Cycle*, The Complete Works of Sri Aurobindo (Vol. 25), Sri Aurobindo Ashram Trust, Pondicherry, 1997, pp. 7-10.

16.4 Sri Aurobindo, *Record of Yoga - I*, The Complete Works of Sri Aurobindo (Vol. 10), Sri Aurobindo Ashram Trust, Pondicherry, 2011, p. 7.

16.5 Sri Aurobindo, *Essays on the Gita*, The Complete Works of Sri Aurobindo (Vol. 19), Sri Aurobindo Ashram Trust, Pondicherry, 1997, p. 515.

16.6 Sri Aurobindo, *The Human Cycle*, The Complete Works of Sri Aurobindo (Vol. 25), Sri Aurobindo Ashram Trust, Pondicherry, 1997, pp. 11-12.

16.7 Sri Aurobindo, *The Mother with Letters on the Mother*, The Complete Works of Sri Aurobindo (Vol. 32), Sri Aurobindo Ashram Trust, Pondicherry, 2012, pp. 18-19.

16.8 M K Gandhi, *Hind Swaraj and Other Writings*, edited by Anthony J Parel, Cambridge University Press, 1997, p. 73.

16.9 Sri Aurobindo, *The Mother with Letters on the Mother*, The Complete Works of Sri Aurobindo (Vol. 32), Sri Aurobindo Ashram Trust, Pondicherry, 2012, pp. 19-20.

16.10 Sri Aurobindo, *Essays on the Gita*, The Complete Works of Sri Aurobindo (Vol. 19), Sri Aurobindo Ashram Trust, Pondicherry, 1997, pp. 515-516.

16.11 Sri Aurobindo, *The Mother with Letters on the Mother*, The Complete Works of Sri Aurobindo (Vol. 32), Sri Aurobindo Ashram Trust, Pondicherry, 2012, pp. 20-21.

16.12 The Mother, *Words of the Mother - I*, Collected Works of the Mother (Vol. 13), second edition, Sri Aurobindo Ashram Trust, Pondicherry, 2004, p. 149.

16.13 Sri Aurobindo, *The Synthesis of Yoga - III*, The Complete Works of Sri Aurobindo (Vol. 24), Sri Aurobindo Ashram Trust, Pondicherry, 1999, pp. 747-748.

16.14 Sri Aurobindo, *The Mother with Letters on the Mother*, The Complete Works of Sri Aurobindo (Vol. 32), Sri Aurobindo Ashram Trust, Pondicherry, 2012, pp. 22-23.

16.15 Sri Aurobindo, *Essays on the Gita*, The Complete Works of Sri Aurobindo (Vol. 19), Sri Aurobindo Ashram Trust, Pondicherry, 1997, p. 164.

16.16 *Ibid.*, p. 149.

17.1 *Ibid.*, pp. 282-287.

17.2 *Ibid.*, pp. 367-368.

17.3 *Ibid.*, pp. 401-405.

18.1 *Ibid.*, pp. 405-406.

18.2 *Ibid.*, pp. 542-557.

18.3 Sri Aurobindo, *Essays in Philosophy and Yoga (1910-1950)*, The Complete Works of Sri Aurobindo (Vol. 13), Sri Aurobindo Ashram Trust, Pondicherry, 1998, pp. 163-166.

About the Author

Devdas Menon is a Professor in the Department of Civil Engineering at IIT Madras, engaged in teaching, research and consultancy in structural engineering. He adopts a holistic approach in education, placing an emphasis on inner development and transformation.

At the age of 25, he underwent a profound inner transformation that left an enduring impression on him. He withdrew from the material world for a brief period, but under the guidance of some Himalayan masters, came to realise that there was no need at all to 'renounce' the world. On their advice, he chose to remain in and practise the profession for which he had been trained.

In engineering, his primary research interests are in the area of structural concrete design, and in the analysis and design of buildings, bridges, towers and chimneys. He has also carried out innovative research and development in affordable and sustainable building systems and in biomechanical orthopaedic devices. He has a special interest in developing codes of practice, and is presently the Chairman of the Bureau of Indian Standards CED 38 Committee on *Special Structures*. He has authored several popular textbooks: *Reinforced Concrete Design*, *Structural Analysis* and *Advanced Structural Analysis*.

Devdas Menon has also authored a book called *Stop sleepwalking through life!* (1998), and has given numerous invited talks and conducted workshops for students, teachers and corporate organisations on finding meaning and fulfilment in life through self awareness and inner transformation. He teaches two uniquely designed and popular elective courses at IIT Madras, *Self Awareness* and *Integral Karmayoga*. For his contributions in engineering and education, he has been conferred several awards. More details are available at www.devdasmenon.com.

For further details, contact:
Yogi Impressions LLP
1711, Centre 1, World Trade Centre,
Cuffe Parade, Mumbai 400 005, India.

Fill in the Mailing List form on our website and receive, via email, information on books, authors, events and more.
Visit: www.yogiimpressions.com

Telephone: (022) 40115981, 22155036
E-mail: yogi@yogiimpressions.com

Join us on Facebook:
www.facebook.com/yogiimpressions

Join us on Instagram:
www.instagram.com/yogi_impressions